AA100
The Arts Past and Present

# Book 1
# Reputations

*Edited by Elaine Moohan*

This publication forms part of the Open University course AA100 *The Arts Past and Present*. Details of this and other Open University courses can be obtained from the Student Registration and Enquiry Service, The Open University, PO Box 197, Milton Keynes, MK7 6BJ, United Kingdom: tel. +44 (0)870 333 4340, email general-enquiries@open.ac.uk

Alternatively, you may visit the Open University website at http://www.open.ac.uk where you can learn more about the wide range of courses and packs offered at all levels by The Open University.

To purchase a selection of Open University course materials visit http://www.ouw. co.uk, or contact Open University Worldwide, Michael Young Building, Walton Hall, Milton Keynes, MK7 6AA, United Kingdom for a brochure. Tel. +44 (0)1908 858785; fax +44 (0)1908 858787; email ouwenq@open.ac.uk

The Open University
Walton Hall, Milton Keynes
MK7 6AA

First published 2008

Edited and designed by The Open University.

Typeset in India by Alden Prepress Services, Chennai.

Printed in Europe by Gutenberg Press Ltd.

ISBN 9780749217006

1.1

**Mixed Sources**

Product group from well-managed forests, and other controlled sources

www.fsc.org Cert no. TT-CoC-002424
© 1996 Forest Stewardship Council

The paper used for this book is FSC-certified and totally chlorine-free. FSC (the Forest Stewardship Council) is an international network to promote responsible management of the world's forests.

INTRODUCTION

Elaine Moohan
page v

1  CLEOPATRA

Trevor Fear
page 1

2  CHRISTOPHER MARLOWE,
   *DOCTOR FAUSTUS*

Anita Pacheco
page 29

3  CÉZANNE

Charles Harrison
page 55

4  FAME AND FARADAY

Isobel Falconer with Frank James
page 85

5  STALIN

Mark Pittaway
page 123

6  THE DIVA

Elaine Moohan with Nick Jones
and Robert Philip
page 161

7  THE DALAI LAMA

Helen Waterhouse
page 197

AFTERWORD

Elaine Moohan
page 230

GLOSSARY

page 231

ACKNOWLEDGEMENTS

page 237

INDEX

page 239

# Contents

Elizabeth Taylor in the title role of *Cleopatra*, dir. Joseph L. Mankiewicz (Twentieth Century Fox, 1963). Photo: Courtesy of Twentieth Century Fox. Coll Pele/Stills/Gamma, Camera Press London.

# INTRODUCTION

*Elaine Moohan*

In this book you will encounter seven different Arts disciplines all linked by the overarching theme of 'reputations'. In considering the notion of reputation we will examine these questions: why are some people widely remembered and others not? Exactly what makes a person famous, or infamous? How does someone acquire a reputation? What is the relationship between a figure's reputation and what we can discover about his or her life from the historical record?

**Activity**
Spend a few minutes noting down some brief, initial answers to these four questions.

**Discussion**
Your thoughts on why some people are remembered and how a reputation – good or bad – can be established will vary. The questions may have prompted you to think of a well-known person you know about from reading newspaper or magazine articles, or from watching and listening to news and current affairs programmes on television and radio. There are no definitive answers to these questions here, but it is important that you try to keep these questions in mind as you work through Book 1 and apply them to each of the case studies examined in the seven chapters. As you work through this book you will probably find your answers developing, and it's well worth keeping a record of your changing attitude to these questions – in your electronic notebook perhaps – and to exchange your ideas with your fellow students, possibly in electronic conferences.

The Arts disciplines you will study in this book are Classical Studies, English, Art History, History of Science, History, Music, and Religious Studies. In Chapter 1 you will consider the reputation of Cleopatra from a Classical Studies perspective. Chapter 2 is a study of Christopher Marlowe's work *Doctor Faustus*, written by an academic from the discipline of English literature. Art History will be studied in the third chapter which is on the work and reputation of the artist Paul Cézanne, and Michael Faraday's fame will be examined in Chapter 4, introducing you to the study of the History of Science. Stalin's reputation will be studied from a historical perspective in Chapter 5, and in Chapter 6 you will be introduced to the discipline of Music as you consider the concept of the 'diva'. The final chapter will introduce you to the study of Religious Studies by looking at the role and reputation of the Dalai Lama.

In addition to this unifying book theme, the chapters contain activities that link some of these seemingly disparate disciplines together. All Arts disciplines are, to a certain extent, history based, relying on a variety of historical writings to build up a picture of a particular person and the period in which they lived, from the ancient historical writings relating to Cleopatra (Chapter 1) to the modern record of the activities of the Dalai Lama (Chapter 7). Many subjects make use of literary texts, most obviously the creative works central to a study of literature (such as Marlowe's *Doctor Faustus*, the subject of Chapter 2), but also biographies and autobiographies that inform our understanding of the person (that of Faraday, for example, in Chapter 4, Stalin in Chapter 5, and the Dalai Lama in Chapter 7), as well as the poetry collections exemplifying the contemporaneous infatuation with the female singing ensemble at the court of Ferrara (Chapter 6). Others rely on specific works of art: Classical Studies in Chapter 1 makes some use of coins and sculpture to establish a contemporary view of Cleopatra; the paintings and drawings of Cézanne are considered in the light of his artistic reputation in Chapter 3. The study of Music (Chapter 6) uses recordings and printed music to assess the vocal ability of singers of various historical periods, a quality that forms the basis of their reputation. By necessity, such works of art are generally studied on university courses largely through reproductions – photographs for Classical Studies and Art History, and recordings for Music – but you are strongly advised to take such opportunities as there may be to see original works of art in galleries and museums, and to attend live performances of music.

Each week's work is designed to occupy the same number of study hours. Within each chapter you will be introduced to some of the specialised language and terminology associated with that discipline and encouraged to start using the appropriate terms in your discussions. Such terms are printed in bold upon their first appearance, and listed in the glossary for future reference. You will find ample opportunity to practise using this language in the activities set out in each chapter and in the tutorial interactions with your tutor and other students in your group. You will also encounter and learn how to interpret a variety of sources – written, visual and audio – which are used to obtain a clearer understanding of a particular topic.

In addition to the teaching contained in the chapters of this book, you will frequently be referred to other materials that comprise the complete range of study materials you need each week, namely readings associated with specific chapters, the Illustration Book, DVDs and Audio CDs, with their accompanying notes. Before you start to study each chapter, make a careful check of the materials that you will need for each study session. You are not expected to work through each chapter in a single study session, but by assembling all the materials required for the complete chapter you will have a better idea of how best to divide each week into several short periods of study. For instance, in Chapter 1 on Cleopatra you are asked to watch some DVD material as part of the first section, so you will need to plan your initial study session to include access to a DVD player. For Chapter 2 you will need to obtain a copy of one of the set books, Marlowe's *Doctor Faustus*, which you will be asked to read during the course of that week's study. In other chapters, for example Section 7.2

of Chapter 7 on the Dalai Lama, you will need access to the internet to complete a particular activity. In contrast, the readings are printed at the end of the relevant chapter. They are printed with a tint in the margin to help you locate them more easily. By taking some time to plan ahead you will be able to get much more out of each study session.

We hope that you find this book an enjoyable and stimulating start to your study of *The Arts Past and Present*.

# 1 CLEOPATRA

*Trevor Fear*

| INTRODUCTION | 3 |
|---|---|
| **1.1 IMPRESSIONS** | **3** |
| **1.2 CLEOPATRA IN HOLLYWOOD** | **4** |
| **1.3 CLEOPATRA AND ROME** | **5** |
| Constructing Cleopatra: 'spin' at Rome | 6 |
| Plutarch's *Antony*: the fallen hero | 9 |
| Cleopatra in Augustan poetry | 11 |
| **1.4 IN SEARCH OF CLEOPATRA** | **15** |
| Who was Cleopatra? | 15 |
| Cleopatra's images of herself | 18 |
| **1.5 REASSESSING CLEOPATRA** | **24** |
| **REFERENCES** | **26** |
| **RESOURCES** | **27** |
| Reading 1.1 | 27 |
| Reading 1.2 | 28 |

**MATERIALS YOU WILL NEED**
- DVD Video: Cleopatra

**AIMS**

This chapter will introduce you to a variety of study skills that are essential for the study of the ancient world and its reception. Once you have read this chapter, you will be able to:

- assess a wide variety of historical evidence (poems, histories, biography, statues, coins and so on)
- bring together into a coherent argument diverse material scattered over long periods of time
- examine and evaluate the context of source material, and the motivations that lay behind its production
- recognise the changing perceptions over time towards the material and figures of classical antiquity
- reflect on how different times and cultures (including our own) make use of the past.

## INTRODUCTION

In this chapter we will be looking at the figure of Cleopatra and investigating the following questions:

1 How has Cleopatra been portrayed in the modern world?
2 How was Cleopatra represented in the ancient world?
3 What is the relationship between modern and ancient images of Cleopatra?
4 Does the evidence available from antiquity suggest that we should reassess our familiar modern images of Cleopatra?
5 How much do the issues of today and our own ways of thinking impact on how we regard Cleopatra?

## 1.1 IMPRESSIONS

Cleopatra is probably one of the most recognised figures from the ancient world. Stop people in the street and there is a good chance that the name will mean something to them and spark off certain associations.

Activity

Pause a minute and think about Cleopatra. If someone were to ask you what springs to your mind when you hear her name, what would you say? Jot down your thoughts.

Discussion

Some of the things that I associate with Cleopatra are the following: 'temptress', 'seduction', 'beauty', 'doomed lover', 'suicide', 'Antony and Cleopatra', 'Egypt', 'Elizabeth Taylor', '*Carry On Cleo*', 'luxury and extravagance'.

Of course, we all bring different backgrounds to our study, and what has sprung into your head will depend on a variety of factors, such as what you heard at school, what you've watched on TV, or how old you are. It is likely though that your perceptions are in some way indebted to the image of Cleopatra that has found its way into the popular culture of our own times. The strongest image I have (as a forty-something male) is that of the actress Elizabeth Taylor in an extravagant and improbably narrow-waisted pseudo-Egyptian costume, but you may have thought of something quite different.

What I want to explore with you in this chapter is where these images of Cleopatra come from. What forces have combined over the last two thousand years to produce our impressions of Cleopatra? In the course of our investigations we shall move across time from the twentieth century to the first century CE, and across space from Hollywood to Rome and then to Egypt, looking at a wide variety of evidence from movies, histories, biographies, coinage, sculpture and poetry. (Note that throughout the course we will use the dates CE and BCE: CE stands for Common Era and is equivalent to AD; BCE stands for Before the Common Era and is equivalent to BC.)

## 1.2   CLEOPATRA IN HOLLYWOOD

Figure 1.1   Poster of Theda Bara advertising the film *Cleopatra*, 1917. Photo: Fox Films/The Kobal Collection.

In this section we will focus on the image of Cleopatra in the popular culture of the twentieth century with particular reference to a series of Hollywood epic movies in this period (see Figure 1.1). This material draws heavily on visual images, and is presented on the DVD Video for Book 1.

Now watch the DVD Video 'Cleopatra'. In the film you will encounter a number of still images and video clips with a running commentary on their significance. Remember you can pause/replay the film at any time to think further about the image/video clip and what is being said, and to make your own notes.

You might find the following questions useful prompts as you go through this material:

- For each movie/TV programme you encounter, think about the type of image of Cleopatra that is being projected. How are the past and the figure of Cleopatra being used to appeal to the audience?

- How does the image of Cleopatra change over the course of the movies and TV programmes shown in the film? How are these differences linked to the changing social habits of contemporary society?

- What do you think this material tells us about the relationship between our popular perceptions of the past and famous figures from antiquity, and the actual events and characters of the past?

There is no discussion of these questions here as these issues are dealt with in the commentary on the DVD Video. You may also find it useful to discuss these issues with your fellow students and your tutor on the online forum or at a tutorial.

## 1.3  CLEOPATRA AND ROME

Figure 1.2   A map of the Mediterranean at the time of Cleopatra, from *Cleopatra, History to Myth*, ed. S. Walker and P. Higgs, London: British Museum Press, 2001. © The Trustees of the British Museum.

Turning away from the glitz of Hollywood and popular culture, we now travel back over two thousand years to Rome and Egypt in the first century BCE to uncover the image of Cleopatra from antiquity.

As a stepping stone to our exploration of how Cleopatra was depicted by the Romans, first let us think about the nature of ancient history and our relationship to the distant past.

**Activity**

We have just considered the problems associated with the relationship between film and the past, how the conventions of certain types of film tend to present the past in their own terms, and how contemporary concerns can colour our perceptions. Now pause for a minute to think about some general obstacles we might face in studying the events of over two thousand years ago. What sort of evidence are we likely to have about a society long past, and what are going to be the difficulties in evaluating it? Jot down your thoughts and then read the discussion below.

**Discussion**

In the DVD material we have spoken about film as though it places obstacles between us and what really happened. The situation, however, is rather more complicated than this. It is true that the conventions of film-making do tend to put their own spin on the past, but what we can't assume is that there is an easy corrective to this problem. The past is never available to us as a simple set of undisputed facts, and this is particularly true of ancient history.

A frequent problem with ancient history is that we really don't know a lot of it with any precision. Trying to draw a picture of what actually went on in Rome and Egypt at the time of Cleopatra is like trying to fit together an enormous jigsaw where most of the pieces are missing. Or, to use a different analogy, we might think of ancient history as being like a string vest; it has an outline and shape, but it is made up of more holes than substance. This is what our view of the ancient world is essentially like. It is fragmentary and puzzling, and piecing it together takes a lot of patience and a certain degree of imaginative creativity.

The material that we do have – poems, biographies, histories, statues and coins – needs careful interpretation. We need to scrutinise the motivations of its authors and their assumptions about the world. We also need to bear in mind that we ourselves are not ancient Romans or Egyptians, and that we bring along our own sets of values, derived from our own cultures, education and upbringing, to our study of this material. It is easy to think of the past as a set of plain facts to be memorised, but history is a lot trickier than this: it is a maze of opinion, contradiction and hearsay. In studying the past, we must be detectives, and we must also suspect our own motives.

## Constructing Cleopatra: 'spin' at Rome

Cleopatra's status as a famous historical figure in the western tradition depends precisely upon her role in the bitter struggles in Roman history in the first century BCE. If Cleopatra had not come into contact with the Roman world, then in the West at least she would be just another peripheral historical figure whose name would mean little. Her fatal interaction, though, with such prominent figures in Roman history as Julius Caesar, Mark Antony and Octavian (who became Rome's first emperor under the name of Augustus), and her various roles as the lover, ally and bitter enemy of these men, have served to define her in the western tradition. According to the Roman historian Cassius Dio (born c.164, died after 229 CE), Cleopatra 'captivated the two greatest Romans of her time, and because of the third, she destroyed herself' (Scott-Kilvert, 1987, p. 76). What has most defined Cleopatra's image is the fact that she ended up on the losing side in these conflicts. After the assassination of Julius Caesar she became the ally of Mark Antony, but their combined forces were defeated by Octavian at the battle of Actium (off the coast of Greece) in 31 BCE, and by the following year both Antony and Cleopatra had committed suicide as Octavian took control of Egypt.

We are familiar in our own time with the manipulation of public opinion by the media and politicians, of how things can be made to look a certain way through putting a 'spin' on them. Cleopatra was the victim of a vicious propaganda campaign that was waged between Octavian on the one hand, and Mark Antony and herself on the other, in the lead-up to the decisive battle of Actium. Unfortunately for Cleopatra she lost and, as the winners in conflicts tend to write history, it is their images of the losers that prevail.

Roman political life was a tough affair and one's own reputation had to be defended continually and that of rivals diminished. Allegations of sexual impropriety and general debauchery were quite normal in the Roman law courts and in political oratory. If you can imagine the sort of stories that appear in our tabloid press about modern celebrities being delivered about rival politicians with the rhetorical skill and gravity of a Winston Churchill in the House of Commons, then you start to get an idea of the verbal brutality of Roman political life. In this climate of vicious satirical exchange, Antony's association with Cleopatra became ammunition for Octavian and his allies to use against him.

**Activity**    To explore the nature of ancient history a little further and to start our investigation into the Romans' characterisation of Cleopatra, turn now to Reading 1.1, which is a condensed version of a speech Octavian is presented as giving to his army before the battle of Actium by the historian Cassius Dio.

As you read through this extract think about:

1    The manner in which this speech presents a negative image of Antony through his association with Cleopatra and Egypt.

2    What this speech tells us about how ancient historians wrote: for example, does Cassius Dio seem to be presenting an impartial picture of the past based on a careful weighting of the evidence available to him?

**Discussion**    1    In this speech Antony is characterised as a shadow of his former, manly Roman self. He has embraced a foreign and decadent way of life and become bewitched and enslaved by Cleopatra to such an extent that he is fighting on her behalf against his own country. Antony has become effeminate, his self-indulgence has made him 'soft' and no longer a threat; he has become a lover and a dancer instead of a fighter.

In addition to the specific abuse of Antony, Octavian also draws a general contrast between Rome and Egypt. Rome is the ruler of the world and its citizens should be embarrassed to be at war with an opponent such as Egypt. What honour is there for them in fighting a nation whose way of life and people (slaves of a woman, worshippers of reptiles and beasts) are so repugnant to Roman tastes and traditions? Egypt and what it stands for, according to Octavian, is contrasted sharply with Rome and its way of life. One only has to look, Octavian says, at what has happened to Antony to see the threat that this strange country poses to Rome and its citizens. What option, he says, do we have but to resist and defend our own way of life and values?

2    In considering this speech as an example of ancient history we can begin to see some of the challenges that this sort of work poses for us as we try to uncover the past. We need to be aware that Cassius Dio was writing about two hundred years after the events he is depicting. This is certainly not an eyewitness account. We also need to realise that ancient historians worked in a rather different way from their modern counterparts. We expect serious historians to undertake painstaking research and back up their points with evidence and references to their source material. It is important for the modern reader to be able to see where a historian gets his or her information from, and to be able to judge how reliable his or her sources are likely to be. (You will learn more about the study of historical sources in Chapter 5 on Stalin.) This sort of transparency of method was less applicable in the ancient world. Ancient historians seldom refer to the sources of their information, and certainly don't feel obliged to justify their assertions.

The speech is a dramatic and engaging piece of rhetoric, but when we start to think about it we are surely justified in being a little suspicious about its authenticity. Writing over two hundred years later, exactly how did Cassius Dio know what Octavian said in this speech? Did Octavian have a historian with good shorthand travelling with him? The explanation is almost certainly that Cassius Dio made up the speech himself. This may, to us, seem a travesty of what history is supposed to be, but this sort of imaginative and inventive colouring of the past – something that we might think more appropriate to a historical novel than history itself – was not unusual in the writing of ancient history. Then historians used their own judgement to put a speech into the mouth of a historical character, gauging what was likely to have been said by such a character in a particular situation. Such speeches are not a record of what was said, but rather plausible fictions.

This particular practice tells us a lot about ancient historical writing, which was often preoccupied with what we might call an ethical approach to history. This approach concentrated on why certain people did certain things in certain circumstances. To the ancient historian, the answer to such questions was inevitably because they were of a particular type of character, and this disposition served to make their actions predictable. In this manner the work of ancient historians can seem to be a bit like a play or novel where what happens is often predetermined by the way the author has presented the make-up of his or her characters.

We will now move on from narrative history to historical biography and look at the presentation of Cleopatra and her relationship with Antony in Plutarch's *Life of Antony*.

## Plutarch's *Antony*: the fallen hero

Plutarch's *Life of Antony* is the principal ancient source for the events surrounding Antony, Cleopatra and Octavian (and also the principal source, through a sixteenth-century translation, for Shakespeare's play *Antony and Cleopatra*). This biography of Mark Antony was one of a larger set of parallel lives of notable Greeks and Romans written by Plutarch (born before 50 CE, died after 120 CE), probably in the early part of the second century CE, some 150 years or so after the events concerning Cleopatra and Antony. This work was not designed as a conventional narrative history, but rather as a series of character studies to illustrate the virtues and vices of the great figures of Greek and Roman history.

Activity    Read the following brief excerpt, in which Plutarch first introduces Cleopatra into his biography of Antony:

> [T]he love for Cleopatra which now entered his life came as the final and crowning mischief which could befall him. It excited to the point of madness many passions which had hitherto lain concealed, or at least dormant, and it stifled or corrupted all those redeeming qualities in him which were still capable of resisting temptation.
>
> (Scott-Kilvert, 1965, p. 25)

What effect does Plutarch say Cleopatra has on Antony?

Discussion    In this passage, as in the extract from Cassius Dio, we can see that Cleopatra is presented as a fatal influence on Antony. She is temptation personified and Antony is incapable of resistance. From Plutarch's point of view, Cleopatra brings out the worst in Antony and suppresses the best. Under her influence Antony is depicted as a man who has lost his mental faculties and with them all sense of responsibility. Love for Cleopatra is depicted as a madness that opened the floodgates keeping in check the baser desires and passions lurking in Antony's soul. Once Cleopatra precipitated this flood of vice, Antony's better nature was irretrievably washed away. Plutarch's account is expressly moralistic: Antony's moral failings lead him to destruction and the agent of his ruin is Cleopatra.

Activity    Read the following short passage on how Plutarch presents Cleopatra's appearance and personality:

> Her own beauty, so we are told, was not of that incomparable kind which instantly captivates the beholder. But the charm of her presence was

irresistible, and there was an attraction in her person and her talk, together with a peculiar force of character which pervaded her every word and action, and laid all who associated with her under its spell.

(Scott-Kilvert, 1965, p. 294)

How does Plutarch's description match your image of Cleopatra?

Discussion    We are used to the most glamorous actresses playing the role of Cleopatra in movies, so we might be a little surprised to read Plutarch's comment that she was not the most beautiful of women (see the discussion of Cleopatra's portrait on coins in Section 1.4), and that her captivating effect relied not so much on the stunning nature of her looks but rather on the sheer force of her personality. What Plutarch does make clear, though, is that Cleopatra was capable of casting a spell over men. The portrait of Cleopatra as somehow bewitching Antony is a constant theme in the Roman sources.

One of the most famous incidents in the relationship between Cleopatra and Antony was their meeting at the ancient Cicilian city of Tarsus (in modern-day Turkey) on the Mediterranean coast in 41 BCE. After Antony arrived in the East, he summoned Cleopatra to meet him and answer charges that she had supported his rivals in the wars that had followed Julius Caesar's assassination.

Activity    Now read the passage below, which is Plutarch's account of this meeting. As you read it, think about what it suggests about Cleopatra's ability to manipulate her appearance to influence others.

> She received a whole succession of letters from Antony and his friends summoning her to visit him, but she treated him with such disdain, that when she appeared it was as if in mockery of his orders. She came sailing up the river Cydnus in a barge with a poop of gold, its purple sails billowing in the wind, while her rowers caressed the water with oars of silver which dipped in time to the music of the flute, accompanied by pipes and lutes. Cleopatra, herself reclined beneath a canopy of cloth of gold, dressed in the character of Venus, as we see her in paintings, while on either side to complete the picture stood boys costumed as Cupids, who cooled her with their fans. Instead of a crew the barge was lined with the most beautiful of her waiting-women attired as Nereids and Graces, some at the rudders, others at the tackle of the sails, and all the while an indescribably rich perfume, exhaled from innumerable censers, was wafted from the vessel to the river-banks. Great multitudes accompanied this royal progress, some of them following the queen on both sides of the river from its very mouth, while others hurried down from the city of Tarsus to gaze at the sight. Gradually the crowds drifted away from the market-place, where Antony awaited the queen enthroned on his tribunal, until at last he was left sitting quite alone.

(Scott-Kilvert, 1965, p. 293)

Discussion    Right at the beginning of this passage Plutarch makes it clear that Cleopatra did not respond to Antony in a subservient fashion. Rather than rushing straight off to Tarsus in response to his summons, she made him wait to the point where her arrival seemed to be on her own terms rather than his. The manner of her arrival is quite spectacular: an exotic display of wealth and luxury combined with a staging of herself and her female crew in the full trappings of mythological regalia as Venus, the goddess of love, and her retinue. Those who watch this spectacle are immediately entranced and Antony finds himself completely upstaged as he goes from being the centre of attention to a forgotten extra as Cleopatra's irresistible show rolls into town. This scene has become a staple of the cinematic versions of the Cleopatra story because Plutarch's vivid description can be staged with great visual impact.

Plutarch presents Cleopatra very much as a cunning manipulator who seduces and out-manoeuvres Antony. She was a master, he says, of a thousand flatteries; she shrewdly measured Antony's desires and appetites and made sure to cater to them. In doing this, Plutarch notes that she turned a veteran statesman and warrior into the equivalent of a spoilt youth content to squander his precious time on idle pleasures.

Plutarch does not preclude there being genuine feeling between Antony and Cleopatra, but for him and the Roman moralising tradition within which he writes, mutual attachment and love are not redeeming qualities. The Roman world did not value romantic love and Antony's infatuation with Cleopatra was simply another indication to Plutarch of self-indulgence and a lack of self-control.

The only aspect of Cleopatra's life that draws grudging admiration from Plutarch is the manner of her death. Cleopatra contrived to have an asp, a poisonous snake, smuggled to her after she had been captured by the Romans following Antony's suicide, and she died from its bite. When her lifeless body was found on a golden couch dressed in her royal robes, one of her dying attendants, in response to the Roman guard's angry question, 'Was this well done?', answered, 'It is well done, and fitting for a princess descended of so many royal kings' (Scott-Kilvert, 1965, p. 347). In this manner she avoided being taken back to Rome to be displayed humiliatingly in Octavian's victory parade.

We turn now from history and biography to poetry. The only written sources that we have that were written fairly close to the time of the actual events surrounding Antony, Octavian and Cleopatra are poems rather than histories or memoirs. In the next section we will look at one particular poetic memorial to this conflict.

## Cleopatra in Augustan poetry

Before we take a close look at one of the surviving Roman poems about Cleopatra, first let us think about poetry in general. Poetry is a special use of language; generally it involves fitting the sound of words to certain rhythmic patterns. This combination is what gives poetry its special effect and beauty, but at the same time this need to marry together sound and rhythm can produce something that is not as easy to read, or as straightforward to understand, as prose writing or everyday speech. We therefore have to be prepared to work a little harder with poetry to tease out the meaning.

What we most often regard as poetry today is a type called lyric poetry. This form of verse usually presents the singular perspective of an individual, the 'I' or speaker of the poem. Most often in modern poetry this 'I' talks about a fairly intense emotional experience or mood. The speaker does not usually address the reader directly, but rather we seem to overhear this voice as it appears to talk to itself about its deepest feelings and experiences.

Ancient lyric poetry is both like and unlike this. In its original state in ancient Greece, lyric poetry was a form of performance art for the community. It was a public event, and the voice of the poet represented an expression of the community rather than that of an isolated individual. This is rather different from what we are used to. For us, reading poetry is generally a private reflective experience where we attempt on our own to commune with the voice of another individual. The Roman poetry that we are about to look at is situated somewhere between these poles of poetic experience. By the time that Horace wrote the ode we will examine below (c. 65–8 BCE), the communal performance of poetry was no longer the norm but the voice of the poet could still be used as the mouthpiece of the larger community.

When we consider the poetry of Horace we need to bear in mind, then, that poetry is a specialised use of language, and that it is generally far less easy to interpret than prose. By its nature, poetry is rarely history. The poem we are going to look at was written in the past near the time of the events that we are considering, but it was written as a poem and not as a historical record of the events. The poem conveys feelings and impressions that may give us some insight into what people at Rome thought of Cleopatra and the events that had transpired, but we must not lose sight of the fact that poems such as this are verbal works of art; they are of historical value, but they are not objective historical records.

### Horace: Ode 1.37

Activity

Read through the translation of Horace's Ode 1.37 (Reading 1.2), bearing in mind the following questions (you might want to jot down your thoughts and read through them before moving on to the discussion that follows):

1    How would you characterise the mood of the opening lines of the poem, set following the news at Rome of the defeat and death of Cleopatra?

2    How does the poet describe Cleopatra and her followers in the first part of the poem?

3    Do you see a change in the mood of the poem and the poet's attitude towards Cleopatra as the poem progresses?

Discussion

1    The opening of this poem is one of the most famous and memorable in Roman literature. In Latin the phrase is 'nunc est bibendum' ('now is the time to drink'). The translation of the poem with its threefold

repetition of 'now' and its double repetition of 'we must' effectively captures a mood of an almost compelling need to celebrate. These lines are full of the imagery of joyous celebration: dancing, feasting, and opening that expensive bottle of wine kept for a special occasion. The enjoyment of the moment is precipitated by the sudden release of the anxiety that has preceded this moment. The sense of it being a 'sin' to enjoy oneself while Rome was under the threat of destruction from Cleopatra is all of a sudden replaced by the urgent need to celebrate the release of the collective anxiety of a nation following the news of Cleopatra's defeat.

2   You may have noticed that Cleopatra is not referred to by name in this poem: she is introduced as the 'queen'. This term in itself would be enough to invoke hostility and suspicion in a Roman audience. Rome had itself once been a monarchy, but its kings had been removed in a bitter struggle and the system of government that replaced it, the Republic, was expressly designed to avoid the concentration of power in an individual's hands. 'King' was a hated term at Rome, and the suspicion that Julius Caesar had aspired to such a title was enough to seal his fate and provoke his assassination on the Ides of March in 44 BCE. The notion of a 'queen' was even worse; it not only had all the negative overtones of 'king', but it stood for royal power being exercised by a woman. For a society such as Rome's in which women generally had no role in political and public life, the idea of a female head of state was abhorrent. Cleopatra is also portrayed as 'mad' and 'crazed with hope unlimited and drunk with sweet fortune' in her wild ambition to destroy Rome and its empire. Her mind is both figuratively drunk (with ambition) and also drunk in actuality (with wine). Her followers in this enterprise are described as a 'contaminated flock of men diseased by vice'. This is strong negative imagery, as we might expect from a Roman poet about an enemy of the state. Cleopatra is characterised as a crazy queen whose unbridled and reckless ambition is supported by a bunch of degenerates. In the first four verses there is little hint of anything but contempt for Cleopatra in the description of her as a mad, drunk queen suffering a crushing naval defeat at the hands of Caesar (Octavian).

3   The negative rhetoric of the poem up to this point is certainly in keeping with the sort of propaganda that appears to have been circulated about Cleopatra and Egypt by Octavian. It is also notable that Antony does not appear at all in this poem. Cleopatra may have been relegated to the status of a mad queen here, but Antony has been erased altogether. This tactic is also in keeping with Octavian's strategy before the battle of Actium, when he was careful to declare war on Cleopatra rather than on Antony, and tried to make the war appear more like a pre-emptive strike against a reckless and dangerous foreign power than a Roman civil war. However, when we come to the second half of the poem we can begin to sense a shift in tone. The image that the poet uses of Octavian's ships pursuing Cleopatra, like a 'hawk' after 'gentle doves', seems to elicit sympathy for her, and though she is soon after described as a 'monster', one has to wonder how monstrous someone could be who has just been compared to a gentle dove. The verses that follow seem to portray

Cleopatra in a very favourable light. She seeks 'a nobler death', does not display 'a woman's fear' and doesn't try to run and hide. Rather, she returns to her palace defeated but with her spirit unbroken, and calmly and bravely chooses death on her own terms. Horace, like Plutarch, describes her suicide as a deliberate and defiant act that prevents her capture by Octavian and her being paraded as a conquered enemy in his triumphal procession back in Rome (Scott-Kilvert, 1965, p. 347).

The second half of the poem is, then, in many ways quite remarkable given the marked hostility that characterises the opening verses. The initial image of Cleopatra as some kind of 'wicked witch' is swept aside in the second half of the poem and replaced by a re-evaluation of her as an admirable figure. She may have been regarded as a 'monster' and an enemy of the state, but the way in which she met her death is sufficient to occasion the poet's admiration, even given his underlying hostility towards her. Her suicide at the prospect of disgrace and humiliation places her on a par with a long list of aristocratic Roman men and women who chose death rather than dishonour. In this way, the Horatian poem suggests a certain ambivalence in the attitude of contemporary Romans towards Cleopatra. On the one hand she is a despised figure, both a threat to Roman security and the embodiment of a foreign, alien and contemptible (from this perspective) culture. Yet at the same time Cleopatra's death serves to redefine her, for in the end this hated female figure acted with a nobility and resolve that was worthy of any Roman aristocrat.

This poem, written by someone in Rome who was never in Egypt and never witnessed the events that lay behind his verses, can't be taken as an objective eye-witness account of what happened at the battle of Actium or of how Cleopatra committed suicide. However, it does tell us something about the sorts of feelings that these events inspired back at Rome and the complex set of emotions that the name of Cleopatra might have evoked.

We have seen, then, that in general the Roman perspective on Egypt and Cleopatra drew sharp distinctions between the two sides. Rome was seen as manly, austere, disciplined and principled, Egypt as effeminate, reckless, indulgent and debauched. This provided authors such as Dio and Plutarch a context for the bewitchment and ruin of Antony, one in which he was drawn out of his better, Roman self and Egyptianised through the seductive wiles of Cleopatra. In Plutarch's version, Antony's involvement with Cleopatra becomes a sort of parable of how the great can be destroyed by their moral flaws.

These Roman views of Cleopatra undoubtedly have their origin in the propaganda of Octavian and his allies. Whether or not he believed his own propaganda, this sort of cultural stereotyping and vilification served a very useful function for Octavian. Not only was it an expedient tool to discredit his most powerful enemy, but it also promoted the conflict as one against a foreign and threatening power.

The war was to be waged against Cleopatra and Egypt, not against Antony. Hence Horace's poem, dating from the Augustan era, raised Cleopatra to the level of a monstrous threat to the state, but failed to even mention Antony. This was a clever way to avoid the appearance of a civil war. Egypt was no direct threat to Rome, but it was a country whose wealth and grain could not be allowed to fall into a rival's hands. At the same time though, Horace's poem allows us to see that the Romans' view of Cleopatra was unlikely to have been as straightforwardly hostile and clear-cut in its condemnation as the accounts of Dio and Plutarch might lead us to suppose.

## 1.4   IN SEARCH OF CLEOPATRA

In this section we turn away from the Roman depiction of Cleopatra and look at this historical figure in her own right, as the last of the **Hellenistic** queens of Egypt and also the last of the pharaohs (Hellenistic is the period of history usually defined as stretching from the death of Alexander the Great in 323 BCE to the battle of Actium in 31 BCE).

### Who was Cleopatra?

It should be noted that in the study of Cleopatra there is typically an emphasis on the Romans' point of view. This is due not only to the primacy of the Roman empire in the western tradition but also to the relative lack of any Egyptian evidence with which to counter this viewpoint. Cleopatra entered the history of the West largely through her incorporation into the written records of Roman authors, and there are no narrative histories or biographies of Cleopatra written by ancient Egyptians that we can set beside the Roman accounts. Even the brief outline of Cleopatra's historical background and life that follows is largely put together from bits and pieces of information from Roman authors. What we do have, however, is some material evidence in the form of statues, inscriptions and coins, which we will examine in the section 'Cleopatra's images of herself' below.

### The last of the Ptolemies

What is often lost in the modern Cleopatra story is an accurate understanding of the real historical figure. Cleopatra has become legendary, but the legends that surround her have a tendency to obscure and distort the actual Cleopatra of history.

One important aspect of Cleopatra, which is underplayed in the Roman sources and also in modern representations of her, is her status not only as an Egyptian but also as a member of a Hellenic (Greek) elite within her own country. Cleopatra was the last ruler of the last dynasty of the pharaohs of Egypt, the Ptolemies (pronounced 'tol-e-mi-z'). The Ptolemies were not native Egyptians, but rather descendants of one of the generals (Ptolemy) of Alexander the Great, a Macedonian Greek who conquered the Persian empire and acquired Egypt in the fourth century BCE. Like all the Ptolemies, Cleopatra was both a pharaoh and a Hellenistic monarch. This is deliberately underplayed in Roman portraits of her which prefer to represent her as the figurehead of a strange and barbarous Egyptian culture. This portrayal is, of course, in itself a deliberate perversion of the ancient and significant culture of Egypt. The reason behind this is that it was much easier for the Romans to draw a picture of radical differences between themselves and Egypt than between themselves and the Greeks, for Rome saw itself as the heir to the intellectual culture of ancient Greece. Modern portraits of Cleopatra have tended to reinforce this promotion of the Egyptian rather than Greek side of Cleopatra. In part this has been an uncritical following of the Roman lead, but it is also because in media such as films it is more dramatically effective: native Egyptian culture simply provides a better visual contrast to the world of ancient Rome.

It is important that we bear in mind that Cleopatra was in fact the head of a Greek-speaking elite that had ruled Egypt for three centuries, but whose members had only ever assimilated themselves to native practices to a certain degree. That these rulers were both kings/queens and pharaohs indicates that they were careful to respect traditional Egyptian practices (for instance, they were crowned in the traditional way as pharaohs, officiated at Egyptian religious cult practices, and even married brother to sister as did the earlier pharaohs) as a means of cementing their own authority and not alienating the native population. Nevertheless, there was a distinct division in this society between a Greek population that was privileged and a native Egyptian population that was largely an underclass. It is well worth bearing in mind that Cleopatra was reputed to have been the first of the Ptolemies who could speak Egyptian, and this was after nearly three hundred years of Ptolemaic rule. We also tend to think of Cleopatra as the unique name of one specific individual and it perhaps comes as a bit of a surprise to discover that 'our' Cleopatra was actually the last of seven Ptolemaic queens who bore that name. The rule of the Ptolemies was centred not at the old sites of Egyptian rule, such as Memphis, but at the city that Alexander the Great had founded in Egypt as its new capital and named after himself, Alexandria. This city was a great metropolis of the ancient world. It possessed stunning architecture – like its famous lighthouse, one of the wonders of the ancient world – and was also a great centre of culture and learning. Its library was famous in antiquity and housed the largest collection of scrolls in the ancient world; it was also a hive of artistic and intellectual activity. The Alexandria of Cleopatra was in many ways a more urbane, sophisticated and intellectually refined place than Octavian's Rome. Although the propaganda of Octavian makes it seem that Egypt was an alien and debased culture, in fact the Egypt of the Ptolemies was a direct heir to the Hellenic culture that was so prized among Rome's aristocratic elite.

ActivityPause here for a minute. Has the information you have just received made you think again about your first impressions of Cleopatra? How might the image of her as a Hellenistic queen of Egypt, at the centre of a sophisticated, intellectual urban culture, serve to upset preconceptions about her which the Roman tradition promoted? There will be no formal discussion of this here, but it is something you might like to talk about in tutorials or online conferences.

## Cleopatra as politician and ruler

Egypt in the time of Cleopatra was the most populous country in the Mediterranean basin and possessed great wealth and resources, but it was nevertheless a power in decline. By the time Cleopatra became ruler of Egypt, the once mighty Ptolemaic kingdom had lost all of its overseas possessions. Egypt was, in fact, officially a possession of the Roman empire. An earlier ruler of Egypt had designated the Roman people as his heir in his will, and only internal wrangling at Rome had prevented its actual annexation into the Roman empire.

The political world that Cleopatra grew up in was one of uncertain and violent intrigue. She had accompanied her own father into exile and seen him bribe his way into the favour of the Romans. She had seen her elder sister set up on the throne in her father's place, and then killed by him when he returned to power. As a member of the ruling family she found herself at the centre of a hotbed of intrigue and sudden violent death. This was a tough world in which to survive.

The traditional Roman viewpoint on Cleopatra tends to emphasise her mad ambition (that she aimed absurdly at supplanting Rome as the principal power in the Mediterranean) or to regard her as a perversely destructive force of aimless sensuality. What is lost here is any realistic appraisal of Cleopatra's actions in the light of her own political reality in Egypt.

Let us take, for instance, one of the most famous incidents associated with Cleopatra, her first meeting with Julius Caesar.

Activity    Read through the following short passage in which Plutarch describes how Cleopatra first met Julius Caesar:

> Cleopatra, taking only one of her friends with her (Apollodorus the Sicilian), embarked in a small boat and landed at the palace when it was already getting dark. Since there seemed to be no other way of getting in unobserved, she stretched herself out at full length inside a sleeping bag, and Apollodorus, after tying up the bag, carried it indoors to Caesar. This little trick of Cleopatra's, which showed her provocative impudence, is said to have been the first thing about her which captivated Caesar, and, as he grew to know her better, he was overcome by her charm and arranged that she and her brother should be reconciled and should share the throne of Egypt together.

(Warner, 1958, p. 290)

How does Plutarch characterise Cleopatra's actions?

Discussion This scene, of course, occurs in every Cleopatra movie. It is a tremendously dramatic event, but what does it tell us about Cleopatra? As we have already seen, Plutarch is in principle hostile to Cleopatra, and the 'spin' that he puts on her actions here is that she behaved in a brazen manner in seeking out Caesar in this way.

However, if we were to consider Cleopatra's actions from a wider perspective, we could choose to portray this action rather differently. Cleopatra was at this time only about twenty-one years of age. She was involved in – and getting the worst of – a civil conflict between herself and the supporters of her young brother, and she had been forced out of Alexandria. The arrival of Caesar in Egypt meant that there was now someone with the authority and resources to make a decisive impact on who would rule Egypt. Faced with being deposed by her brother's supporters who were in control of Alexandria, Cleopatra acted swiftly and decisively to seize the initiative and impress the man best able to help her secure her future. This was not simply a flirtatious whim on her part, but a matter of both political expediency and self-preservation.

The Roman tradition of Cleopatra as a destructive sexual predator must be set against a counter view that would see her associations with Julius Caesar and Mark Antony as astute political alliances. Through her children with Caesar (one son) and Antony (two sons and a daughter), Cleopatra forged dynastic ties with the most powerful nation in the Mediterranean. Whatever the personal feelings of those involved, these were pragmatic and political decisions and unions. These alliances promised to bring stability to the region and to restore the power of Ptolemaic Egypt (both Caesar and Antony restored territories to Egypt that had been lost). These ties also suited both Caesar and Antony, who were not naively seduced by Cleopatra. Caesar was already moving on to campaign elsewhere, and he needed stability in Egypt; he also needed the wealth and grain of Egypt. In Cleopatra he saw the best means to this end. The same was true for Antony. Egypt's support was an important cog in his power base in the East and a needed resource in his conflict with Octavian. On her part, through her liaisons with Caesar and Antony, Cleopatra attempted to steer a shrewd path among the shifting sands of the violent civil conflicts of Rome.

## Cleopatra's images of herself

Cleopatra left behind objects (coins, statues, sculptures) which present images of herself. These have not really made much impression on the mainstream reception of her, yet it is vitally important to consider these images because through them we gain a greater insight into how Cleopatra wanted others to see her. By looking at these artefacts we can try to restore some of Cleopatra's own 'voice' as a counterpoint to how she has been represented by others. Of the various artefacts that survive we are going to limit ourselves to just a few examples, a sculptural relief, two coins and two marble portraits. It is most likely that Cleopatra herself authorised these images, and in this respect they should give us some insight into her strategies for self-representation.

The first example we will consider is a sculptural relief that situates Cleopatra firmly within the traditional practices and modes of the portraiture of ancient Egypt.

Figure 1.3   A portion of the relief sculpture on the southern exterior wall of the Temple of Hathor at Dendera in Egypt. Photo: akg-images/Erich Lessing.

**Activity**

Look now at Figure 1.3, a portion of the relief sculpture on the southern exterior wall of the temple of Hathor at Dendera in Egypt. Take a few moments to write down your thoughts on what you see. How would you describe this sort of art, and what sort of words spring into your mind as you look at it? Two of the four figures are those of Cleopatra and her son by Caesar, Caesarion. Which figures do you think they are, and why?

**Discussion**

The temple of Hathor at Dendera was an ancient religious site. The remains of the temple still standing date to a rebuild of the complex started by Cleopatra's father and largely completed by Cleopatra herself. Her own involvement in this project is a likely indication that these relief sculptures were approved by the queen herself.

The temple is very much architecture on a grand scale. It is hard to get a sense of scale from Figure 1.3 but these figures are around twice life size.

The sculpture is unquestionably a piece of art in the style of ancient Egypt: the hieroglyphic symbols form a dense graphic backdrop to the figures, which are depicted with the stiff formality of this type of archaic art. The images display a sort of timeless, frozen impersonality, which helps to suggest the continuity of the pharaohs through the ages. In this sculpture, Cleopatra deliberately places herself and her son within this artistic tradition stretching back thousands of years.

Cleopatra is the figure on the right. She wears a headdress with horns on either side of a disc representing the sun and she carries a *sistrum* (rattle) and *mnet* (crescent-shaped necklace), some of the objects usually associated with the Egyptian goddesses Hathor and Isis (who are often linked with one another). The figure in front of her is Caesarion. He wears a kilt and the double-crown headdress of Upper and Lower Egypt, and is holding out an offering of incense. The diminutive figure between Cleopatra and Caesarion is a representation of Caesarion's *ka* (the royal life force that was passed from one pharaoh to the next). Facing Cleopatra and her son Caesarion are the goddess Hathor and her son Ihy. (Don't worry: you don't need to remember the names of these deities or any of the Egyptian terms.)

You might well have thought that the figures on the left were Cleopatra and her son (Caesarion was, after all, probably only in his early teens at most when these sculptures were carved), and it might well be supposed that Cleopatra herself would be represented as the more significant of the two. But in this relief Caesarion is placed in the more important position (closest to the gods) and he is depicted as a fully adult male pharaoh. This suggests the importance Cleopatra placed on the promotion of Caesarion as a legitimate pharaoh and ruler of Egypt. Representing her son in the timeless fashion of traditional portraits of the pharaohs was a means to establish his legitimacy. In promoting her son, Cleopatra could be suggesting her integration with the traditional practices of Egypt, where women exercised power only with, or on behalf of, their male relatives. At the same time she is also emphasising her own status and authority as not only a pharaoh, but also as the mother of a pharaoh. You can see the similarities between the headdress that Cleopatra wears and that of the goddess Hathor facing her. Hathor was a goddess associated with a wide range of activities, which included fertility, motherhood and love. She was also equated with the Greek goddess Aphrodite (known as Venus to the Romans) and the Egyptian goddess Isis (Plutarch mentions that Cleopatra dressed on occasion as both these deities). As Cleopatra and her son face Hathor and her son, an obvious parallel seems to be drawn between the fertility and power of the mother goddess and those of her human counterpart.

This piece of grand architecture, then, shows Cleopatra embracing the ancient traditions of Egypt. She appears in a timeless portrait as an integral cog in the line of the pharaohs. She also displays herself as dutifully providing a link between the divine and the human worlds. In doing so she not only expresses her adherence to Egypt's past but also uses this past to stress her own authority and legitimacy. However, at the same time that she uses this traditional form of expression to link herself to the past, she also employs it to look to the future by investing Caesarion with all the authority of a pharaoh. If there was any question of whether the illegitimate son of Cleopatra and the Roman Caesar could be the pharaoh of Egypt, there is no sign of it in the emphatic message on this piece of monumental sculpture. It was important for Cleopatra to be seen to respect the traditional ways of her country (remember she was supposedly the first Ptolemy to speak Egyptian, and she also used the title of *philopatris*, fatherland-loving), but she also knew how to make those traditions work to promote her own designs and ambitions.

### Cleopatra on coins

**Activity**

Let us now turn to Figures 1.4 and 1.5. On both of these coins there is an image of Cleopatra. What immediate impression do these portraits make on you? How would you say Cleopatra is being depicted?

**Discussion**

We seem here to be a long way from the larger-than-life portraits in the timeless tradition of the pharaohs on the temple walls at Dendera. For one thing, we are dealing with radically different material objects here, made for a different audience. The monumental sculptures at Dendera are a static display of Cleopatra's allegiance to Egyptian tradition. Coins, however, circulate in everyday life and hence are seen by more people over a wider geographical area. These coins were minted in the East and would have circulated throughout Antony's and Cleopatra's territories and possibly beyond. Unlike the Dendera sculptures, they were not designed primarily for an Egyptian audience.

Figure 1.4   *Coin portrait of Cleopatra*, silver tetradrachm *c.* 37–32 BCE, collection of the American Numismatic Society, 1977.158.621 reverse. Photo: courtesy of the American Numismatic Society.

Figure 1.5   *Coin portrait of Cleopatra*, silver denarius, 32 BCE reverse. British Museum, London. Photo: © The Trustees of the British Museum.

As you look at the images on the coins, you will probably be struck by how they don't appear to be very flattering portraits of Cleopatra. If you picture her as a famous beauty, then these images are quite jarring. On the coins, she doesn't appear youthful; her neck is thick set and she has a rather unflattering roll of skin under the chin (particularly in Figure 1.5); the nose is prominent and hooked; the jaw juts out (again, more so in Figure 1.5) and the eyes are almost bulbous. In fact, nose, jaw and eyes all look rather exaggerated, perhaps more in keeping with a caricature than a portrait. It is perhaps hard not to stifle an initial impression that such an image is a negative rather than a positive image of the queen.

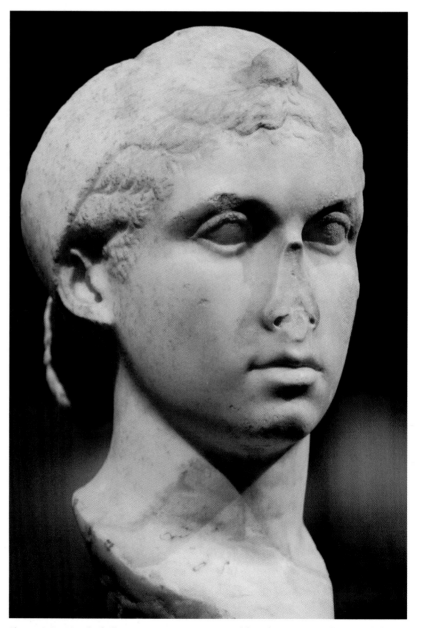

Figure 1.6    Head of Cleopatra, c. 51–30 BCE, marble. Photo: © Sandro Vannini/ CORBIS.

Aside from the facial features Cleopatra is represented very much in the manner of a Hellenistic queen. Her hairstyle, with pulled-back braids and a bun, usually referred to as a 'melon' hairstyle (because the braids are like the stripes on a melon), was typical of female members of the royal Ptolemy family. The hairband too is a traditional part of the portrait of Ptolemaic queens. The hairband is in fact the *tainia*, a sort of diadem and an emblem of royalty. In the images on these coins, however, the portrait of a Hellenistic queen is allied to what seems like a harsh realism. For comparison look at Figure 1.6, a marble portrait of Cleopatra. Here the same features of diadem and melon hairstyle complement a serene and more timelessly youthful image of the queen. The almond-shaped eyes and small mouth are similar to those on the coins, but the coin images are altogether harsher and more incisively realistic.

The coin portraits are very much in the Roman style of portraiture of the day known as *verism*. This was a style of sculpture that aimed at a realistic, or even overly realistic, depiction, often referred to as 'warts and all' portraiture. The style appears to aim not at flattering the subject or assimilating it into an almost timeless continuum, as traditional Egyptian and Hellenistic representations tend to do, but rather to project powerful and striking individuality.

Another notable thing about the images on the coins is Cleopatra's jewellery. In Figure 1.4, where the upper part of the torso is visible, you can see a sizeable and elaborate pearl necklace (just the top of this is visible in Figure 1.5), and in both images you can see a large pearl-drop earring. The visual impact of the pearls, particularly in Figure 1.4, impresses on the viewer the wealthy status of the subject and hence serves to reinforce the projection of power in this image.

On the other side of each of these coins is an image of Mark Antony, similarly depicted in a veristic style (see Figures 1.7 and 1.8; the coin shown in Figure 1.7 is the other side of the coin shown in Figure 1.4, and the coin in Figure 1.8 is the other side of that shown in Figure 1.5). The forceful presentations of each figure and the way that they even look like each other suggests a natural symmetry and resemblance between these figures which mirrors their political and personal alliance. (It is also possible that the ostentatious pearls that Cleopatra wears were a well-known gift from Antony.)

These particular coins, then, represent an image of Cleopatra that was perhaps primarily intended for the audience of the Roman empire. On them she is depicted as a strong and forceful leader, a natural female counterpart to the Roman general Mark Antony, and a figure worthy of alliance with Rome and of ruling with Rome (in Figure 1.5, if you trace a vertical line down from Cleopatra's nose to the bottom of the coin, you can just make out a ship's prow which is used to indicate the strength of the royal Egyptian fleet).

Figure 1.7    *Coin portrait of Antony*, silver tetradrachm, *c.* 37–32 BCE, collection of the American Numismatic Society, 1977.158.621 obverse. Photo: courtesy of the American Numismatic Society.

Figure 1.8    *Coin portrait of Antony*, silver denarius, 32 BCE obverse. British Museum, London. Photo: © The Trustees of the British Museum.

If the sculptures at Dendera were intended to impress on the Egyptian population the legitimacy of Cleopatra and Caesarion to rule as pharaohs in Egypt, then these coins were similarly designed to present Antony and Cleopatra as viable rulers of the Roman empire. For the Egyptians, Cleopatra appears as a timeless female pharaoh; for the residents of the Roman empire she appears as a powerful and formidable dynast.

There were many different Cleopatras, which existed simultaneously and served various functions, but each was deliberately designed by Cleopatra herself to appeal to a certain segment of her audience. In this she appears to have been a shrewd manipulator of public opinion and a skilled promoter of her own image.

## 1.5    REASSESSING CLEOPATRA

In this final section of the chapter, let us take stock of the different strands of Cleopatra's representation and reception that we have looked at. We have seen Cleopatra in a variety of poses, from a glamorous Hollywood star to a depraved foreign tyrant, to a determined stateswoman and patriot. She has been many things to many people: 'Age cannot wither her, nor custom stale/ Her infinite variety' (Shakespeare, *Antony and Cleopatra*, Act 2, Scene 2, l. 244). To some extent we all create our own version of Cleopatra and what we see in her tends to reflect our own cultural traditions.

As I mentioned earlier, to work out the details of ancient history we need to act like detectives. We must remember that new evidence from the past may always appear, and there is always the possibility that new clues will take us in new directions. This is one reason why our work on Cleopatra is never likely to be definitive or finished. Another reason is that as a powerful, historical, female figure from the African continent, Cleopatra is always likely to remain a controversial figure. We might say that there are simply too many important issues (gender, race, colonialism and so on) invested in this figure for there ever to be an agreed assessment. Such issues are fundamental to how we see the world, but the way that we see these issues continually changes over time. As our relationship to such issues changes over time, so too the reputation of Cleopatra will continue to evolve.

Recently, Cleopatra has been caught up in the academic debate on Afrocentrism. Afrocentrism is not the easiest term to define and many would describe it in different ways. For some it has involved a subjective and partisan reassessment of history in an attempt to promote the primacy of African civilisation. For others it is a necessary readjustment to an intellectual history of the world that has always privileged white, European culture, and hidden and deliberately misrepresented the fundamental contributions of African civilisation. It is a debate that calls for us to think about our general perceptions of the past, about who has written our history, and about what biases they have brought to the process.

Cleopatra serves as a famous figure in this debate, as some have argued that she was black (a notion that is part of Afro-American oral history). The traditional historical view of Cleopatra, however, is that she was a descendant of one of the Macedonian generals of Alexander the Great, and so her roots and racial origin lay in Europe rather than Africa. Nevertheless, although Cleopatra is claimed by the European intellectual and cultural tradition, it is also clear that her ancestors were not simply Greeks intermarrying generation after generation, but were also very probably the product of relationships between Ptolemaic kings and Egyptian/African concubines (Elizabeth Taylor's Cleopatra in the 1963 movie describes herself as 'an almost all-Greek thing'). Part of the specific argument regarding Cleopatra has rested on a question mark over the exact identity of her grandmother, and whether she was Egyptian/African. However, whatever skintone and features Cleopatra actually may have had, surely there is some basis for treating someone whose family had lived in Egypt for three hundred years as Egyptian and African. The Ptolemies may have clung on to their Macedonian heritage and spoken Greek, but they also practised the ways of the pharaohs. The fact that history has generally viewed Cleopatra as Greek and not African is a clear indication to the proponents of Afrocentrism that the writers of history wanted to promote European culture over African. In this manner Cleopatra has become a symbol of the suppression of African heritage. The way in which Cleopatra has become part of the Afrocentric debate demonstrates how historical figures are always likely to be re-evaluated according to the terms of contemporary cultural and social debates.

We can, of course, try to be objective and say that we are approaching the ancient material with an eye to simply extracting the truth about what really happened, but in practice this is far harder than it sounds. We are all so imbued with our own values that they tend to creep in even when we are determined to shut them out, and the concept of 'truth' (or 'the facts') is notoriously slippery. On the one hand we have so few facts from the ancient world, and on the other we have different versions of the 'truth'. Was the real Cleopatra the one the Romans saw, the one Egyptians saw, the one Shakespeare wrote about, or the one we see in the movies? There is no simple formula in the study of history that inevitably uncovers the truth or the real story of what happened in the past. That said, this doesn't mean that what we are doing is of no value. Our explorations of the past do have meaning. What we bring to the past can cast it in a new light and help to bring out aspects of that history that have previously remained in the shadows, or been deliberately distorted in the explorations of those who have gone before us. Our own explorations will in turn by reassessed by others, and our own shortcomings, which we might not be able to see ourselves, exposed. This is what makes history alive and significant. Its shape is always changing and, as we look at the past, it tells us about ourselves and our own values.

Activity    Your final task for this chapter is to reassess Cleopatra for yourself. Have you read or seen anything in this chapter that has changed your way of thinking about her? Do you think your own ways of looking at issues such as gender, race, sexuality and politics allow you to see the historical Cleopatra clearly, or with any more authenticity than other ages and cultures have viewed her? What significance do you think this historical figure has in the early twenty-first century?

There is no formal discussion of this final task here but you might want to share your thoughts with, and compare them to, those of your fellow students in tutorials or online.

## REFERENCES

Scott-Kilvert, I. (trans.) (1965) *Plutarch: Makers of Rome*, Harmondsworth, Penguin.

Scott-Kilvert, I. (trans.) (1987) *Cassius Dio: The Roman History: The Age of Augustus*, Harmondsworth, Penguin.

Warner, R. (trans.) (1958) *Plutarch: Fall of the Roman Republic*, Harmondsworth, Penguin.

West, D. (trans.) (2004) *Horace: The Complete Odes and Epodes*, Oxford, Oxford University Press.

## RESOURCES

Reading 1.1   **Augustus on Cleopatra**

We Romans are the rulers of the greatest and best parts of the world, and yet we find ourselves spurned and trampled upon by a woman of Egypt.

[...]

Would we not utterly dishonour ourselves if, after surpassing all other nations in valour, we then meekly endured the insults of this rabble, the natives of Alexandria and of Egypt, for what more ignoble or more exact name could one give them? They worship reptiles and beasts as gods, they embalm their bodies to make them appear immortal, they are most forward in effrontery, but most backward in courage. Worst of all, they are not ruled by a man, but are the slaves of a woman ...

Who would not tear his hair at the sight of Roman soldiers serving as bodyguards of this queen? Who would not groan at hearing that Roman knights and senators grovel before her like eunuchs? Who would not weep when he sees and hears what Antony has become? [...] [He] has abandoned his whole ancestral way of life, has embraced alien and barbaric customs, has ceased to honour us, his fellow-countrymen, or our laws, or his fathers' gods.

[...]

He is either blind to reason or mad, for I have heard and can believe that he is bewitched by that accursed woman, and therefore disregards all our efforts to show him goodwill and humanity. And so, being enslaved by her, he plunges into war with all its attendant dangers which he has accepted for her sake, against ourselves and against his country. What choice, then, remains to us, save our duty to oppose him together with Cleopatra and fight him off?

[...]

And even if at one time he showed some valour when he served with our army, you can rest assured that he has now lost it beyond recall through the change in his manner of life. It is impossible for anyone who indulges in a life of royal luxury and pampers himself as a woman to conceive a manly thought or do a manly deed, since it cannot but follow that a man's whole being is moulded by the habits of his daily life.

[...]

To sum up, if it were a matter of being called upon to cavort in some ridiculous dance or cut some erotic caper, Antony would have no rival – for these are the specialities in which he has trained. But when it comes to weapons and fighting what has anyone to fear from him?

Source: Scott-Kilvert, 1987 pp. 52, 53, 54 and 55.

Reading 1.2    **Horace, Ode 1.37**

Now we must drink, now we must
beat the earth with unfettered feet, now,
    my friends, is the time to load the couches
        of the gods with Salian feasts.

Before this it was a sin to take the Caecuban
down from its ancient racks, while the mad queen
    with her contaminated flock of men
        diseased by vice, was preparing

the ruin of the Capitol and the destruction
of our power, crazed with hope
    unlimited and drunk
        with sweet fortune. But her madness

decreased when scarse a ship escaped the flames
and her mind, which had been deranged by Mareotic wine,
    was made to face real fears
        as she flew from Italy, and Caesar

pressed on the oars (like a hawk
after gentle doves or a swift hunter
    after a hare on the snowy plains
        of Thrace) to put in chains

this monster sent by fate. But she looked
for a nobler death and did not have a woman's fear
    of the sword, nor did she make
        for secret shores with her swift fleet.

Daring to gaze with face serene upon her ruined palace,
and brave enough to take deadly serpents
    in her hand, and let her body
        drink their black poison,

fiercer she was in the death she chose, as though
she did not wish to cease to be a queen, taken to Rome
    on the galleys of savage Liburnians
        to be a humble woman in a proud triumph.

Source: West, 2004.

# 2 CHRISTOPHER MARLOWE, *DOCTOR FAUSTUS*

*Anita Pacheco*

| INTRODUCTION | 31 |
| --- | --- |
| **2.1** | **CHRISTOPHER MARLOWE** | 31 |
| | *Doctor Faustus* | 34 |
| | Reading a Renaissance play | 34 |
| **2.2** | **READING *DOCTOR FAUSTUS*** | 36 |
| | Act 1, Scene 1: 'Yet art thou still but Faustus, and a man' | 36 |
| | Act 2, Scene 1: Faustus and God | 44 |
| | Acts 3 and 4: What does Faustus achieve? | 46 |
| | Act 5, Scene 2: Faustus's last soliloquy | 49 |
| | Morality play or tragedy? | 51 |
| **2.3** | **HERO AND AUTHOR** | 52 |
| **REFERENCES** | 54 |
| **FURTHER READING** | 54 |

## MATERIALS YOU WILL NEED

- *Doctor Faustus: The A Text*, ed. John O'Connor (set book)
- Audio CDs: *Faustus – Part 1*; *Faustus – Part 2*

## AIMS

This chapter will:

- provide you with practice in close reading (how to analyse a passage from the play)
- encourage you to think about genre (what *kind* of play is *Doctor Faustus*?)
- ask you to consider themes (what are the main themes or issues explored in the play?)
- demonstrate how to read historically (what are some of the connections between *Doctor Faustus* and the historical period in which it was written?)
- help you to read biographically (what, if any, insights does *Doctor Faustus* give us into the character and reputation of its author?).

## INTRODUCTION

In this chapter I will discuss the question of reputation in relation to a literary text, *Doctor Faustus* by Christopher Marlowe, which was written sometime between 1588 and 1592 and was first published in 1604 (the A text). We will start by considering the literary reputation of Marlowe (1564–93), who lived and wrote at the same time as Shakespeare and is probably the most famous of his many gifted fellow writers.

We will then look at *Doctor Faustus*, Marlowe's best-known play. The main aim of this section of the chapter is to introduce you to the study of literature at undergraduate level. We will discuss several aspects of the play, and engage in some of the main skills and techniques involved in the analysis and interpretation of literary texts.

Let's begin by looking at the life and reputation of the play's author.

## 2.1 CHRISTOPHER MARLOWE

> Marlowe's touch was in my *Titus Andronicus*, and my *Henry VI* was a house built on his foundations ... I would give all my plays to come for one of his that will never come.

These lines come from John Madden's 1998 film *Shakespeare in Love*. Shakespeare, played by Joseph Fiennes, has just heard that Marlowe has been stabbed to death in a tavern in Deptford and believes, mistakenly, that he is responsible for his death. Stricken with guilt and grief, he acknowledges the immense artistic debt he owes his great contemporary, without whose works he feels he could never have written two of his own early plays.

This scene from the film gives us a reasonably accurate picture of the kind of reputation that Marlowe now enjoys as a writer: he is seen both as an important dramatist in his own right, and as a pioneer whose achievements on the stage made possible the considerable accomplishments of his successors, most especially the plays of Shakespeare. What *Shakespeare in Love* only hints at in its mention of Marlowe's sticky end is that he is as famous for his life and death as for his works.

**Activity** If you have not already done so, please read the short biography of Marlowe ('Marlowe's life and career') on pages 119–20 of the Longman edition of *Doctor Faustus*, the set text for this chapter.

**Discussion** You will see from this brief account that Marlowe lived a short and exceptionally turbulent life, rising from humble origins to attend Cambridge University, working (probably) as a government spy, and combining an astonishingly productive career as poet and playwright with regular run-ins with the authorities. O'Connor mentions the counterfeiting and the street

ANNO . DNI    ÆTATIS SVÆ. 21
7 5 8 5

QVOD ME NVTRIT
ME DESTRVIT

Figure 2.1    Unknown artist, 'The Corpus Christi portrait', 1585. Corpus Christi College, Cambridge. Photo: By permission of the Master and Fellows of Corpus Christi College, Cambridge. Known as the Corpus Christi portrait, this is thought to be a portrait of Marlowe (Corpus Christi was Marlowe's college at Cambridge).

fight that ended in a man's death, but the historical record affords us two further glimpses of Marlowe's apparent penchant for violence and lawbreaking. In May 1592, Marlowe was in court in London for making threats against two local constables and was bound over to keep the peace; in September that year he attacked a tailor in Canterbury with a stick and dagger – this time the case was settled out of court. Then there is his early, violent and mysterious death at the age of twenty-nine, at the time that he was under investigation for heresy.

Marlowe's posthumous literary reputation was heavily influenced by several hostile contemporary accounts of his character and beliefs. His fellow playwright Thomas Kyd accused him of holding a variety of 'monstrous opinions', of being 'intemperate' and of having 'a cruel heart' (Maclure, 1979, pp. 35, 33), though it's important to realise that

Kyd made these claims under torture. The spy Richard Baines, who had already informed on Marlowe during the counterfeiting affair, submitted a report to the authorities which portrayed him as a scoffer and heretic who, for example, mocked religion as a tool used by the powerful 'to keep men in awe' and said 'Christ was a bastard and his mother dishonest [unchaste]' (ibid., p. 37). Baines also accused Marlowe of what we would call homosexuality (the word did not exist in the sixteenth century, though buggery was punishable by death) when he attributed to him the view that 'all they that love not tobacco and boys were fools' (ibid., p. 37). The puritan Thomas Beard charged Marlowe with 'atheism and impiety', with denying 'God and his son Christ' (ibid., p. 41). He also interpreted Marlowe's violent death as God's judgement upon his sins, or, as Beard put it rather more colourfully, as the 'hook the Lord put in the nostrils of this barking dog' (ibid., p. 42). It's only fair to add that Marlowe was also admired and celebrated as a poet and dramatist during and immediately after his lifetime; for example, fellow dramatist George Peele called him 'the Muses' darling' (ibid., p. 39), while another playwright, Thomas Heywood, writing in 1633, described him as 'the best of poets in that age' (Cheney, 2004, p. 3).

Given such spectacular biographical material, it's not surprising that Marlowe the man has always been as famous as Marlowe the writer. Moreover, the correlations between the work and the life (both the facts and the gossip) are undeniably striking: all of Marlowe's dramatic protagonists are in some significant sense rule-breakers, who challenge religious, political or sexual orthodoxies, much as he was accused of doing. Two of his best-known heroes, Tamburlaine and Doctor Faustus, share with their creator their rise from low-class origins to fame and success, while another protagonist, King Edward II, is sexually infatuated with his favourite Piers Gaveston.

Marlowe's literary reputation has depended to a considerable extent on how different historical periods have viewed his life and his unconventional protagonists. Those critics in the eighteenth century who had some knowledge of Marlowe were generally scandalised by the biographical accounts that survived and repelled by what they perceived to be the intemperate nature of his protagonists. It was not until the nineteenth century that a more favourable view of Marlowe's artistic accomplishments began to emerge. The establishment of English Studies as a distinct academic discipline in the second half of the nineteenth century brought with it the construction of a canon of great writers and a history of English literature which accorded Marlowe the crucial groundbreaking role he plays in *Shakespeare in Love*.

Changing views of the artist consolidated his integration into the literary canon. Viewed in the light of the biographies of Romantic poets like Percy Bysshe Shelley (1792–1822), an avowed atheist, and

George Gordon, Lord Byron (1788–1824), surrounded through much of his career by sexual scandal, Marlowe's tumultuous life and early death, along with his sensational plays, began to look less like culpable immorality and more like evidence of poetic genius. As the figure of the artist became increasingly associated with rebellion and excess, so the life and work that once disqualified Marlowe from literary celebrity came virtually to guarantee it.

## *Doctor Faustus*

Critics who have studied Marlowe's work have for the most part been inclined to take on trust the picture of him provided by Kyd, Baines, Beard and others, and to read the plays as statements of the author's own radical beliefs. But there is an obvious problem with this approach to Marlowe's work: we simply don't know whether these hostile accounts of his opinions are accurate or, as seems likely, deeply compromised by their writers' own motives and circumstances.

*Doctor Faustus* is the most famous of Marlowe's plays, and its hero, who sells his soul to the devil in return for twenty-four years of power and pleasure, is by far the best known of his rebellious protagonists. Marlowe based the plot of his play on *The History of the Damnable Life and Deserved Death of Doctor John Faustus* (1592), an English translation of a German book (now known as the *Faustbuch*) about an actual historical figure who gained notoriety in early sixteenth-century Germany by dabbling in the occult. This story rapidly became the stuff of legend and, like most legends, it has been subject to numerous retellings, including the two-part play *Faust* (1808; 1832) by the German writer Goethe, the novel *Doctor Faustus* (1948) by Thomas Mann, and Peter Cook's and Dudley Moore's 1967 film *Bedazzled* (remade in 2000), which adapted the legend for comic ends.

Why did Marlowe choose to adapt the Faust legend for the stage? Was the free-thinking dramatist, as numerous critics have speculated, attracted to a story about a man who rebelled so flagrantly against the Christian God? One of the interesting questions to ask about *Doctor Faustus* is whether the play seems to strengthen or undermine the long-standing view of Marlowe as a maverick artist, and we will return to this question at the end of the chapter.

## Reading a Renaissance play

If you have never read a Renaissance play before – and even if you have – you may well find *Doctor Faustus* a challenging read. This is chiefly because, like the plays of Shakespeare, *Doctor Faustus* was written during the historical period known as the Renaissance (or the early modern period), when the vocabulary was significantly different from twenty-first-century English. It is also written largely in

**blank verse**, a term that requires a few words of explanation. Look for a moment at the four opening lines of *Doctor Faustus*:

> Not marching now in fields of Trasimene
> Where Mars did mate the Carthaginians,
> Nor sporting in the dalliance of love
> In courts of kings where state is overturned ...

(Prologue, ll. 1–4)

If you count the syllables in these lines, you will find that each one contains ten. If you read the lines aloud, you will hear that for the most part every other syllable carries a particularly marked accent:

> Not **march**|ing **now** | in **fields** | of **Tra**|simene
> Where **Mars** | did **mate** | the **Car**|thagi|nians,
> Nor **sport**|ing **in** | the **dal**|liance | of **love**
> In **courts**| of **kings**| where **state**| is o|ver**turned**

The second line doesn't fit all that comfortably into the overall pattern because it feels a bit awkward giving a strong stress to the last syllable of 'Carthaginians'. But we can still say that, roughly speaking, each line of verse has five stressed and five unstressed syllables, and that these are arranged in a fairly regular pattern of unstressed/stressed. In poetry this pattern, or metre, is called **iambic pentameter**, which is generally thought to be the poetic metre that most closely reproduces the cadence of English speech. This is also *blank* verse because, in addition to being written in iambic pentameter, the lines are unrhymed. (There is more information on metre on pages 144 to 147 of your set text.) Marlowe was known and admired by his contemporaries for the skill with which he used blank verse in his plays.

Don't worry if this discussion of metre is new to you: its purpose is just to make you aware that the play's verse has an underlying rhythm. This rhythm is mainly determined by the metre which, as we have just seen, is more regular at some points than others, but it is also affected by punctuation, which can slow the verse down (if there are a lot of stops and pauses) or speed it up (if there are few of these).

*You will need to allow 1 hour 40 minutes to listen to the whole recording of* Doctor Faustus *on the Audio CDs.*

Everyone has their own way of reading, but I would suggest, especially if this is your first encounter with Renaissance drama, that when reading the play you focus on the story: try to get the gist of what happens, who the main characters are and what they do. Don't worry if you find this hard going or feel that you do not understand it all. Remember that reading early modern English *is* challenging, and that in the second part of this chapter we will be looking more closely at particular parts of the play and discussing them together. It might also be a good idea to listen to the version of the play on the Audio CDs as you read. This will add to your understanding and enjoyment of the play and make it much easier for you to hear the rhythm of the verse.

The edition of *Doctor Faustus* that we are using offers a lot of help with the play's language and themes in notes that are conveniently located on pages facing the text. You should use these as and when you feel you need them, but do keep in mind that the important thing at this stage is just to grasp the broad outlines of the plot. The edition also contains a wide-ranging selection of information relevant to the study of *Doctor Faustus*. Apart from the biography of Marlowe, which we have already discussed, none of this material is required reading, though you should of course read it if you wish to.

If you have not already done so, please read *Doctor Faustus* now.

## 2.2    READING *DOCTOR FAUSTUS*

### Act 1, Scene 1: 'Yet art thou still but Faustus, and a man'

#### The morality play

Before looking at the play's opening scene I should add a brief note on the medieval **morality play**, the type of drama on which Marlowe draws in adapting *The Damnable Life* for the stage. After the Prologue and Faustus's long opening speech, you may have been startled by the appearance of the Good and Evil Angels. Even if you had expected to find supernatural beings in a play about a man who sells his soul to the devil, the Good and Evil Angels may have struck you as strange, perhaps because they are not what we expect characters in literary texts to be like. Their names tell us pretty much everything we need to know about them for, rather than having individualised personalities, they represent abstract moral qualities – in this case, goodness and evil. At this point and throughout the play they are engaged in a struggle for the soul of Faustus, the Good Angel warning him of the danger of arousing 'God's heavy wrath' (1.1.74) by practising black magic, the Evil Angel egging him on by reminding him of the power that necromancy will bring him.

This way of creating characters, or **characterisation**, is typical of morality plays, which are fundamentally religious dramas that enact the conflict between good and evil, each of which is embodied in supernatural figures (like Mephistopheles and Lucifer) or personified abstractions (like the Good and Evil Angels and the Seven Deadly Sins). They are shown fighting for the soul of a central human character who often represents humanity itself, hence the title of one of the best-known morality plays, *Everyman*. The aim of the morality play was primarily didactic; that is, it sought to teach its audience, and to offer moral and spiritual lessons about how to live a good Christian life. In *Doctor Faustus*, this didactic element can be seen most clearly in Marlowe's use of a **Chorus** to present a Prologue and Epilogue that, rather like the Choruses of ancient Greek tragedies, express traditional attitudes and guide the audience's response to the play. (As you will see when you study Seamus Heaney's translation of Sophocles' *Antigone* later in the course, in Greek tragedy the Chorus was a group of people, whereas in *Doctor Faustus* and Elizabethan drama generally, it is one person.) Yet morality plays also sought to entertain their audiences; they are full of clowning and knockabout comedy, just as is the case in *Doctor Faustus*.

Morality plays were prevalent in England during the late Middle Ages, but were still popular when Marlowe was writing. The fact that he turned to the morality play when he came to dramatise *The Damnable Life* raises questions about the **genre** of *Doctor Faustus*: what kind of play is this? Is it essentially a late sixteenth-century morality play, warning its audience of the dire consequences of practising black magic? Or is its attitude to the story it tells more complicated than this? How does the play encourage us to respond to the central character who sells his soul to the devil?

**Activity**

*You can listen to the Prologue on the Audio CD 'Faustus – Part 1', track 2.*

We can begin to answer these questions by looking at the Prologue. Reread the speech now, and then write a brief summary of it in no more than four or five sentences. What main points would you say the Chorus is making here?

**Discussion**

Here is what I've come up with:

1   The Chorus spends several lines telling the audience what the play is *not* about – war or love or martial heroism – before he tells us what it *is* about: 'Faustus' fortunes, good or bad' (l. 8).

2   Then he tells us about Faustus's childhood, specifically that although he was born to 'parents base of stock' (l. 12), he went on when he was older to study divinity at the University of Wittenberg, where his intellectual brilliance led swiftly to his being awarded a doctorate.

3   In line 20, the tone of the speech seems to change, as the Chorus speaks of Faustus's 'cunning of a self-conceit', which your edition of the play explains as 'intellectual pride engendered by arrogance'.

4   The Chorus goes on to explain that his intellectual pride led Faustus to take up the study of magic, or 'cursèd necromancy', despite the fact that it jeopardises 'his chiefest bliss' (l. 27); that is, his chance of being granted eternal salvation when he dies.

The Chorus, then, is kicking things off by giving us a brief biography of the play's protagonist. I hope you agree that the picture of Faustus it offers us is a mixed one. The Chorus undoubtedly condemns Faustus's study of magic and encourages us to disapprove of it too. But the speech also registers the greatness of a man who, through his own merit, overcame the considerable disadvantage of lowly birth to rise to the pinnacle of his profession.

Let's look a little more closely now at the last eight lines of the Prologue. When the tone of the speech changes in line 20, the Chorus says not just that Faustus is full of intellectual pride and arrogance, but that he is 'swollen' with it. This is easy for us to understand, for we still use the expression 'swollen head' to describe someone who thinks too highly of themselves. We also understand that the Chorus is not using the adjective 'swoll'n' literally; it is not that Faustus is actually swollen up, but that he has an inflated opinion of himself. In other words, 'swoll'n' is used in a *figurative* rather than a literal way. **Figurative language** describes one thing by comparing it with something else. The two most well-known types of figurative language are **similes** and **metaphors**. Similes make a direct comparison by using the word 'like' or 'as'. If Marlowe had written 'Till, swoll'n like a balloon with cunning of a self-conceit', he would have made a direct comparison between Faustus's pride and an inflated balloon. But he chose to use not a simile but a metaphor, with the result that rather than being likened to a particular inflated object, pride is identified more broadly with the condition of being swollen.

This metaphor is followed by the lines: 'His waxen wings did mount above his reach,/ And melting heavens conspired his overthrow' (ll. 21–2). This is an allusion to the ancient Greek myth of Icarus, who attempted to escape from Crete with a pair of waxen wings, but flew too near the sun and plunged to his death when the sun melted the wax. He became the symbol of the 'overreacher', of the man who tries to exceed his own limitations and comes to grief as a result. Like Icarus, in the Chorus's view, Faustus tried to 'mount above his reach' and was punished for his presumption: 'heavens conspired his overthrow' (l. 22). This is an intriguing twist on the Icarus myth; for whereas Icarus's pride seems to be self-destructive, Faustus's sparks the intervention of a deity who 'conspires' to destroy him (see Figures 2.2 and 2.3).

What happens to the language when the Chorus starts to talk about Faustus's study of magic? In the two lines 'And glutted more with learning's golden gifts, / He surfeits upon cursèd necromancy' (ll. 24–5), 'glutted' means 'overfull', or 'stuffed', and 'surfeits' means 'to eat too much', 'to gorge oneself'. Why is the Chorus referring to eating, specifically to eating too much? It seems that once again the language is not working literally; instead, it is drawing metaphorical links between Faustus's intellectual curiosity and a kind of greedy self-indulgence. He is portrayed as a glutton who, stuffed full of 'learning's golden gifts', turns to magic and gorges himself on that as well.

So, by looking closely at the language of the Prologue, we can see more clearly what the Chorus is saying about Faustus – that it associates his intellectual ambition with an immoderate appetite, with an inflated sense of his own value, and with a dangerous, Icarus-like overreaching that brings him into conflict with the Christian God. So even though the Prologue praises Faustus for his intellectual brilliance, it also insists that this brilliance is not an unqualified good; if it pushes

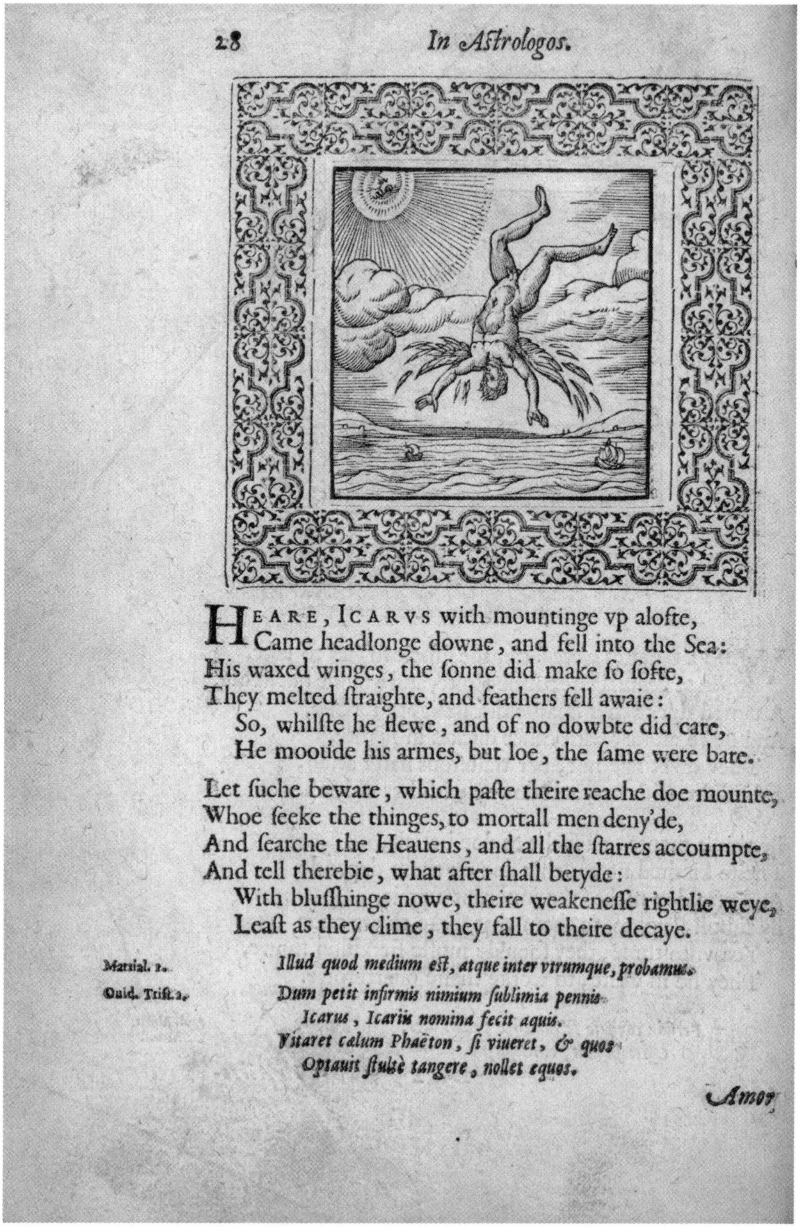
28 *In Aſtrologos.*

HEARE, ICARVS with mountinge vp alofte,
Came headlonge downe, and fell into the Sea:
His waxed winges, the ſonne did make ſo ſofte,
They melted ſtraighte, and feathers fell awaie:
So, whilſte he flewe, and of no dowbte did care,
He moou'de his armes, but loe, the ſame were bare.

Let ſuche beware, which paſte theire reache doe mounte,
Whoe ſeeke the thinges, to mortall men deny'de,
And ſearche the Heauens, and all the ſtarres accoumpte,
And tell therebie, what after ſhall betyde:
With bluſſhinge nowe, theire weakeneſſe rightlie weye,
Leaſt as they clime, they fall to theire decaye.

Martial. 2. *Illud quod medium eſt, atque inter vtrumque, probamus.*
Ouid. Triſt. 3. *Dum petit infirmis nimium ſublimia pennis*
*Icarus, Icariis nomina fecit aquis.*
*Vitaret cælum Phaëton, ſi viueret, & quos*
*Optauit ſtultè tangere, nollet equos.*

*Amor*

Figure 2.2 Unknown artist, 'Fall of Icarus', from Geoffrey Whitney's *Choice of Emblemes*, 1586. Stirling Maxwell Collection, Glasgow University Library, SP.coll S.M.1667. Photo: By permission of the department of Special Collections of the University of Glasgow Library. Whitney's text extracts a similar moral from the myth of Icarus as the opening Chorus of *Doctor Faustus*. In both cases, Icarus illustrates the dangers attendant on humans seeking 'the thinges, to mortall men deny'de'.

Figure 2.3    Pieter Brueghel, *Landscape with the Fall of Icarus*, 1555, transferred from panel. Musées Royaux des Beaux-Arts, Brussels. Photo: © 1990, Scala, Florence. It is interesting to compare Brueghel's treatment of the myth with that of Marlowe's Chorus and Whitney's emblem. Icarus, just visible in the bottom right of the painting as he sinks to his death in the sea, is unnoticed as the rest of the world goes about its business.

past certain boundaries, it becomes sinful and provokes divine punishment. The Prologue tells us, in short, that the play's protagonist lives in a Christian universe that places limits on the pursuit of knowledge.

### Faustus's first speech

*You can listen to Faustus's first speech on the Audio CD 'Faustus – Part 1', track 3.*

The Chorus now introduces Faustus, who delivers his first speech of the play. The way the speech is staged and written serves to emphasise Faustus's position as an eminent scholar. It is set in his study, and he is surrounded by books, from which he reads in Latin. The works he consults, written by such great thinkers of classical antiquity as the Greek philosopher Aristotle, the Greek medical authority Galen and the Roman emperor and jurist Justinian, were central texts in the sixteenth-century university curriculum. The first impression the speech gives us, then, is of the breadth of Faustus's learning.

The American poet William Carlos Williams (1883–1963) wrote the following poem about Brueghel's painting:

**Landscape with the Fall of Icarus**
According to Brueghel
when Icarus fell
it was spring

a farmer was ploughing
his field
the whole pageantry

of the year was
awake tingling
near
the edge of the sea
concerned
with itself

sweating in the sun
that melted
the wings' wax
unsignificantly
off the coast
there was

a splash quite unnoticed
this was
Icarus drowning

William Carlos Williams, from *The Collected Poems*, II: 1939–1962. © by William Carlos Williams.

There is no one on stage with Faustus as he delivers these lines, which means that it is a **soliloquy**, a speech in which a dramatic character, alone on stage, expresses his or her thoughts, feelings and motives. The soliloquy is an ideal device for establishing a strong relationship between a character and an audience, for it seems to give us access to that character's mind at work. In Faustus's opening soliloquy, we notice right away that he is addressing himself in the third person – 'Settle thy studies, Faustus, and begin' (l. 1) – which creates the impression that he is talking to himself. We listen as he tries to make up his mind, now that he has been awarded a doctorate in Theology, what subject he wants to specialise in. He declares that he will be a 'divine' only in appearance ('in show'), while aiming to achieve expertise in every academic discipline. Immediately, then, we hear a note of dissatisfaction and restlessness in Faustus's voice; despite his dazzling academic success, he is impatient for more knowledge.

Yet as he runs through the four main academic disciplines he has studied – Philosophy, Medicine, Law and Theology – he dismisses each of them as an intellectual dead-end. Faustus feels that he has already achieved everything that the study of philosophy and medicine has to offer. He then rejects the law as suitable only for a 'mercenary drudge' (l. 34). For a moment, he returns to divinity as the most worthy profession, but then rejects that as well, as the passages he reads from Jerome's Bible stress only human sinfulness and the damnation that awaits it.

So what is it that Faustus wants that these traditional fields of study fail to supply? When contemplating his own remarkable achievements in medicine, he laments that although he can cure illness he is unable either to give his patients eternal life or to raise them from the dead: 'Yet art thou still but Faustus, and a man' (l. 23). What he wants, then, is to transcend his human limitations, to break through the boundaries that place what he sees as artificial restrictions on human potential. He has gone as far as his human condition will allow him to go, but wants to go further still, which means transforming himself into a 'mighty god', 'a deity' (ll. 64, 65), a goal he feels only magic will enable him to realise.

When Faustus declares that he wants to achieve something that '[s]tretcheth as far as doth the mind of man' (l. 63), he expresses an intense optimism about human ability that has often been seen as characteristic of the Renaissance, and as the quality that most distinguishes it from the more religious Middle Ages. Historical periods are too complex to be boiled down to a single, defining essence; nor are there clear breaks between them. Nevertheless, there were developments in Europe from the fourteenth to the eighteenth centuries that, broadly speaking, encouraged a newly secular view of the world: the growth of scientific investigation into the structure of the universe and the laws of the physical world; the voyages of exploration, expansion of trade routes and colonisation of the Americas; the new technology of printing, which allowed for the rapid dissemination of new ideas and discoveries; and the development of a **humanist** educational programme, based on the study of ancient Greek and Latin authors, and dedicated to the restoration of classical ideals of civic virtue and public service. When Faustus fantasises that 'All things that move between the quiet poles/ Shall be at my command' (ll. 58–9), his speech is inflected with the scientist's and coloniser's desire for control over the natural world (Hopkins, 2000, p. 62). When he tells Mephistopheles that he is not afraid of damnation because he believes instead in the classical Greek afterlife (see 1.3.60–1), he voices a humanist reverence for classical culture.

It is highly unlikely, though, that any sixteenth-century humanist would have countenanced this kind of explicit challenge to Christian doctrine, so if Faustus represents the secular aspirations of the Renaissance, he does so in an extreme or exaggerated form. Moreover, the fact that *Doctor Faustus* is set in a Christian universe and affirms the reality of hell and damnation should warn us not to overstate the secular values of Renaissance England. Indeed, what the play explores – its principal **theme** – is the conflict between the confidence and ambition its protagonist embodies, and the Christian faith, which remained a powerful cultural force when Marlowe was writing and required humility and submission to God's will.
The play's two opening speeches set up an opposition between the Prologue's view of boundless ambition as sinful presumption and Faustus's implicit claim that the Christian universe places unjust restrictions on human potential.

Which side in this conflict do you think the play encourages us to take? We saw earlier that the Prologue seeks to discredit Faustus's interest in necromancy by portraying it in terms of an intemperate appetite. Is there more evidence in the opening scene to support this claim?

**Activity**    Have another look at Faustus's speech on page 9, lines 80–101, in which he imagines the power that magic will bring him. What is it he wants to achieve with this power? What kinds of motives or desires do you think he expresses in these lines?

**Discussion**    The Good and Evil Angels have just made their first appearance, and in response to the Evil Angel's promise that magic will allow him to be 'on earth as Jove is in the sky' (l. 78), Faustus exclaims, 'How am I glutted with conceit of this!' (l. 80). Right away, then, he echoes the language of the Prologue and so identifies his own longing for godlike power with a gluttonous craving. A few lines later he thinks of the gold and precious jewels the magical spirits will bring him, along with 'pleasant fruits and princely delicates', or delicacies (l. 87). You may have noticed as well how often Faustus repeats the phrase 'I'll have', which makes him sound a bit like a greedy child in a sweet shop. Yet alongside these acquisitive and hedonistic impulses he expresses a genuine thirst for knowledge, for example, when he says he wants the spirits to 'resolve' him 'of all ambiguities', or to answer all his questions (l. 82), and to read him 'strange philosophy' (l. 88). His desire to overturn the university dress code by filling the universities with silk 'Wherewith the students shall be bravely clad' (l. 93) strikes me as a harmless, even appealing, expression of social rebellion.

Faustus's motives in this speech seem to be mixed, neither all good nor all bad, rather like the Chorus's initial portrait of him. I'd like to say a bit more at this point about Faustus's desire to levy soldiers to 'chase the Prince of Parma from our land' (l. 95). In this line he is voicing antipathy to an Elizabethan hate-figure. *Doctor Faustus* was written during a protracted period of military conflict with Catholic Spain. The Prince of Parma was the Spanish governor of the Netherlands, and in the 1580s he was closely involved both in Spain's plans to invade England and in the suppression of a Protestant rebellion in the Netherlands which England supported. It's true that the pro-Protestant force of Faustus's statement is somewhat weakened by the fact that he seems to want rid of the Prince of Parma so that he himself might 'reign sole king of all our provinces' (l. 96); still, the play's original audience is likely to have warmed to the picture of this representative of Spanish Catholic military might being ignominiously chased out of northern Europe.

This is a good example of the way in which reading literary texts with their historical context in mind can help to shed light on their meaning. The mention of the Prince of Parma in this speech strongly suggests that Marlowe was, at least to some extent, seeking to arouse audience support for Faustus.

## The comic scenes

*You can listen to Act 1, Scene 4 on the Audio CD 'Faustus – Part 1', track 6.*

There is no doubt, though, that the play keeps drawing our attention to its protagonist's weaknesses. The comic scenes in Act 1 serve to reinforce the connection between magic and appetite. In Act 1, Scene 4, Wagner tells us that Robin is so poor that 'he would give his soul to the devil for a shoulder of mutton, though it were blood raw' (ll. 9–11) and Robin adds: 'Not so, good friend. By'r Lady, I had need have it well roasted, and good sauce to it, if I pay so dear' (ll. 12–15). Coming directly after the scene in which Faustus first conjures Mephistopheles, the joke glances at Faustus's own 'hunger' and drives home the absurdly high price he is paying for comparatively trivial pleasures. This is one of the main functions of the play's comic scenes – to comment on the serious action. Time and again, Marlowe juxtaposes scenes so that the later comic one comments on the preceding serious one by re-presenting Faustus's ambitions in their lowest form, stripped of the power of his own speeches. With techniques such as these the play diminishes its hero by exposing the triviality and foolishness of his aims.

## Act 2, Scene 1: Faustus and God

*You can listen to Act 2 on the Audio CD* 'Faustus – Part 1', *tracks 7–9.*

By the end of Act 1, Faustus appears to have made up his mind to sell his soul to the devil in exchange for twenty-four years in which he will 'live in all voluptuousness' (1.3.94). Act 2, Scene 1 opens with another soliloquy.

**Activity**

Now look at this soliloquy (page 33, lines 1–14). How would you describe its mood? Jot down any points you think are important about the way the language helps to create this mood.

**Discussion**

I would say that the mood of this speech is one of self-doubt and inner division. Just as in the first soliloquy, Faustus is talking to himself, but on this occasion the voice we hear sounds markedly less confident. One possible reason for this is that the speech is peppered with questions which seem to betray his uncertainty about his chosen course of action; for example, in line 3 he asks himself, 'What boots it [what use is it] then to think of God or heaven?' The question is followed by a series of commands: 'Away with such vain fancies and despair!/ Despair in God and trust in Beelzebub./ Now go not backward. No, Faustus, be resolute' (ll. 4–6). Faustus is ordering himself not to backtrack, but to no avail, as his next question makes clear: 'Why waverest thou?' (l. 7). Suddenly another voice appears, urging repentance: 'Abjure this magic and turn to God again!' (l. 8). This voice seems to get the upper hand briefly, but Faustus silences it with an extreme statement of his commitment to the devil.

Faustus appears to be wrestling with his conscience in this soliloquy. He clearly feels the urge to repent, so why doesn't he? It is interesting that although he delivers this speech *before* he has signed his contract with Lucifer, he tells himself in the first line that he must 'needs be damned'; in other words, he sees his own damnation as unavoidable. So what's the point, he asks himself, of thinking of God or heaven? The repetition of the word 'despair' in lines 4 and 5 emphasises Faustus's hopeless state of mind. If you count the syllables in lines 2 and 10, you will see that each line has only six. This means that in performance the actor would have to pause for a moment because the lines are shorter than normal, and this would have the effect of drawing attention to the sentiments expressed in the two lines – that is, to Faustus's despairing conviction that he cannot be saved and that God does not love him.

Why should Faustus feel so strongly that he is damned, when at this point in the play there seems to be every reason to believe that repentance will secure God's forgiveness? Some critics, most notably Alan Sinfield (1983) and John Stachniewski (1991), have argued that Marlowe is exploring the mental and emotional impact of the form of Protestantism that prevailed in England during the late sixteenth century, based on the doctrines of the French-born Protestant reformer Jean Calvin. Calvinist theology developed and changed over time, but at this historical juncture it stressed the sinfulness and depravity of human nature. In contrast to the traditional view of salvation as something that an individual could earn by living a virtuous Christian life, Calvinism argued that salvation is entirely God's gift rather than the result of any human effort. Moreover, according to the doctrine of predestination, God gives that gift only to a fortunate few whom he has chosen; everyone else faces an eternity of hellfire.

This theology formed the official doctrine of the Elizabethan Church. However bleak it sounds, its effect on believers was often positive; for those persuaded by their own virtuous impulses that they were chosen by God, it proved an enormous source of comfort and well-being, perhaps especially for poorer members of society, for whom the conviction of divine favour could be empowering. But for some, these doctrines provoked a sense of powerlessness and anxious fear about their spiritual destiny. It is possible to argue that Marlowe's Faustus is a depiction of one of these casualties of Calvinist doctrine, and that this helps to explain not only his opening dismissal of Christianity as obsessed with sin and damnation, but also his repeated inability to repent. As in the soliloquy that opens Act 2, he cannot bring himself to believe that God favours him and has granted him salvation. The desire for repentance is overwhelmed by a still stronger belief, consistent with Calvinist doctrine in its early modern form, that the chances are that God does not love him at all.

However, it isn't necessary to believe that *Doctor Faustus* is specifically about Calvinism to feel that its portrait of the Christian God who vindictively 'conspires' Faustus's overthrow is not entirely flattering. Numerous critics have been troubled by a particular episode in the play that seems to cast doubt on the presence of divine mercy and benevolence. This is the moment in Act 2, Scene 3 when Faustus makes his most serious attempt at repentance. He quarrels with Mephistopheles, the Good Angel (unusually) gets the last word in the debate with the Evil Angel, and Faustus calls out to Christ 'to save distressèd Faustus' soul' (2.3.85). And what happens? Lucifer, Beelzebub and Mephistopheles enter. Why does God not intervene to save Faustus? The stony silence that greets his plea for divine assistance seems to call into question the traditional Christian notion of a loving and merciful God.

Other critics have argued that God is silent on this occasion because Faustus's repentance is insincere, and that he consistently fails to repent not because he is suffering from theologically-induced despair, but because he is afraid of the devils and constantly distracted by the frivolous entertainments they stage for him, like the pageant of the seven deadly sins which follows this episode. One could argue as well that the play *does* represent the Christian God as loving and merciful, and shows human beings to be free to shape their own spiritual destinies. The Good and Evil Angels, after all, seem to give dramatic form to Faustus's freedom to choose: he has a choice between good and evil, and he chooses evil in full knowledge of what the consequences will be. As late as Act 5, Scene 1, the Old Man appears on stage to drive home the availability of God's mercy if only Faustus will sincerely repent his sins. Looked at from this perspective, it is Faustus and not God who is responsible for the terrible fate that greets him at the close of the play.

This critical debate serves to remind us that it is difficult to evaluate how much sympathy the play arouses for its protagonist without taking into consideration its treatment of the Christian God. If you think the God of the play is fundamentally benevolent then you are less likely to feel favourably disposed towards Faustus than if you think he comes across as a harsh and punitive cosmic despot. It is clear, though, that the play offers textual evidence in support of both views. Once again, we find Marlowe refusing to be pinned down to one interpretation.

## Acts 3 and 4: What does Faustus achieve?

*You can listen to Act 3 on the Audio CD 'Faustus – Part 1', tracks 10–12. Act 4 is on the second Audio CD, 'Faustus – Part 2', tracks 1–3.*

Act 2 points repeatedly to the failure of Faustus's attempt to secure power and autonomy through his pact with Lucifer: in Act 2, Scene 1 Mephistopheles declines his request for a wife, and in Act 2, Scene 3 he refuses to tell him who made the world. Acts 3 and 4 cover the bulk of the twenty-four-year period that Faustus purchased with his soul. How do they make us feel about what he actually achieves through his embracing of black magic? Are we encouraged to feel it was worth it?

**Activity**

Have another look at Act 4, Scenes 1 and 2. On the basis of these scenes, would you say that Faustus has realised his dreams of power and pleasure? What evidence would you offer in support of your view?

**Discussion**

These two scenes show us Faustus in the role of court magician, entertaining the emperor Charles V and then the Duke and Duchess of Vanholt with conjuring tricks. Many critics have felt that these scenes highlight the hollowness of Faustus's achievements; far from realising his grand dreams of immense power, all he manages to become is the entertainer of the established ruling elite. Marlowe certainly makes a point in Act 4, Scene 1 of stressing the limitations of his protagonist's conjuring powers. Because Faustus is still unable to raise people from the dead, he can do no more than summon spirits who resemble Alexander and his paramour. In Act 4, Scene 2 the point seems to be not that Faustus lacks the power to fulfil the request made of him by his aristocratic employer, but that the Duchess of Vanholt can think of nothing more challenging to ask for than a dish of ripe grapes, to which Faustus replies, apparently with some regret, 'Alas, madam, that's nothing' (4.2.14). He seems at this point to share the view of many critics that he is squandering his abilities on trivial activities.

Yet is this all there is to say on this matter? As usual with this play, there is another side to the story, especially if we consider Act 3. Earlier we looked at Faustus's desire to 'chase the Prince of Parma from our land', and speculated how, in a climate of military conflict with Spain, this might have endeared him to the play's original audience. At the time of the play's first performances, the Catholic Church would have been viewed by many with comparable hostility. In 1570 the

Pope had excommunicated Elizabeth I and released her Catholic subjects from their allegiance to the Protestant heretic queen; in 1580 he proclaimed that her assassination would not be a mortal sin. Read with this context in mind, Act 3, Scene 1, in which Faustus makes a fool of the Pope under cover of his magician's cloak of invisibility, looks like a bid for audience approval, by its portrayal of the Catholic Church as decadent and corrupt and mired in absurd superstitions like the ceremony of excommunication. By casting Faustus in the role of Protestant hero, this scene seems designed to elicit a favourable response to his conjuring skill.

We need to remember as well the limitations of the theatre, and in particular of Marlowe's open-air theatre, where plays were performed in broad daylight with little in the way of props, scenery or artificial lighting (for more information, see pages 130–3 of the set text, and Figure 2.4). In these conditions, it is not hard to grasp why so many of Faustus's adventures as a magician are reported rather than enacted: the Chorus to Act 3, for example, tells us that in order to learn 'the secrets of astronomy' (l. 2), Faustus scaled Mount Olympus 'in a chariot burning bright/ Drawn by the strength of yoky dragons' necks' (ll. 5–6). This sounds anything but a hollow experience, and when discussing Acts 3 and 4 we should give due weight to the descriptions Marlowe provides of activities he was unable to enact on stage, especially given that these descriptions probably had a powerful impact on the play's original audience, who were much more accustomed to listening to long and often complex speeches (sermons, for example) than we tend to be nowadays.

The mention of the play in performance leads us to an important characteristic of drama, which makes it different from other literary forms such as the novel and poetry: plays are written to be performed whereas novels and poems are written to be read. This means that a play is not so much a fixed and finished literary text as a blueprint for actors and directors who will have to make decisions about how it is going to be translated from the page to the stage. They will have to ask themselves questions, such as what is actually happening on stage at any given moment? How should a particular speech be spoken by the actor playing the part, and which actor is best suited to play the part? A director will also need to make decisions about set design, costumes, lighting, music and other sound effects. All of these aspects of performance will contribute to the meaning of the play, and they will differ from one production to another. You will be thinking again about performance-related issues when you study Seamus Heaney's translation of Sophocles' play *Antigone* later in the course.

**Activity**  So how might consideration of *Doctor Faustus* as a text intended for performance affect our response to Faustus's career as a magician? A moment ago we discussed the way in which Act 4 in particular seems to emphasise the gap between Faustus's aspirations and his actual

Figure 2.4   William Dudley, *The 1587 Rose Theatre: A Cutaway View*, 1999, created for the onsite exhibition designed by Dudley. Used with the permission of William Dudley. The Rose was the site of the first recorded performance of *Doctor Faustus* on 30 September 1594. (For more information about the Rose and Elizabethan playhouses, see pp. 130–3 of the set text.)

achievement. Does thinking about these scenes in terms of performance open up different possibilities?

**Discussion**   It strikes me that Act 4, Scene 1, for example, in which Faustus conjures up the image of Alexander the Great and his paramour, could easily, with the skilful use of music and lighting, be turned into a thrilling stage spectacle. It might then be possible to perform Act 4 in such a way as to create the impression not of the emptiness, but of the wonder of Faustus's magical powers.

*You can listen to Act 5, Scene 1 on the Audio CD 'Faustus – Part 2', track 4.*

The same might be said of the two appearances of Helen of Troy in Act 5, Scene 1. This scene is structured in such a way as to establish a clear contrast between Faustus's two encounters: with the Old Man, who urges piety and repentance, and with the legendary beauty Helen of Troy (Figure 2.5). Faustus chooses Helen, and many critics have echoed the Old Man's stern disapproval. Yet the critic Thomas Healy points out that in the theatre Helen is usually represented as so 'strikingly beautiful' that even if one agrees on a rational level that Faustus would be better off with the Old Man, on a visual level the Old

Man loses out to Helen, who engages what Healy calls the audience's 'emotional and aesthetic sympathy' (Healy, 2004, p. 183). By the same token, a director might choose to portray Helen instead as a malign influence on the hero.

## Act 5, Scene 2: Faustus's last soliloquy

*You can listen to Faustus's last soliloquy on the Audio CD 'Faustus – Part 2', track 5.*

The play draws to a close with Faustus's final soliloquy, which is supposed to mark the last hour of his life.

**Activity**

Reread this speech now, thinking as you read about how Marlowe uses sound effects to heighten the emotional impact of the soliloquy.

**Discussion**

The soliloquy represents an attempt to imagine and dramatise what the last hour of life feels like to a man awaiting certain damnation. Of course, the speech doesn't really take an hour to deliver, but Marlowe uses the sound of the clock striking to create the illusion that the last hour of Faustus's life is ticking away and so heightens the sense of impending doom. It strikes eleven at the start of the speech, then half past the hour ninety-six lines later, then midnight only twenty lines after that. Why does the second half hour pass much more quickly than the first? Is this Marlowe's way of conveying what the passage of time feels like to the terrified Faustus: it seems to be speeding up as the dreaded end approaches? The thunder and lightning that swiftly follow the sound of the clock striking midnight announce the final entrance of the devils.

Critics have often commented on how skilfully Marlowe uses rhythm to underline the passage of time. Look, for example, at the second line: 'Now hast thou but one bare hour to live' (l. 67). Because this is a sequence of monosyllabic words, it is not entirely clear which of them are stressed. It would certainly be possible for an actor to give a more or less equally strong stress to each word, which is why O'Connor points out that the line seems to echo the striking clock we have just heard (p. 108). This echo effect is strengthened by the internal rhyme between 'Now' and 'thou'. The monosyllabic words continue into the next line until the last word: 'And then thou must be damned perpetually' (l. 68). The sudden appearance of a long five-syllable word focuses our attention on it and alerts us to what it is that Faustus most fears: an infinity of suffering. This sparks his desperate and futile plea for time to stand still, and Marlowe underlines the futility through the use of **enjambement**, or run-on lines:

> Fair nature's eye, rise, rise again, and make
> Perpetual day; or let this hour be but
> A year, a month, a week, a natural day ...

(ll. 71–3)

Faustus wants time to stop or slow down, but the way one line of verse tumbles into the next, accelerating rather than slowing down the

Figure 2.5    Dante Gabriel Rossetti, *Helen of Troy*, 1863, oil on panel, 33 × 28 cm. Photo: Hamburger Kunsthalle, Hamburg/ The Bridgeman Art Library. A representation of Helen of Troy, reputed to be the most beautiful woman in the world, by the pre-Raphaelite artist Dante Gabriel Rossetti.

rhythm, seems to signal the inevitable frustration of that wish. Faustus himself grasps this: 'The stars move still; time runs; the clock will strike;/ The devil will come, and Faustus must be damned' (ll. 76–7).

Time really is the essence of this soliloquy, not only because the clock is ticking for Faustus, but because, as we have seen, what most horrifies him is the prospect not of suffering but of endless suffering. After the clock strikes the half hour, Faustus pleads with God to place a limit on his time in hell – 'Let Faustus live in hell a thousand years,/ A hundred thousand, and at last be saved' (ll. 103–04) – only to come back to the awful truth: 'O, no end is limited to damnèd souls' (l. 105).

One of the most striking aspects of the speech is the way it reverses the dreams of power and glory that Faustus expressed in his first soliloquy. In that speech he declared his desire to be more than human, to be a 'mighty god', but now, as he faces an eternity in hell, he wishes that he were less than human: he longs to be transformed into 'some brutish beast' whose soul would simply dissolve into the elements when it dies (ll. 109–12), or that his soul might 'be changed into little waterdrops,/ And fall into the ocean, ne'er be found' (ll. 119–20). In his final soliloquy, Faustus's self-assertive spirit collapses into a desire for extinction; his aspiration to divinity into a longing for annihilation as he seeks desperately to escape from 'the heavy wrath of God' (l. 86).

Does this final humbling of Faustus encourage a feeling of satisfaction that he has got what he deserved? That seems to be how the Epilogue sees things. As in the Prologue, the Chorus begins by acknowledging Faustus's greatness, but in essence it is issuing a warning to the audience that his terrible fate is what awaits all those 'forward wits' who 'practise more than heavenly power permits' (ll. 7–8). Yet it is arguable that the final soliloquy's powerful evocation of Faustus's agony, coupled with its stress on the horrors of the never-ending suffering to which he has been sentenced, are designed to make us wonder whether the savage punishment really fits the crime. Feelings of pity and fear might seem a more appropriate response to Faustus's end than the Epilogue's tidy moral in its concluding rhyming couplet.

## Morality play or tragedy?

Pity and fear are the emotions that, according to the Greek philosopher Aristotle, are aroused by the experience of watching a tragedy. At the start of this chapter we asked whether *Doctor Faustus* is a late sixteenth-century morality play, designed to teach its audience about the spiritual dangers of excessive learning and ambition. When the play was published, first in 1604 and then in 1616, it was called a 'tragical history' (see Figure 2.6); if we take 'history' here to refer not to a particular dramatic genre but more generally to a narrative or story, then the publisher described the play as a tragic tale. So what is a tragedy? In fact, 'tragedy' is a notoriously difficult literary term to define, for it seems to take various forms in different historical periods. But for the sake of discussion, we can fall back on the broad strokes of Aristotle's description (in the *Poetics*) of the tragedies he had seen in Athens in the fourth century BCE: tragedies are plays that represent a central action or plot that is serious and significant. They involve a socially prominent main character who is neither evil nor morally perfect, who moves from a state of happiness to a state of misery because of some frailty or error of judgement: this is the tragic hero, the remarkable individual whose fall stimulates in the spectator intense feelings of pity and fear. You will be thinking more about the definition of tragedy and the tragic hero when you come to study *The Burial at Thebes* in Book 3.

To what extent does *Doctor Faustus* conform to this description of a tragic play? Well, it follows the classic tragic trajectory in so far as it starts out with the protagonist at the pinnacle of his achievement and ends with his fall into misery, death and (in this case) damnation. From the beginning the play identifies its protagonist not as 'everyman', the morality play hero who 'stands for' all of us, but as the exceptional protagonist of tragic drama. Moreover, it is certainly possible to argue that Faustus brings about his own demise through his catastrophically ill-advised decision to embrace black magic. Perhaps most importantly, we have seen in the course of this chapter that Faustus is consistently presented to us as an intermediate character, neither wholly good nor wholly bad: both brilliant and arrogant, learned and foolish, consumed with intellectual curiosity and possessed of insatiable appetites for worldly pleasure, a conscience-stricken rebel against divine power. We have seen as well how skilfully Marlowe uses the soliloquy to create a powerful illusion of a complex inner life: from Faustus's first proud rejection of the university curriculum and his exuberant daydreams of unlimited power, to his anguished self-questioning and final terrified confrontation with the divine authority he defied, the play gives us access to the thoughts and feelings of a dramatic character whose fall, whether or not we feel it is deserved, seems to call for a fuller emotional response than the Epilogue's moralising can provide.

## 2.3   HERO AND AUTHOR

What, if anything, does *Doctor Faustus* tell us about its notorious author? Having read the play, do you feel that it supports or invalidates the dominant view of Marlowe as the bad boy of Elizabethan drama? There is certainly no doubt that the play has a defiant streak, that it calls into question the justice of a universe that places restrictions on human achievement and demands the eternal suffering of those who disobey its laws. On this level, it does seem to be the work of an author disinclined to take orthodox beliefs on trust, who bears some

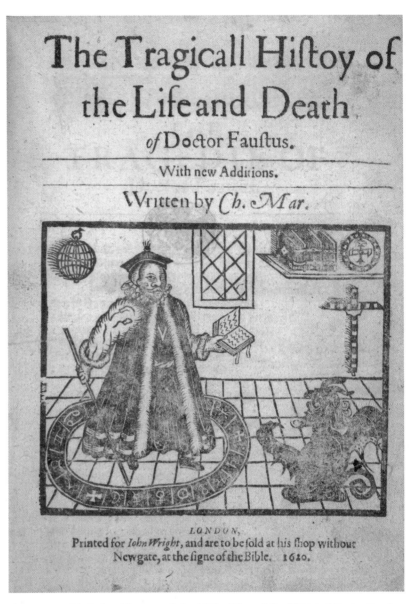

The Tragicall Hiftoy of
the Life and Death
*of* Doctor Fauftus.

With new Additions.

Written by *Ch. Mar.*

LONDON,
Printed for *Iohn Wright*, and are to be fold at his fhop without
Newgate, at the figne of the Bible.  1620.

Figure 2.6   This is the title page of the 1620 edition of the 'B' text of *Doctor Faustus*, first published in 1616: *The Tragicall History of the Life and Death of Doctor Faustus*. British Library, London. *c.* 1891–6 C.39.c.26. Photo: By permission of the British Library. (For the differences between the 'A' text and the 'B' text, see pp. 121–2 of the set text.)

resemblance to the restless, irreverent personality described and decried by the likes of Baines and Beard. However, we have seen throughout this chapter that this allegedly rebellious figure produced a play that, if it questions divine justice, also insists on the egoism and sheer wrong-headedness of its erring protagonist, and powerfully conveys his feelings of guilt and remorse. Perhaps the play's ambiguity is a measure of how risky it would have been for Marlowe to write a more overtly subversive drama; yet one could also argue that the play's orthodox sentiments are too deeply felt to be dismissed as camouflage for the author's heretical opinions. In the end, all we can say is that Marlowe's treatment of the Faust legend is neither simply orthodox nor simply radical. With its stubborn resistance to single, fixed meanings, *Doctor Faustus* leaves the character and beliefs of its author in shadow. Yet if we cannot finally assess the accuracy of Marlowe's reputation as a rebel and outsider, I hope that your reading of the play has made clear why he also has a reputation as a pioneer of English drama.

## REFERENCES

Cheney, P. (2004) 'Introduction: Marlowe in the twenty-first century', in Cheney, P. (ed.) *The Cambridge Companion to Christopher Marlowe*, Cambridge, Cambridge University Press, pp. 1–23.

Healy, T. (2004) '*Doctor Faustus*', in Cheney, P. (ed.) *The Cambridge Companion to Christopher Marlowe*, Cambridge, Cambridge University Press, pp. 174–92.

Hopkins, L. (2000) *Christopher Marlowe: A Literary Life*, Basingstoke, Palgrave.

Maclure, M. (1979) *Marlowe: The Critical Heritage*, London, Routledge and Kegan Paul.

Sinfield, A. (1983) *Literature in Protestant England*, London, Croom Helm.

Stachniewski, J. (1991) *The Persecutory Imagination: English Puritanism and the Literature of Religious Despair*, Oxford, Clarendon Press.

## FURTHER READING

You may find it interesting to look at one or more of the following:

Dabbs, T. (1991) *Reforming Marlowe: The Nineteenth-Century Canonization of a Renaissance Dramatist*, London, Associated University Presses.

Kuriyama, C.B. (2002) *Christopher Marlowe: A Renaissance Life*, Ithaca, NY, Cornell University Press.

Levin, H. (1954) *The Overreacher: A Study of Christopher Marlowe*, London, Faber and Faber.

Sales, R. (1991) *Christopher Marlowe*, New York, St Martin's Press.

# 3 CÉZANNE

*Charles Harrison*

| 3.1 | CÉZANNE'S RENOWN | 57 |
|-----|------------------|----|
| 3.2 | TERMS AND TECHNIQUES | 63 |
| 3.3 | TRADITION AND MODERNITY | 66 |
| 3.4 | THE MODERN NUDE | 68 |
| 3.5 | THE ARTISTS' ARTIST | 71 |
| 3.6 | PAINTING THE LANDSCAPE | 72 |
| 3.7 | 'SUCH PURE THINGS' | 76 |
| 3.8 | A STILL LIFE AND ITS VALUE | 78 |
| 3.9 | SCHOLARS AND OWNERS | 81 |
| REFERENCES | | 84 |
| FURTHER READING | | 84 |

## MATERIALS YOU WILL NEED

- Illustration Book (this contains the 'Plates' referred to in the chapter)
- Though we shall necessarily be considering reproductions of the painter's works, it is important to bear in mind that there is no real substitute for first-hand encounter with the paintings themselves.

## AIMS

This chapter will:

- introduce you to the work of the French artist Paul Cézanne
- encourage you to consider the reasons for his reputation
- provide some general introduction to the art of painting and some grounding in relevant technical terms and concepts
- encourage you to consider relevant principles of composition
- help you discover meaning and value in the relationships between works of different kinds.

## 3.1  CÉZANNE'S RENOWN

Paul Cézanne lived from 1839 to 1906. Figure 3.1 illustrates a work in the category known as still life, painted when Cézanne was in his fifties. In May 1999 it was sold for $60.5 million (or £36.9 million). At the time this was the fourth highest price ever paid at auction for a painting. Where sums of this magnitude are at stake, other kinds of value become hard to hold on to. To ask whether or not this is 'a good painting' seems somehow beside the point. It is not a particularly large work. Its subject matter is unremarkable. But it does seem that the name of Cézanne must stand for something extraordinary in the history of art if its attachment to so apparently humble a picture can attract so gross an investment. In what follows we will consider the nature and formation of the artist's reputation over the course of his working life and since. We will return to the still life shown in Figure 3.1 at the end of the chapter (for a higher quality reproduction of this figure, see Plate 1.3.1 in the Illustration Book).

Figure 3.1   Paul Cézanne, *Still Life, Curtain, Jug and Compotier. c.*1893–94, oil on canvas, 59 x 72 cm. Private collection, USA. Photo: akg-images/Erich Lessing.

Cézanne was born in Aix-en-Provence in the south of France. His father achieved some prosperity in a business making hats, and in 1848 became one of two partners in a small bank. His mother was a former worker in the hattery, whom his father married five years after their son was born. At the end of 1858, following a successful career at school, Paul Cézanne was obliged by his father to enrol as a student of law, a course he pursued for over two years. At the same time, however, he was taking classes at the free school of drawing in Aix. In 1861 he travelled to Paris, following a path marked out by his childhood friend, the novelist Emile Zola, who had left for Paris three years earlier. His aim was to establish himself as a painter. The sense of vocation that the two friends fostered in each other can be measured in their surviving correspondence. Responding in the spring of 1860 to an expression of frustration on Cézanne's part, Zola wrote:

> There are two men inside the artist, the poet and the worker. One is born a poet, one becomes a worker. And you, who have the spark, who possess what cannot be acquired, you complain when all you have to do to succeed is exercise your fingers, become a worker.

(Letter of 16 April 1860, in Zola, 1978, p. 146)

The roots of this kind of distinction between the poet and the worker lie in the Romantic movement of the late eighteenth and early nineteenth centuries. The legacy of that movement shows in the assumption, shared between the young writer and the aspiring painter, that true artists are born with the spark of imagination and have only to 'exercise [their] fingers' – with its corollary that technical accomplishment alone cannot make an artist. No doubt this same assumption also served as the means to assert a youthful ambition against the rigours of academic training. What is distinctive about the career of Cézanne is that to the end of his life and beyond he was to be regarded by the majority of both his admirers and his detractors in terms consistent with this typically adolescent self-image: as someone possessed of an authentic 'artistic temperament', who continued to struggle with the problems of technique. (The term technique refers to those – typically manual – procedures for performing an operation that tend to require practice, and that improve with practice. In this context the relevant procedures were drawing, especially drawing from nature and from the model, and painting, involving not simply the controlled application of paint but also experience in the mixing and interrelating of colours. The possibility of development in an artist's work will normally depend upon some change or extension of technique. It could therefore be said that the only artists who *don't* encounter technical problems are those who are content simply to repeat themselves.)

At the time during the 1860s and 1870s when Cézanne was working largely in Paris, the French art-world was dominated by the annual Salon. This was a large public exhibition to which anyone could submit work, but which was heavily influenced by the traditional values of the Academy of Fine Arts, with entries vetted by a jury of senior professionals. Before the late nineteenth century, those who failed to get noticed in the Salon had little prospect of establishing any kind of career, since there were then few independent dealers' galleries where aspiring artists might hope to be shown. Cézanne's first recorded submissions to the Salon were probably made in 1863, but it was not until 1882 that he managed to have a work admitted. In 1874 he took part in the first exhibition of an independent group of artists who banded together to share the expenses of showing their work outside the Salon. This was the group that came to be known as the Impressionists. The formation of this group is of particular importance to the history of art in the modern period. It serves to mark a growing division in the wider world of European culture at the time: a separation between traditionalists, who looked to established principles of training, technique and composition, and modernists who believed that art should represent and stimulate a specifically contemporary sensibility. The artists involved included Claude Monet, Camille Pissarro, Auguste Renoir, Berthe Morisot, Alfred Sisley and Edgar Degas. Plate 1.3.2 (in the Illustration Book) illustrates a representative work by Pissarro that was included in 1874. The Impressionist exhibitions continued sporadically until 1886, though Cézanne only showed with the group once more when he submitted a group of works to the third exhibition in 1877.

Figure 3.2   Paul Cézanne, *The House of the Hanged Man at Auvers,* 1872–73, oil on canvas, 55 x 66 cm, Musée d'Orsay, Paris. Photo ©: RMN/Hervé Lewandowski.

Figure 3.2 illustrates one of the paintings that Cézanne showed with the independents in 1874 (this is also reproduced as Plate 1.3.3). Published reviews of the exhibition varied from moderate support to scathing dismissal. A reviewer signing himself 'Jean Prouvaire' was one of several who singled Cézanne out for particular ridicule.

Shall we mention Cézanne, who, by the way, has his own legend? No known jury has ever, even in its dreams, imagined the possibility of accepting a single work by this painter, who came to the Salon carrying his paintings on his back, like Jesus Christ carrying his cross.

('Prouvaire', 1874, in Moffat, 1966, p. 126)

Reviewing the Impressionist exhibition three years later, however, another writer named George Rivière compared Cézanne's work to some of the most prestigious works from the classical canon:

M. Cézanne's works are those of a Greek of the classical period; his canvases have the tranquil and heroic serenity of antique painting and pottery, and the fools who laugh at *les Baigneurs*, for instance, make me think of barbarians criticizing the Parthenon. M. Cézanne is a painter, and a great painter. Those who have never wielded a brush or pencil have said that he can't draw, and they have identified 'flaws' in his work which are in fact deliberate refinements, the result of his enormous skill.

(Rivière, 1877, in Harrison et al., 1998, p. 596)

A work similar to the picture Rivière referred to is illustrated in Plate 1.3.4. This is one of the earliest in a long series of paintings of bathers that the artist produced between the 1870s and his death in 1906. These show nude or near-nude figures – usually females – in outdoor settings. To label these works as 'bathers' is not necessarily to imply that the pictured figures have actually been swimming or washing. Rather, it is to identify a type of subject-matter or genre. **Genre** is a conventional term meaning 'kind', originally used in the late seventeenth century to refer to different classes of subject-matter in painting, such as history painting, landscape, portraiture, still life and scenes from everyday life. Cézanne's pictures of bathers occupy a substantial proportion of his total output. In 1989 an exhibition was mounted in Basle that was devoted entirely to his works in this vein. It included some 130 pictures in oil and watercolours from over 200 that survive (see Krumrine, 1990). Plate 1.3.5 illustrates one of the last and largest of these. Cézanne was probably working on this painting up to the time of his death in 1906.

**Activity**  Make some brief notes now in order to describe this picture and to record your initial response to it. (It may help if you imagine that you are doing this for the benefit of a friend who doesn't have access to the work.) The purpose of this activity is twofold: the task of description will help you to concentrate on the painting's appearance; and what you write will provide you with a point to which you can return towards the end of the chapter, when you will be able to assess whether what you have learned about Cézanne's work has made any difference to your initial impressions. Be assured that there is no 'correct' response to the picture. So long as you take the trouble to examine it carefully, you will gain most at this stage by being as straightforward as possible about your view of the work.

The genre of bathers has a long history in European painting. In the Italian Renaissance during the late fifteenth and sixteenth centuries, most paintings and sculptures were devoted to the illustration of biblical and other religious texts. But the surviving literature of Latin poetry and prose provided some justification for works of a different kind. A picture of an attractive nude woman could be a 'Venus', the goddess of love; a collection of nudes imagined in an outdoor setting could be nymphs, the spirits that peopled the landscape in classical mythology – and notably in the work of the Latin poet Ovid – as personifications of different aspects of the natural world. From the point of view of the painters and their patrons, the most popular of nymphs were the Naiads, the spirits of rivers, who could most reasonably be expected to appear unclothed. Plate 1.3.6 illustrates a picture of bathing nymphs by the Venetian painter Palma Vecchio ('Vecchio' means 'the older'). Stories of the loves of the gods provided further justifications for displays of nudity. Plate 1.3.8 shows a painting by Antonio Allegri, known as Correggio, on the theme of Leda and the Swan. In classical mythology, Leda was one of the various mortal women seduced by the god Zeus, who adopted a different disguise in each case. He appeared to Leda in the form of a swan and the union produced two pairs of children, one of whom was the future Helen of Troy. (Cézanne painted a picture of Leda and the Swan, probably in the late 1880s; see Plate 1.3.9.) By the end of the sixteenth century, paintings such as Palma Vecchio's and Correggio's – large pictures of nymphs in landscape settings, of the various loves of the gods, or of Venuses – were to be found in princely collections throughout Europe.

For the purposes of art, reference to such classical themes as these gave a kind of respectable cultural gloss to the natural connection between bathing and nudity, a connection that artists continued to exploit over the next two centuries. Plate 1.3.7 reproduces a work painted in 1765 by the French artist Jean-Honoré Fragonard. By the mid nineteenth century the term 'baignade' – meaning a scene of bathing – had become firmly established in France as the label for a certain type of ambitious painted scenario. In enterprises such as these, artists measured their practical skills against the comparable achievements of their predecessors in two respects that were both central to the art of painting and pleasing to the (generally male) spectator: by managing a coherent illusion of broad and deep pictorial space, and by providing plausible representations of the nude figure in a variety of poses.

But if this is the context in which we should be considering Cézanne's large *Bathers* (Plate 1.3.5), there seems to be something of a problem – or a paradox at least. On the one hand, if we take our measures of artistic achievement from such traditional examples of the genre as Palma Vecchio's or Correggio's, or even Fragonard's, his painting appears deficient in both the supposedly crucial respects I have cited.

It would be quite understandable if your observations on Cézanne's picture have been less than enthusiastic. Where the compositions of the earlier works present an open and measured passage from foreground into depth, allowing the absorbed spectator to imagine some interaction with their figures, the picture space of Cézanne's work seems dense and hard to read, while his nudes appear relatively lumpy and unconvincing. When this painting was acquired by the National Gallery in London in 1964 there was certainly considerable public disagreement about its merits. Ninety years after the artist was singled out among the Impressionists for particular attack by Prouvaire, sections of the British press ridiculed the later painting of *Bathers* of *c*. 1900–06, and responded with expressions of incredulity at the price that was paid for it. (The money was raised with a gift of £225,000 from the Max Rayne Foundation and with a special subvention from the Treasury.)

At the same time, Cézanne's *Bathers* occupies a virtually unequalled position in the history of art as this is represented in the national collections in Britain. The National Gallery contains one of the world's most celebrated accumulations of paintings devoted to the development of the western tradition since the late thirteenth century. With the opening of Tate Modern at London's Bankside in 2001, an agreement was reached whereby the more established museum would restrict its collecting to the period before 1900, leaving the period since – the period of the 'modern' – to be covered by the newer institution. (The old Tate Gallery at Millbank, renamed Tate Britain, is now primarily reserved for the collection and display of British art of all periods.) It is an open question whether Cézanne's *Bathers* was ever finished to his satisfaction, but it was certainly worked on well into the twentieth century. In being retained by the National Gallery it thus seems more markedly than any other single work in the national collections to be positioned as a bridge between one epoch of art and the next. It both marks the very end of the long tradition of figurative painting represented in the National Gallery, and serves as a potential point of entry to the **avant-garde** art of the modern period represented at Bankside. (In the French military vocabulary from which it is borrowed, the term 'avant-garde' designates an advanced fighting force. When applied to artists, writers and musicians it serves to identify those considered pioneers in the development of specifically *modern* forms.) Pablo Picasso and Henri Matisse – both featured at Tate Modern – were among the major artists of the twentieth century who responded to the *Bathers* in 1907 when it was shown in Paris in a memorial exhibition following Cézanne's death. Plate 1.3.10 reproduces one of the many sketches of bathers in the open air that Picasso made in the period 1907–08. Plate 1.3.11 reproduces one of the largest of several paintings Matisse made on the same theme.

## 3.2 TERMS AND TECHNIQUES

In exploring the paradox that Cézanne's *Bathers* presents we gain some understanding of the complex nature of his reputation, for it was in the context of heated arguments about the very nature of skill and ambition in art that that reputation developed. The arguments in question were largely conducted between the defenders of certain traditional values and the supporters of what became known as modern art. It is clear from the reviews of the Impressionist exhibitions cited earlier that of all the young independent artists, Cézanne was the one around whose work critical opinion tended to polarise. As Rivière noted in 1877,

> The artist who has been most maligned and misjudged over the last fifteen years by press and public alike is M. Cézanne. There is no epithet so vile that it has not been used to describe him, and his works have been rewarded with the hysterical laughter that we still hear today.

> (Rivière, 1877, in Harrison et al., 1998, p. 596)

In the view of hindsight, the wide differences of opinion about his work serve vividly to demonstrate the gap that had already grown between traditional and 'modern' views on art.

To those who viewed Cézanne's paintings with an eye to traditional standards of artistic skill and competence, they appeared simply worthless. Yet for the English critic Clive Bell, writing in 1914 and speaking for a gathering army of supporters of the modern movement in art, the painter was 'the Christopher Columbus of a new continent of form', the person who 'In so far as one man can be said to inspire a whole age ... inspires the contemporary movement' (Bell, 1914, pp. 207, 199). In fact, it would be a mistake to regard Cézanne as 'the first modern artist'. No one person alone could be held responsible for initiating the kinds of change in artistic values and priorities that are now associated with the concept of modernism. But to examine what is distinctive about Cézanne's painting is to learn a great deal about the more general tendencies that led the 'avant-garde' art of the later nineteenth and early twentieth centuries to diverge from an established tradition traceable back to the early Renaissance.

At the heart of the early disagreements between modern and traditional views of Cézanne lay a significant misunderstanding. Imagine a panel of jurors at the French Salon around 1884. So far as these jurors are concerned, a well-painted picture of bathers will look something like the work illustrated in Plate 1.3.12. This is by William-Adolphe Bouguereau, a regular and popular exhibitor in the Salon, the recipient of some prestigious public commissions and, after 1888, professor at the Academy of Fine Arts in Paris. Let us say that what Cézanne submits is the work illustrated in Figure 3.3 (also reproduced as Plate 1.3.13). The two pictures are clearly very different.

Figure 3.3    Paul Cézanne, *The Three Bathers, c.* 1879–82, oil on canvas, 52 x 55 cm. Musée de la Ville de Paris, Musée du Petit Palais, Giraudon/The Bridgeman Art Library.

In the next section I shall suggest that you make a comparison between the two pictures. First, though, in order to give added purpose to this comparison, I will introduce some terms and definitions, and offer a basic practical lesson in technique. After working through this section you should be better equipped to sort out specific aspects of the paintings we are looking at.

**Delineation** refers to the representation of shapes and details by means of drawing.

**Modelling** refers to the technical means used to represent figures and objects as three-dimensional. In drawing and painting, modelling involves assuming a direction and fall of light, normally from the side. (An object lit from directly in front tends to appear relatively flattened, whereas an object lit from behind tends to appear as a silhouette.) A given fall of light, whether observed or assumed, will distinguish lit from unlit surfaces, and will impart a particular quality to the transition from one to the other: gradual when the light is subdued and diffused, abrupt when it is bright and concentrated. The technique used to convey the quality of this transition is known as **shading**. Plate 1.3.14 shows a shaded drawing of a posed male model, made by Cézanne at the Académie Suisse in Paris around 1865.

In standard academic practice, modelling involves establishing relations of **tone**. Tone is the range from lightest light (pure white) to darkest dark (pure black). In painting, the more that black is mixed with a given colour, the darker its tone will be. An artist may exploit dramatic contrasts of tone, or may use a relatively even range of tones.

**Activity**
*You don't need to be able to draw for this. The point is simply to help you to see how shading and tone work to establish modelling.*

Take a pencil and a sheet of paper and draw two small circles some distance apart. On the first circle, gently shade the left-hand side, making the transition from dark to light as gradual as you can. On the second circle, shade the left-hand side much more firmly, leaving a more marked division between the darkest tone (black) and the lightest (white). Your two circles have now been 'modelled' into two spheres, both lit from the right, one appearing as though seen in a soft and diffused light, the other implying a brighter and more concentrated light source. With such simple differences in shading, differences in mood and atmosphere may already be suggested. Finally, draw a plain rectangular frame round each sphere, so that each forms part of a simple picture – as it might be of a ball hanging in space.

You now have a pair of elementary figures in simple spatial grounds. This illusion of space is the result of the modelling. You would not be able to see either circle *as* a sphere unless you could imagine the surrounding surface of white paper as having depth sufficient to contain it. This kind of imaginary depth is known as **picture space** – the virtual world within which all of a picture's represented contents are contained.

The frontier between this virtual world and the actual world in which the viewer stands is known as the **picture plane**. This is a virtual vertical surface that defines the nearest extent of the picture space and includes all that the painting's spectator is imagined as seeing. It is thus a crucial element of **composition.** (In the language of computing technology, a virtual surface is one that does not physically exist but is made by software to appear as though it does.) The picture plane works much like the proscenium arch in a theatre, which serves to mark a conventional divide between the real world of the audience and the fictional world of the play. Imagine a painting of a man seen near-to, who is pointing an outstretched arm and finger towards you, so that the finger seems to come as near as it can without poking through the surface. Now imagine that you reach out to touch that finger. The picture plane is like a sheet of glass that runs through the point where the fingers would touch if they could. In fact, of course, what you would actually touch is the **literal surface** of the canvas, and in doing so you would – as it were – be breaking a spell cast by the painting's illusionistic properties. To recover the power of the illusion you would need to step back and adopt a viewing distance appropriate to the picture. The point to remember is that while literal picture surface and picture plane normally coincide, the one is real and tangible, the other virtual and visual. (We will return to consideration of the relationship between picture plane and picture surface in Section 3.6.)

**Brushwork** is the evidence of the means of application of paint that is left on the literal surface of the painting. It is one of the factors that most clearly define the individual artist's style and technique. During the period we are considering, artists' oil-painting brushes varied greatly in texture, from very soft to bristly, and in size from a few hairs' width to several centimetres. Whereas artists working in classical styles tended deliberately to smooth over the evidence of application of paint, typically the Impressionists applied their paint with comparatively stiff square-ended brushes, leaving the separate coloured touches often unblended on the surfaces of their pictures. One effect of this was to make it harder for the spectator to ignore the coincidence of the literal surface with the picture plane, so that however appealing the represented content of the *picture* might be, the *painting* would always also be experienced as a decorated surface.

## 3.3   TRADITION AND MODERNITY

Activity

Now make some notes on the differences between the two paintings of bathers (Plates 1.3.12 and 1.3.13). Consider particularly the treatment and expressions of the figures, the relationship of figures to surrounding space and background, and the evidence of brushwork.

Discussion

There are three particular differences that strike me as important. The first is in the delineation and modelling of the figures. Though Bouguereau has not given his women an explicitly classical setting, they are clearly studied from models adopting conventional statuesque poses, they are proportioned according to traditional notions of female beauty, and they are smoothly and gradually modelled. The light is directed into the picture from the left, so that the right-hand side of the figures is cast into a soft shade. The basic organisation of the picture is tonal; that's to say Bouguereau has mixed various amounts of black and white into his colours to produce the graduations of tone that suggest rounded forms in an even light. Cézanne's women, on the other hand, are more robust – the one at the right in particular being far from the classical ideal – and they are painted as though caught in motion. The light is directed onto the figures from the near left; that is to say from this side of the picture plane – the imaginary screen that is supposed to separate the world of the picture from the world of the imagined spectator. The modelling is much rougher than in the Bouguereau. In accordance with Impressionist practice, Cézanne has eliminated black from his palette, using a deep blue for the darkest areas, and contrasting this with a bright yellow where the sun catches the trees in the middle distance.

This leads me to the second major difference I observe, which is in the quality of the brushwork, and in the relations between figure and background that result. Bouguereau has worked for a smoothly graduated surface, blending one touch into another, and has projected his figures against a deep and relatively empty space. But Cézanne leaves each mark of the brush distinct, so that the entire surface has a mosaic-like quality. Even the figures are clearly composed of separate touches, with a considerable range of colours being used to convey the sensation of flesh tones in full sunlight. Though Cézanne's pictured women have a kind of sculptural solidity, the space within which they are placed seems relatively shallow and densely filled.

The third difference is in what I think of as the emotional or psychological qualities of the pictures. Bouguereau particularises the expressions of his two women, giving them a self-consciously absorbed and abstracted air that colours the mood of the picture as a whole. In the case of Cézanne's picture, on the other hand, two of the women have their backs to the spectator, while the features of the third are so sketchily indicated that it would be hard to attribute any specific emotional state to the woman represented.

Now imagine our jurors reflecting upon these differences in 1884. Given the professional standing of Bouguereau and the public success of his work, I think it likely that each significant departure from the type of work that his 'baignade' represents would have been read as a sign of incompetence. That's to say, the jurors would probably have seen Cézanne's picture not as a successful attempt to paint the picture that actually emerged, but rather as a failed attempt to paint a picture like Bouguereau's – the failure being attributable to a sheer lack of technical skill. How, after all, could any professional painter *mean* to produce a work in which the figures were so roughly modelled and so unbeautiful, in which the picture space was so shallow and uncertainly defined, and in which the spectator was deprived of any prospect of emotional engagement with the women represented?

To say that the appearance of Cézanne's picture was a consequence of incompetence – that it was not what he *meant* to produce – was, in effect, to say that his work was meaning*less*. (Over the course of the next century, criticism in these terms was often to be levelled at the artists of the modern movement by the defenders of traditional values.) In fact, if evidence is needed of Cézanne's ability to produce faithful and delicate likenesses, it is there in abundance. Look, for example, at the drawing reproduced in Plate 1.3.15 of his partner Hortense with a spray of hydrangeas. (The French word for hydrangea is hortensia. Cézanne had met Hortense Fiquet in 1869. Though their son Paul was born in 1872, the couple were not married until 1886, Cézanne being sure that his father would not approve of the match.) We also know that far from meaning to emulate Bouguereau's work, Cézanne hated and despised everything it stood for. In 1874 he had written to his mother that he had to work hard in order *not* to acquire that 'final perfection which earns the admiration of imbeciles'. Echoing his earlier correspondence with Zola, he added, 'and this thing which is commonly appreciated so much is merely the effect of craftsmanship and renders all work resulting from it inartistic and common' (Letter of 26 September 1874, in Harrison et al., 1998, p. 549).

So what the Salon jurors no doubt took for the unintentional signs of involuntary incompetence were actually the intentional consequences of the artist's determination to do things differently. He *meant* his painting to look as it did. To put the point another way, it was in its very difference from the prevailing academic standard that the meaning of the painting was to be found. And it was central to that 'meaning' that artistic quality was somehow at odds with, or was inhibited by, the acquisition of academic technique and the exercise of craftsmanship as conventionally understood.

What is clear is that in the late nineteenth century there was considerable and growing disagreement over the matter of how 'artistic quality' was to be defined and measured (and it has certainly become no clearer since then). The one thing that Cézanne's contemporary defenders were sure of was that it was produced by an unusual strength of feeling in the painter. This was the clear sign of the artist's authenticity. In the view of Rivière, 'In all his pictures the artist moves us, because he himself has already experienced violent emotions when confronted with nature, and used his skill to transfer them to canvas' (Rivière, 1877, in Harrison et al., 1998, p. 597). But how is this to be reconciled with the observation that the figures in Cézanne's bathers are given none of the expressive features that in Bouguereau's largely serve to establish the emotional aspect of the picture? To address this question is to get to the very heart of the case against traditional art as it was made by the defenders of the modern.

## 3.4   THE MODERN NUDE

What was at issue was the relationship between three crucial factors: the imagined world represented by the work of art, the physical and technical character of the work – the paint on canvas of which it was composed – and the experience of the spectator. The criticism the modernists levelled at such work as Bouguereau's was that its supposed emotional content was unoriginal and bogus. Its effects were achieved by playing on the thoroughly conventional associations evoked by certain poses and situations and types of likeness, so as to draw the spectator into a thoroughly familiar range of sentiments. To support the idea of a *modern* art was to regard the work of art as something made out of the materials of the present: drawing on the sensation of real rather than literary or mythological scenes and figures, executed in an original style so as to engage the spectator actively with its actual colours and forms, and stimulating to a fresh emotional response rather than a reassuring sentimentality. (By sentimentality I understand a tendency to cultivate and to respond to the *appearance* of emotion. It is associated with a tendency to coerce the feelings of others. Think of the effect the dreamy expressions of Bouguereau's painted women were no doubt intended to have on the spectator.)

The idea of a specifically '*modern* beauty' had been raised in a review of the Salon as early as 1846 (Baudelaire, 1846, in Harrison et al., 1998, pp. 301–4). Its author was the poet and critic Charles Baudelaire (1821–67), who played an early and dominant role in establishing the imagery and vocabulary of modernity in art and

literature. Seventeen years later he published a long and highly
influential essay in which he characterised 'The painter of modern
life', using as his exemplar – or as the cat's paw of his argument – a
then little-known watercolourist and illustrator called Constantin Guys
(see Plate 1.3.18). Baudelaire conceived of the artist as a kind of
receptive surface, whose consciousness registered the distinctive
flavour of the present as he passed through the typical locations of the
modern city. In a crucial passage on 'Modernity', Baudelaire
proposed that art demands a kind of tension between its abiding
traditional values and its preoccupation with the fleeting aspects of
the present. 'By "modernity" I mean the ephemeral, the fugitive, the
contingent, the half of art whose other half is the eternal and the
immutable.' Reviewing the works then being exhibited in Paris,
he diagnosed a tendency among painters to 'dress all their subjects
in the garments of the past', as though by this means they could evade
the contrasting demands of the present – or of 'Realism', to use a term
that was prevalent in the art and literary criticism of the 1850s and
1860s (Baudelaire, 1863, in Harrison et al., 1998, p. 497).

If we return to our comparison with Baudelaire's strictures in mind we
may get a better understanding of what was at issue at the time in the
contrast between two paintings such as these. It was in part a matter of
just *how* the balance between tradition and modernity was to be struck.
Of course, a nude woman is always by definition *un*dressed, and thus
might be thought always potentially timeless, unless, that is, she is
somehow set within a recognisable context. In fact, the 'proper'
context for the nude in academic practice was an idealised classical
world. To set an undressed figure in the present was to imply some
immorality – on the part of the pictured figure, or of the artist, or of
both. One such explicitly *modern* nude was exhibited in the Paris
Salon in 1865 by the French artist Edouard Manet, and it caused a
considerable scandal (see Plate 1.3.16). By combining a pose
associated with representations of Venus with a setting that
unmistakably referred to the world of the contemporary prostitute,
Manet brought the traditional and the modern into a collision with
which very few commentators at the time could cope. The prevailing
response, as with Cézanne's early submissions to the Salon, was to
accuse Manet of incompetence; that's to say, to defuse the critical
effect of the painting by implying that it was actually accidental and
unintended.

Cézanne later referred to *Olympia* as marking the beginning of 'our
Renaissance' (as reported by Joaquim Gasquet, in Gasquet, 1991
[1921], p. 71). He had shown his own version of the subject in the first
exhibition of the independent artists in 1874, including a self-portrait
in the position of the prostitute's assumed client and giving it the title
*A Modern Olympia* (Figure 3.4 and Plate 1.3.17). It is significant,
however, that his own painted nudes tend almost always to avoid the
kind of direct confrontation with the gaze of the viewer that is so

dramatic in Manet's *Olympia*. They also tend to be arranged in landscape settings, and to be devoid of the kind of cues that would pin them down to a given present. What makes Cézanne's bathers appear relatively 'modern' is the simple fact that they *don't* appear classical either in setting or in style. Remove from the nude figures the insulating illusion of a golden age, allow their bodies to be possibly imperfect, and it is as though the whole scenario is forcefully projected into the here and now. At the same time the inescapable fact that this is an image constituted out of dabs of paint on canvas makes it very much harder for the spectator to project himself in fantasy into a world established on the other side of the picture plane, and thus to escape from the critical demands of the present. (My use of the masculine form for the spectator is deliberate, chosen with the coy self-consciousness of Bouguereau's pictured nudes in view. What I mean by this is that Bouguereau's carefully staged nudes seem to assume the kind of interest that a male spectator would bring to bear. By contrast, if Cézanne's painting was made with a largely male audience in mind, there is nevertheless nothing about his picture to suggest that a man is likely to be *better qualified* to enjoy it than a woman.)

There is one possible contradiction that you may have noticed. Given that modernism is generally associated with a rejection of the classical tradition, how is this claim for the relative 'modernity' of Cézanne's work to be reconciled with Rivière's assessment, quoted above, that

Figure 3.4    Paul Cézanne, *A Modern Olympia,* 1873, oil on canvas, 46 x 55 cm. Musée d'Orsay, Paris. Photo ©: RMN/Hervé Lewandowski.

the painter resembles 'a Greek of the classical period'? The answer lies in the nature of the resemblance Rivière had in mind. He was not suggesting that Cézanne was painting in a classical style, which in the 1870s he evidently was not; rather that his painting had 'the indefinable attraction of biblical and Greek antiquity' and that his figures were 'as simple and as noble' as those of classical sculpture (Rivière, 1877, in Harrison et al., p. 597). What he was trying to convey, I think, was that rather than conforming to a certain style, Cézanne's work appeared like a point of origin for what might come after. For the spectator, the measure of this 'originality' was the emotion the work gave rise to – an emotion deriving ultimately from the strength and freshness of the artist's own feelings before nature.

Baudelaire had made a related point about the ideal 'painter of modern life':

> The child sees everything in a state of newness; he is always *drunk*. Nothing more resembles what we call inspiration than the delight with which a child absorbs form and colour ... Genius is nothing more nor less than *childhood recovered* at will – a childhood now equipped for self-expression with manhood's capacities and a power of analysis which enables it to order the mass of raw material which it has involuntarily accumulated.
>
> (Baudelaire, 1863, in Harrison et al., 1998, pp. 495 6)

This image of the modern artist as someone who preserves a childlike strength and freshness of response was to persist in criticism and theory over the next hundred years – and Cézanne was to retain a prominent place among those from whose work this image was constructed. Its corollary was the idea of the hide-bound traditionalist, in thrall to the past and restricted by convention and precedent, whose work might reassure but could never provoke and challenge the viewer. This is how Bouguereau was widely viewed at the end of the nineteenth century. By that time the supporters of the modern were in the ascendant, at least in Paris.

## 3.5   THE ARTISTS' ARTIST

It was a sign of that ascendancy that a public exhibition of Cézanne's work was arranged in 1907, the year following his death. This was the exhibition that made such an impression on Picasso and Matisse. It was held not in the main Salon, however, which had by then largely lost its prestige and authority, but in the Salon d'Automne (Autumn Salon), the newest of four competing Salons founded between 1881 and 1903. For Matisse this was by no means a first acquaintance with Cézanne's paintings of bathers. The *Three Bathers* we have been examining had been in his own possession since 1899, when he had purchased it from the dealer Ambroise Vollard at what was for him then a considerable expense. In 1936 he donated the picture to the Musée du Petit Palais in Paris, where it still hangs. In an accompanying note to the curator he wrote, 'I know this canvas rather well, although I hope not completely; it has provided me with moral support at critical moments in my adventures as an artist; I have drawn from it my faith and my perseverance' (quoted in Cachin et al., 1996, p. 168).

It seems that Cézanne's paintings of bathers exercised a particular hold over other artists as well. Among those besides Matisse who at one time or another owned such works are four fellow members of the Impressionist group – the painters Gustave Caillebotte, Degas, Pissarro and Renoir – together with Pierre Bonnard, a leading French painter of the next generation. In 1957 Picasso was to purchase a work similar to the one owned by Matisse. The English sculptor Henry Moore bought a small composition of bathers in 1960 (see Plate 1.3.19), and the American painter Jasper Johns a small painting of a solitary male bather in 1989. No other group of works by a single painter could be said to have held a comparable fascination for other artists over the entire course of the past century.

One other spectator at the Salon d'Automne in 1907 left a significant record of his interest in Cézanne's work. The German poet Rainer Maria Rilke (1875–1926) paid several visits over the course of the exhibition, registering his growing fascination with the paintings in a series of long letters to his wife (subsequently compiled into a small book). Of the task of understanding the painter's work, he wrote, 'it all takes a long, long time. When I remember the puzzlement and insecurity of one's first confrontation with his work, along with his name, which was just as new. And then for a long time nothing, and suddenly one has the right eyes' (Letter of 10 October 1907, in Rilke, 1988 [1944], p. 43). Rilke had been working as secretary to the French sculptor Auguste Rodin, and was an experienced viewer of the modern art of his day. That he found it necessary to devote time and concentration to Cézanne's work is confirmation of its demanding nature. What he was trying to capture, I think, was the moment at which the painter's work *made sense* to him; when the initial strangeness of its form and technique seemed to be justified by its *effect*.

## 3.6   PAINTING THE LANDSCAPE

One contributory factor in Cézanne's reputation as it developed at the end of the nineteenth century was his apparent attachment to his native Provence. 'When one is born down there ... nothing else means a thing', he wrote to a friend in 1896 (Letter of 23 July 1896 to Philippe Solari, in Smith, 1996, p. 20). The Impressionism of the 1870s was largely an art of the city, its suburbs and its rural surroundings, and those who remarked on the modernity of the Impressionists' paintings tended to attribute it as much to their subject-matter as to their technique. But from the mid 1870s to the end of his life, much of Cézanne's work was devoted to the rural scenery of Provence, which, like his bathers and his still lifes, appeared largely untouched by the social and technological processes of modernisation. After the late 1870s his visits to Paris were to become increasingly short and infrequent, though he maintained relations with several of the principal painters of the Impressionist circle, and especially with Camille Pissarro, in whose company he had learned the Impressionist technique of painting in light touches of relatively pure colour (see Plate 1.3.2). On the one hand his absence from the occasions of the Parisian art-world fed the image of him as a reclusive genius, the strength of whose work derived from a kind of authentic and primitive vigour; on the other, the 'timeless' character of his subjects led other sympathetic critics to discover the kind of 'classical' purity that Rivière had claimed for his paintings.

There is one particular feature of the Provençal landscape that appears in over thirty of Cézanne's paintings. This is Mont Sainte-Victoire. The paintings in question are divided into two groups. The distinctive shape of the mountain appears in some twenty oil paintings from the 1880s, all based on viewpoints that could be reached by a long walk from the painter's childhood home. It is also the dominant motif in eleven canvases and a number of watercolours from 1901 to 1906. These were painted in a studio that Cézanne occupied on a hillside facing the mountain. Plate 1.3.20 illustrates a work from the first series, painted around 1887.

At the time when Cézanne was exhibiting with the independent group in the 1870s, the guiding principle of Impressionism was to achieve a kind of realism in the visual *effects* of nature and of modern life; to capture the fleeting appearance either of the landscape, or of urban or suburban life under specific conditions of light and atmosphere. But while this principle conformed well to the sense of modernity that Baudelaire had associated with 'the ephemeral, the fugitive, the contingent', it tended to be less favourable to those 'eternal and immutable' values that furnished the other half of his recipe for art. Cézanne was to remain committed to the aim of truth to the immediate *sensation* of nature, but he is reported as having said near the end of his life, 'What I wanted was to make of Impressionism something solid and durable, like the art of the museums' (in Harrison and Wood, 2003, p. 42). He also told the younger painter Emile Bernard, 'Imagine Poussin entirely remade from nature, that's what I understand by classical' (quoted in Smith, 1996, p. 28).

The French painter Nicolas Poussin was the major figure in the establishment of a classical style of painting in the mid seventeenth century. He worked principally in Rome, using studies of the actual buildings of Roman and Renaissance Italy and of the surrounding countryside as material for lucid and ordered compositions. Typically peopled with figures from the world of classical and biblical mythology, his landscapes furnished a powerful visual imagery for the idea of a golden age. Plate 1.3.21 illustrates a work of the kind Cézanne is likely to have had in mind.

**Activity**    Bearing in mind the discussion of terms and techniques in Section 3.2, make a brief note of what you see as the principal similarities and differences between Cézanne's landscape reproduced in Plate 1.3.20 and that of Poussin (Plate 1.3.21).

**Discussion**    The principal similarities I notice are all in the basic compositions of the two paintings. Both have tall trees framing the space at the left, both have buildings catching the light slightly further back on the same side, both represent extensive views over a large enclosed area, and both have projecting mountains in the far distance. As to differences, there are marked variations in the scenes depicted – for instance, the absence of any human or animal life in Cézanne's picture, whereas the goatherd and flock provide a point of entry to Poussin's painting – but the main contrasts I notice are in technique, and particularly in the ways in which the two painters handle the relationship between virtual picture plane and actual surface.

This last is a complicated point. Even if you observed the kind of contrast I'm trying to describe, I would not have expected you to express it in quite this way. But the issue is central both to the general study of painting as an art, and to the specific matter of Cézanne's reputation and standing in relation to subsequent art. It is therefore deserving of careful explanation. Looking at the printed reproduction of a landscape set on its white page it is easy to forget that what the painter starts with is a flat textured surface of canvas – a surface that has a clear physical edge. To paint a picture is to do something to that surface so that it will appear *other than flat* – and so that it can then become a self-sufficient imaginative world. Not only must the artist fill the rectangular shape with figures or objects of one kind or another, but in order that those figures and objects can be seen as existing in plausible relation to each other, he or she must produce the illusion of a coherent picture space sufficient to contain them. And if the finished painting is to have the power to affect and to absorb its spectator, as part of this process the artist must establish an imaginary position from which the whole makes sense. Another way to put this is to say that what the artist must do is not only to conceive the scene as something that an imagined spectator is seeing, but also to conceive it *as that* spectator sees it – as if to accord the spectator a certain identity and disposition.

This last point is perhaps easiest to understand in relation to the genre of portraiture and to other pictures in which individual figures are given some appearance of psychological life. Part of what made Manet's *Olympia* so shocking at the time it was first exhibited was the fact that the prostitute's challenging outward stare appeared to presuppose an answering regard from *this* side of the picture plane, where the actual spectator stands. And whose regard could that be but that of her client? In imagining *Olympia* as she might be seen by the other party in an alienated exchange of money for sex, Manet had put the actual spectator in that imaginary client's place – which, of course, was not where the respectable visitors to the Paris Salon wished to be, at least not when anyone else was watching them. This casting of the imaginary spectator as client is the point that Cézanne had clearly appreciated and had made explicit in his own *Modern Olympia* (Plate 1.3.17).

The picture plane, as I mentioned earlier, defines the nearest vertical point of the represented space that the picture contains. Everything on the other side of it is part of the picture's represented content, everything on this side part of the world we inhabit. In traditional classical paintings such as Poussin's, that plane is made more or less transparent. What I mean by this is that the artist customarily works to make spectators forget that what is actually being looked at is a flat surface covered with more or less expensive varieties of pigment. Thus the spectators may the more easily become absorbed in the pictured scene, and in whatever incidents it may contain. In the case of Cézanne's picture, on the other hand, the paint never quite ceases to look like paint, the canvas to appear as a canvas, however compelling the illusion of breadth and distance may be, and however pungent the sense of spatial division created by such incidents as the point at the left where a sharp yellow wall stands out against a deep blue shadow. It is in part this strange tension between represented depth and literal surface that makes Cézanne's painting seem initially so perplexing.

Though the resulting tension was certainly not new to painting, there had been no painting before Cézanne's in which it was tuned to quite so high a pitch, or in which the sheer *transparency* of classical painting's picture plane was so robustly questioned. The implication was that the difficult relationship between the virtual and the actual might be what Cézanne's painting was really about – that it might in some sense be its 'content' or philosophical meaning. This realisation in turn both served to stimulate the interest of critics and art historians in the wider development of modernist technique in painting, and encouraged such younger painters as Picasso and Matisse to place an increased stress on the relationship between virtual content and literal surface. It could even be said that from this point on no painting could properly be conceived as *modern* unless it involved some evident tension between the two.

Plate 1.3.22 illustrates a work from the second series of Cézanne's views of Mont Sainte-Victoire. It is dated to the years 1904–06. What makes this work so intense is the fact that every brushstroke he applied had to satisfy two very different demands. It had to be true to Cézanne's sense of the relative values of light and colour as these defined his intense sensation of the real landscape he was looking at; it had thus to play its part in the composition of colours and tones by which the sense of substance and distance and atmosphere would be reproduced in the eye of the spectator. At the same time, however, each touch of colour had to be adjusted to the dynamic pattern that developed on the literal flat surface of the canvas. It was only through the vividness and autonomy of this artificial decorative thing – the painting in its aspect as an independent, self-sufficient whole – that Cézanne could be assured of some adequate match with the reality and harmony of the natural world as he perceived it.

## 3.7  'SUCH PURE THINGS'

This late picture of the Mont Sainte-Victoire was painted at a time when Cézanne was probably also working on the large picture of bathers reproduced in Plate 1.3.5. It is time now for you to return to this and to look back over your initial description and response to it. Whether or not your liking for the work has increased, I hope you will now have a better understanding of the difficult and conflicting demands that the artist was trying to meet, and thus of why the painting looks the way it does.

One important consideration to bear in mind is that none of the figures in the painting was posed from life. According to his dealer Vollard:

> For his nude compositions, Cézanne used drawings from nature made previously at the Atélier Suisse [see Plate 1.3.14], and, for the rest, he called upon his memories of museums. His dream would have been to have models pose in the open air; but that was unfeasible for many reasons, the most important being that women, even when clothed, frightened him.

> (Vollard, 1914, p. 96)

The Atélier Suisse was the studio where the artist had worked while studying in Paris. The 'memories of museums' to which Vollard refers would have taken the form of poses recalled and sometimes transcribed from the work of earlier painters he admired. In the large *Bathers*, the group of eleven women – with ten in the foreground and one apparently pacing in the middle-distance at the right – was composed from a repertoire of figures that Cézanne assembled and reused over the course of his entire working life, occasionally changing them from one gender to the other. The woman lying diagonally on her stomach at the right centre, for example, can be traced back to a study of a diving figure from the late 1860s (see Plate 1.3.23).

That Cézanne suffered from a fear of women, and in general of being touched, is a well-established component in the mythology of his life. What is perhaps more important for our purposes is that in the imaginary worlds he worked to establish for them, his figures appear compellingly tactile and solid. If the spectator is to be involved with the represented world, however, it will not be by means of an unreal continuity between that world and the actual one in which the spectator stands – a continuity that might be suggested by some such device as an arch outward glance directed through the picture plane by one figure or another. Rather, it is notable that, as in the great majority of Cézanne's paintings of bathers, the figures as a group convey an air of completeness and self-sufficiency. The spectator's imagination may be exercised, but it is not *pandered to*. The very absence of sentimental appeal is a telling feature both of the pictured women and of the painting as a whole.

Following successive visits to the Salon d'Automne in 1907, the poet Rilke attempted to put into words for his wife this particular quality of dispassionateness – the marked absence of sentimentality – that he found in Cézanne's mature works.

**Activity**

Read the following extract from Rilke's letter. This is a difficult passage, partly because Rilke is feeling his way to an understanding as he writes. Approach your reading as a kind of exercise in comprehension, and then test your understanding of its main points against the suggestions I offer in the discussion that follows.

> Without looking at a particular one, standing in the middle between the two rooms, one feels their presence drawing together into a colossal reality. As if these colours could heal one of indecision once and for all. The good conscience of these reds, these blues, their simple truthfulness, it educates you; and if you stand beneath them as acceptingly as possible, it's as if they were doing something for you. You also notice, a little more clearly each time, how necessary it was to go beyond love, too; it's natural after all to love each of these things as one makes it; but if one shows this, one makes it less well; one *judges* it instead of *saying* it. One ceases to be impartial; and the very best – love – stays outside the work, does not enter it, is left aside, untranslated: that's how the painting of sentiments came about [Rilke means painting with merely sentimental appeal] ... It may be that this emptying out of love in anonymous work, which produces such pure things, was never achieved as completely as in the work of this old man ... With this disposition, which was completely developed now, thanks to his strangeness and insularity, he turned to nature and knew how to swallow back his love for every apple and put it to rest in the painted apple forever. Can you imagine what that is like, and what it is like to experience this through him?
>
> (Letter of 13 October 1907, in Rilke, 1998 [1944], pp. 50–1)

**Discussion**

The key point that I think Rilke is trying to make is this: that it is not through the mere sentimental 'showing' of one's emotions that the strong sensation of the world – the 'love for every apple' – becomes invested in the finished painting; rather, it is through the impartial discipline of artistic work. When the sensation is thus 'put to rest' in the work, it becomes possible for it to be recovered and experienced by the spectator who approaches the painting 'as acceptingly as possible' (and who thus has 'the right eyes').

## 3.8   A STILL LIFE AND ITS VALUE

With Rilke's mention of the painted apple it is time finally to return to the still life reproduced in Plate 1.3.1. The types of element from which it is composed are familiar from a number of others of Cézanne's pictures: the ordinary kitchen table with a single drawer, the patterned dark blue cloth, the glazed stoneware jug, the plain rustic fruit dish and white cloth, and, of course, the lemons, oranges, apples and pears that provide such intense concentrations of colour across the horizontal expanse of the canvas (see, for instance, Figure 3.5 and Plate 1.3.24). The *Still Life, Curtain, Jug and Compotier* reproduced in Plate 1.3.1 would certainly have been made in the presence of the assembled motif. In fact, the intensity of Cézanne's attention can be deduced from certain slight but significant variations in the consistency of his viewpoint. Note how the profile of the large apple just in front of the fruit dish has grown outward at the upper right, presumably as the artist leaned forward as though to see round it, anxious to capture the full richness of its volume. Similarly, the pyramid of apples and oranges in the fruit dish at the right appears to rise from its logical horizontal position and to advance towards the picture plane, invested with strange independence and vitality by the singular attention Cézanne must have devoted to it in the process of its depiction. Notice also how assiduous he has been in finding the minutest variations of texture and tone in his account of the wall behind the table, lest it be reduced to a simple flat background plane.

In comparing the two pictures of bathers in Plates 1.3.12 and 1.3.13, I noted how, where Bouguereau used a tonal basis for the modelling of his figures, Cézanne organised the spatial relations of his paintings

Figure 3.5   Paul Cézanne, *Jug and Fruit,* 1885–87, oil on canvas, 43 x 63 cm. Private collection. Photo © Lefevre Fine Art Ltd., London/The Bridgeman Art Library.

by means of modulations of colour. There is a clear case of this technique at the extreme right of the still life in Plate 1.3.1, where a brightly painted orange stands out against the contrasting deep green of a cooking apple behind. Though this contrast cannot be representing more than a minimal spatial distance between the one object and the other, the effect is to create a powerful *sense* of depth at that point in the composition – or rather, perhaps, to project the orange forward so that it *feels* almost graspable. Similarly the green apple poised on the corner at the lower right is so placed and delineated as virtually to engage the spectator's sense of reach and of touch.

The important and difficult issue that remains to be considered is just why such observations as this should matter. How is it that a painting of ordinary fruit on a table can be taken to *mean* so much? The question may be best approached by considering some other examples of the still-life genre. Still life emerged as a fully independent type of subject for painting around 1600 and became prominent during the ensuing century, especially among painters in the Protestant Low Countries. It was common for still-life pictures to be designed as allegories: collections of objects and motifs that could all be read symbolically. The commonest allegories were those that encouraged philosophical reflection on human mortality and on the transience of sensory pleasures and material possessions. A painting of this type is referred to as a 'Vanitas', after a verse from the biblical book of Ecclesiastes: 'Vanity of vanities, all is vanity saith the preacher' (Eccles. 1:2). The most easily interpreted Vanitas paintings are those featuring objects that have clear associations with the passage of time and with death. (Such works are often referred to by the Latin tag *memento mori*, 'remember that you must die'.) The work by Harmen Steenwyck reproduced in Plate 1.3.25 includes a skull, an empty shell, a watch, an extinguished and smoking taper and a lute placed face down (possibly implying the silencing of music). The trumpet may refer to the worthlessness of worldly fame, the Japanese sword to military power, and the books to another passage from Ecclesiastes: 'Of making many books there is no end, and much learning is a weariness of the flesh.'

Other still lifes from the same period appear to record exotic possessions and to celebrate the delights of the senses. For example, in the small work by Jacob van Hulsdonck (Plate 1.3.26) an appetising collection of fruit is arranged in and around a Chinese porcelain bowl from the reign of Wan Li (1573–1619) – a recently imported item to which a very special value would have been accorded. (It was to be another century and a half before porcelain was made in Europe that approached anything like this degree of refinement.) If this second still life seems to suggest a more hedonistic and less philosophical way of life than the first, we should bear in mind – as its contemporary viewers would no doubt have done – that porcelain is fragile, that fruit decays and that orange blossoms wither.

My point is that for all the appeal that still-life paintings may have as apparently straightforward pictures, that appeal has traditionally been supplemented by a certain complexity in the responses that the works invite. On the one hand, they mount a determined appeal to the senses – an appeal sustained by conspicuous displays of artistic virtuosity in the representation of complex three-dimensional forms, of subtle surface textures, and of demanding effects of transparency and reflection. On the other hand, they may suggest religious and philosophical reflection on the brevity of life and on the emptiness of worldly achievements and material possessions. The appeal is generally *no less* seductive where the objects depicted are suggestive of mortality. If there are some still-life paintings that offer their spectators images of themselves as consumers of opulent banquets, these are balanced by others that encourage us to admit the simpler priorities of the austere kitchen. The works reproduced in Plates 1.3.28 and 1.3.29 were both painted by Jean-Siméon Chardin, the most accomplished French still-life painter of the eighteenth century, whose work Cézanne certainly knew well.

If, as I believe, paintings have the potential to offer us different kinds of imaginative experience and identification, then we might say that what largely characterises the genre of still life is its playing on differences of *way* of life – differences, that's to say, in the way one's life may be lived. With this view in mind I return to Plate 1.3.1, Cézanne's *Still Life, Curtain, Jug and Compotier*. I don't mean to suggest that the elements represented should be read as symbols in quite the way that a skull may signify death. Nor does the picture appear to *stage* a way of life other than the one from which the painting itself must have emerged. Rather, the very *lack* of potential for symbolic reading requires us to concentrate the more closely on the distinctive qualities of the composition and technique. However intense this concentration, I don't believe that it is likely to yield the kind of moralistic reading that a painting such as Steenwyck's enables. But my own feeling is that the more I focus on the way the individual fruits are represented in Cézanne's painting, and on the ways in which they are related one to another, the more it seems that individuality and relationship are here being given substance as values in themselves – or at least as values in some larger sense than can be restricted to a world of apples and pears and lemons.

If this seems a slightly far-fetched idea, the way to test it is try to find words for the properties of the objects as they are painted, and for the relationships between them as established by the artist. Unless we simply resort to an alien arty jargon, in the process of trying to describe such effects and relations we tend inevitably to set up associations with a wider world in which the words we use have a more customary meaning and value. Rilke found himself writing of the 'good conscience' and 'simple truthfulness' of Cézanne's paintings, and felt 'educated' by them. For my part, I find it hard to describe the way in which the elements in this particular still life are arranged without resorting to the kinds of term that might be applied to a grouping of people in some kind of social world. I think of the differences of meaning between keeping one's distance and allowing a person their own space, or between edging up and making contact. The world I'm led to imagine is one in which various individuals might be gathered together in a complex harmony without compromising their different values. What I am saying, I think, is that the painting *feels* like a kind of model or metaphor for the way of life such a social world might permit. The art historian Paul Smith has gone further and suggested that 'seeing and interpreting Cézanne involves a challenge to our politics' (Smith, 1996, p. 75).

It seems fair to say that a painting with potential of this order must indeed be a quite special kind of object. Whether that makes it possibly worth $60.5 million is quite another matter. For most of us the relevant calculations remain entirely unreal. We can probably in any case assume that it was first and foremost the still life's status as a kind of compact gilt-edged security that led to its inflated price. Ironically, security of the relevant kind tends to be associated with more or less unchallenged political conditions. But it is a possibly consoling thought that a high proportion of works accorded these kinds of financial value tend to end up in museums, where members of the public can visit them, get to know them and learn to derive pleasure from their company. Of the works by Cézanne illustrated in connection with this chapter, only a minority remain in private hands.

## 3.9  SCHOLARS AND OWNERS

If it seems strange that Cézanne's work might involve some form of challenge to one's politics, it would perhaps not have seemed so at the time when he was embarking on his career as a painter. In France from the 1860s to the 1880s, substantial disagreements occurred between different factions concerning the virtues of the work of Manet and the Impressionists, and particularly of the work of Cézanne. Where such prolonged and violent controversies are provoked, there is always likely to be more at stake than simple differences of taste. At moments such as these, disagreements on artistic matters tend actually to betray much wider divisions between the value systems that define the social order. This point had been forcefully made by the critic Jules-Antoine Castagnary, writing a review of the Salon exhibition of 1863:

> The purpose of painting is to express, according to the means at its disposal, the society that produces it ... Painting is not an abstract concept, raised above history, alien to human vicissitudes, to the revolutions in morals and notions; it is part of social consciousness, a fragment of the mirror in which each

generation in its turn contemplates itself, and as such, it must follow society step by step and describe its incessant transformations.

(Castagnary, 1863, in Harrison et al., 1998, p. 411)

In this case, I suggest, the transformations that really mattered were not those associated with conflicts between the aristocracy – or what remained of it in France after the major revolution in 1789 – and the middle class, or even between middle class or bourgeoisie and working class. Following further revolutions in 1830 and 1848, the bourgeoisie was without question the dominant class in France and the one that largely shaped its literary and artistic culture. What was not quite so clear was how membership of the bourgeoisie was to be defined, or the precise values that it represented. Was it one's taste and culture that served to establish class status, or was one's property and financial standing the deciding factor?

As early as 1846 Baudelaire had prefaced his review of that year's Salon with an ironic dedication – 'To the Bourgeoisie' – and had made clear the possible grounds for a conflict of values *within* the class in question – a conflict that he symbolised in terms of the different powers and interests of 'scholars' and 'owners'.

> You are the majority – in number and intelligence; therefore you are the force – which is justice.

> Some are scholars, others are owners; a glorious day will come when the scholars shall be owners and the owners scholars. Then your power will be complete, and no one will protest against it.

> Until that supreme harmony is achieved, it is just that those who are but owners should aspire to become scholars; for knowledge is no less of an enjoyment than ownership ...

> But the monopolists have decided to keep the forbidden fruit of knowledge from you, because knowledge is their counter and their shop, and they are infinitely jealous of it.

(Baudelaire, 1846, in Harrison et al., 1998, p. 301)

What Baudelaire was pointing to was a conflict between those whose class-status was secured by heredity, by education and by culture (the 'scholars' who claimed a monopoly on knowledge), and those who had acquired status through industry and the acquisition of property (the 'owners'). It was the latter that he pretended particularly to address, warning them, in effect, that those who saw themselves as the *already* cultured were not about to hand over their privileges. It was from its rooting in this larger social context that modernist art's characteristic conflict of values drew its animating tension: was the work of art something to be esteemed for its own sake – for its 'aesthetic quality'; or were such things as paintings and sculptures properly regarded as specialised kinds of commodities, the value of which could always be tested in the market place?

As an accomplished poet and critic, Baudelaire was, of course, a 'scholar' rather than an 'owner'. But it was a part of the complex social and moral condition under which writers and artists worked during the period in question that few of them were able or willing straightforwardly to identify themselves as bourgeois, or to identify with the typical interests of the class in either of its divisions. Cézanne maintained a kind of dissident 'scholarly' ambition against the admonitions of his 'owner' father, while continuing to challenge accepted notions of what a 'cultured' and professionally produced picture should look like. It was this apparent compulsion to drift free from the prevailing identifications of the dominant class that largely accounted for the emergence of an 'avant-garde' in the world of art – a community of artists whose primary identification was with the idea of art itself, as the point of most certain critical moment in a modernising world.

That Cézanne's work showed him to be the most advanced of the avant-garde was a view widely held during the later nineteenth century both by his supporters and by his – and the avant-garde's – detractors. The quality of extreme impartiality that Rilke had noted in his work – the purging of sentiment and the transferring of worldly emotions and attachments to the *forms* of his pictures – was seen as demonstrating the priority of aesthetic values over the material and the commercial. During the early twentieth century, as avant-garde movements came to occupy an increasingly central role in the development and business of the art-world, Cézanne's reputation grew accordingly. He was to remain for a considerable time both the artists' artist *par excellence* and – until finally supplanted by Picasso – the favoured Aunt Sally of modern art's professional opponents.

If Cézanne's reputation has now finally stabilised, it does not necessarily follow that the individual paintings are any the less demanding. I still recall my own experience as a student of modern art history, eager to get to know the painter's notorious work, feeling an intense sense of disappointment – and something like rejection – when the pictures I had travelled to Paris to see initially left me cold. My point is that if what is required is that one gain 'the right eyes', then respect for Cézanne's *reputation* alone will not suffice. I could not have written this text unless I believed that a better understanding of his work can be taught and can be learned. But in the end the only *right* eyes are one's own.

# REFERENCES

Baudelaire, C. (1846) 'Salon of 1846' in Harrison, Wood and Gaiger (eds), 1998, pp. 301–4.

Baudelaire, C. (1863) 'The painter of modern life', *Le Figaro,* Paris, 26 and 28 November and 3 December 1863, in Harrison, Wood and Gaiger (eds), 1998, pp. 495–6.

Bell, C. (1914) *Art,* London: Chatto & Windus.

Cachin, F., et al. (1996) *Cézanne,* London, Tate Publishing (exhibition catalogue).

Castagnary, J.-A. (1863) 'The three contemporary schools', originally published as 'Salon de 1863', *Nord,* Brussels, 14 May–12 September; trans. in Harrison, Wood and Gaiger (eds), 1998, pp. 410–13.

Denis, M. (1907) 'Cézanne', in *L'Occident,* Paris, September (trans. R. Fry, 1910, *Burlington Magazine,* vol. 16, London, January–February); in Harrison and Wood (eds), 2003, pp. 39–46.

Doran, M. (ed.) (1978) *Conversations avec Cézanne,* Paris, Macula.

Gasquet, J. (1991 [1921]) *Cézanne: A Memoir with Conversations* (trans. C. Pemberton), London, Thames and Hudson.

Harrison, C. and Wood, P. (2003) *Art in Theory 1900–2000,* Oxford, Blackwell.

Harrison, C., Wood, P. and Gaiger, J. (1998) *Art in Theory 1815–1900,* Oxford, Blackwell.

Krumrine, M.L. (1990) *Cézanne: The Bathers,* London: Thames and Hudson in association with Kunstmuseum Basle (exhibition catalogue).

Moffat, C. (ed.) (1996) *The New Painting: Impressionism 1874–1886,* Oxford, Phaidon (exhibition catalogue).

Prouvaire, J. [Pierre Toloza] (1874) review of the Independents Exhibition of 1874, *Le Rappel,* 20 April; in Moffat, 1996, p. 126.

Rilke, R.-M. (1988 [1944]) *Letters on Cézanne* (ed. C. Rilke, trans. J. Agee), London, Jonathan Cape (first published 1944 as *Lettres sur Cézanne,* trans. and intro. M. Betz, Paris, Editions Correa; original German text first published 1952 as *Briefe über Cézanne,* ed. C, Frankfurt, Insel Verlag).

Rivière, G. (1877) *L'Impressioniste,* no. 2, Paris, 14 April, in Harrison, Wood and Gaiger (eds), 1998, pp. 593–8.

Smith, P. (1996) *Interpreting Cézanne,* London, Tate Publishing.

Vollard, A. (1914) *Paul Cézanne,* Paris, Galerie A. Vollard.

Zola, E. (1978) *Correspondance,* vol. 1: *1858–1867* (ed. E.H. Bakker), Montreal, Presses de l'Université de Montréal.

# FURTHER READING

You may find it interesting to look at one or more of the following:

Harrison, C. (2005) *Painting the Difference: Sex and Spectator in Modern Art,* Chicago, University of Chicago Press.

Rewald, J. (1976) *Cézanne Letters,* New York and Oxford, Oxford University Press.

Shiff, R. (1984) *Cézanne and the End of Impressionism,* Chicago and London, Chicago University Press.

# 4 FAME AND FARADAY

*Isobel Falconer with Frank James*

| INTRODUCTION | | 87 |
|---|---|---|
| 4.1 | FOUNDATIONS OF A CAREER | 89 |
| 4.2 | A CAREER IN SCIENCE | 90 |
| 4.3 | THE ROYAL INSTITUTION: HOME | 93 |
| 4.4 | THE ROYAL INSTITUTION: LABORATORY | 97 |
| 4.5 | THE ROYAL INSTITUTION: PUBLIC FORUM | 109 |
| CONCLUSION | | 113 |
| REFERENCES | | 114 |
| RESOURCES | | 115 |
| | Reading 4.1 | 115 |
| | Reading 4.2 | 117 |
| | Reading 4.3 | 118 |
| | Reading 4.4 | 119 |
| | Reading 4.5 | 120 |
| | Reading 4.6 | 121 |
| | Reading 4.7 | 121 |

## MATERIALS YOU WILL NEED

- DVD ROM: Faraday
- Illustration Book

## AIMS

This chapter will:

- introduce you to the life of Michael Faraday and his important discoveries
- explore the context of these discoveries
- explore the relationship between Faraday's experiments and his scientific ideas
- explore the role of the Royal Institution in advancing Faraday's career
- show the relationship between Faraday's public and private life
- assess how Faraday's reputation was built on both scientific discoveries and his public lecturing
- give an insight into the aims and methods of historians of science
- introduce you to the use of visual sources in the study of history.

## INTRODUCTION

Albemarle Street, London, 8.30 p.m. Friday 23 January 1846. On this cold, wet, dark evening the carriages of the rich and famous are drawing up outside an imposing classical-fronted building located in the only one-way street in London. On entering, the men and women, in evening dress, pass up a grand staircase. Turning right at the top, they walk through a portrait-hung room into a steeply raked semi-circular lecture theatre. This evening there will be more than one thousand people crammed into this space, many standing on the stairs and passageways; so crowded indeed that at least one journalist will complain that he could not get in. Why are they here in all their finery in such cramped and stuffy conditions? The clock approaches nine, a hush falls over the theatre, the clock strikes once and through the door enters Michael Faraday, for twenty years the master of the Royal Institution's lecture theatre. For the next hour he describes and demonstrates his recent discoveries showing the connection between light and magnetism, and that magnetism affects all matter. These discoveries are so important that the following week he is portrayed in the *Illustrated London News* delivering his lecture (Figure 4.1).

Figure 4.1    Unknown engraver, 'Faraday delivering his Friday Evening Discourse "Magnetism and Light" on 23 January 1846', engraving from the *Illustrated London News*, 31 January 1846, vol. 8, p. 77. Photo: The Illustrated London News Picture Library.

In the nineteenth century the **natural philosopher** Michael Faraday (1791–1867) was incredibly famous. (He never called himself a scientist; indeed, the term 'scientist' did not come into general use until the end of the nineteenth century, after Faraday's death. However, it is a useful shorthand and I use it ahistorically later in this chapter.) He was feted in the scientific world and his name was widely recognised by the public. But how did this man who was born into a working-class family become so famous? How did the public learn about his work? In this chapter I try to answer these questions by taking a biographical approach that emphasises the relationship between the private and the public spaces in Faraday's life. In doing so, I hope you will get a flavour of some of the topics that interest historians of science, such as the following questions:

- How did people make careers for themselves in science in different eras?
- What is the process by which scientific ideas develop?
- What is the relationship between science and religion?
- How has the nature of science and the scientific method changed over time?
- What is the relationship between the public and science at different times?

In studying Faraday, we raise two further important questions – those of **interpretation** and **generalisation**. Many of the facts of Faraday's life are well documented. *Interpretation* means suggesting explanations for these facts, and relationships between them: for example, how did Faraday's religious views affect his scientific views? (Interpretation is discussed further in Chapter 5 on Stalin.) Faraday, though, is just an individual. However fascinating he may be, does studying his life and work put us in a better position to understand any of the general topics in the history of science? Can any of our interpretations be *generalised*? These are large and open questions that I am alerting you to here. I make no attempt to answer them within this chapter, but I do try to make clear where I am interpreting the facts by using words such as 'may have', 'perhaps' or 'it seems that'. I also try to show where Faraday was typical of, or unlike, other scientists. Where we find that he seems typical we might say that we can generalise our conclusions.

Activity    Read Faraday's obituary in *The Times* (Reading 4.1), and jot down a list of the things the obituary mentions that show that Faraday was famous. You might like to divide your list into facts that show he was famous to other scientists, and others that suggest he was famous among the public. What does the author of the obituary particularly admire about Faraday? What does the author pinpoint as the most important reasons for Faraday's fame?

**Discussion**  Obituaries in *The Times* were less common in Victorian times than they are now, and the very fact that Faraday had a lengthy obituary is an initial indication of his fame.

In my first list, showing that Faraday was famous to other scientists, were: his election to scientific societies all over the world, his being given medals by scientific societies all over the world, his appointment as the first Professor for the new **Chair** of Chemistry at the Royal Institution, and his honorary degree from the University of Oxford. In my second list, showing Faraday's fame among the public, were: crowds coming to hear his lectures, his recommendation by Lord Melbourne (the Prime Minister) for a government pension, his receiving honours from foreign governments, and his being granted a house to live in by Queen Victoria.

I noticed that the author admired Faraday's lecturing style, which was vivacious and showed a mastery of his subject, and his experimental skill. But above all, the obituarist seems to admire Faraday for being a self-made man and for the 'lofty purity of [his] life', which was apparently free from any ambition for public acknowledgement or wealth. I get the impression that the reasons for Faraday's fame were his scientific discoveries, his lectures and his books. Faraday made his outstanding discoveries in the privacy of his laboratory, and no one would have known about them were it not for his lectures and publications, which told the world what he had done.

We have noted that his contemporaries admired Faraday for being a self-made man and for the purity of his life, which was exactly how the Victorians thought scientists ought to be. They should be motivated entirely by curiosity about the world and uninterested in rewards. In this sense they were supposed to keep their scientific lives and their private lives separate. Although later in the chapter we will question the extent to which Faraday's scientific and private lives were, in fact, separate, there seems little doubt that he was uninterested in rewards in the most obvious sense of wealth and high position. We see here how it was easy for contemporaries to admire Faraday because his attributes coincided with the values of the society in which he lived. More generally, perhaps we might gain broader insights into nineteenth-century history, politics and culture as we begin to study how Faraday's reputation was constructed.

## 4.1   FOUNDATIONS OF A CAREER

Michael Faraday was born on 22 September 1791 in Newington Butts, now the Elephant and Castle area of London. His father, James Faraday (1761–1810), was a blacksmith from Westmorland who had married a domestic servant, Margaret Hastwell (1764–1838), in 1786. They already had two children by the winter of 1788 when they moved to London looking for work. Michael's birth was followed by that of a much younger sister in 1802.

Little is known of Faraday's early life. His father was a member of the **Sandemanian Church** and Michael grew up within a small, close-knit

Christian community, which was to shape much of his life, as discussed later in this chapter. His education 'was of the most ordinary description, consisting of little more than the rudiments of reading, writing, and arithmetic at a common day-school' (Jones, 1870, vol. 1, p. 9). When he was thirteen he became an errand boy for the bookseller George Riebau, whose shop in Blandford Street was a couple of minutes' walk from Faraday's home. In October the following year (1805), two weeks before the battle of Trafalgar, Riebau took him on as an apprentice bookbinder and he went to live above the shop. Riebau may have provided Faraday with a second father figure, particularly following James Faraday's protracted ill health and death in 1810.

At Riebau's Faraday was exposed to a wide variety of new influences. Riebau was a political activist and linked to various non-conformist religious sects. Some of London's leading artists were his customers, and Faraday began to take notice of illustrations, being particularly interested in new methods of reproducing pictures. Books were sold without covers in the early nineteenth century and Faraday learned to bind them for customers, reading them at the same time. In this way he came across books such as Jane Marcet's *Conversations in Chemistry* (1809), which gave instructions for home experiments, and the scientific parts of the *Encyclopaedia Britannica*. He read Isaac Watts's *Improvement of the Mind* (1741) and attempted to follow its advice, for example, by writing letters to clarify his ideas. Riebau encouraged Faraday to experiment, to travel about London to see the new machinery of the Industrial Revolution in action and, from 1810, to attend weekly lectures at the City Philosophical Society. This was one of the many small self-improvement societies which flourished in London at the time. There Faraday formed lifelong friendships with a small group of men and women with whom he earnestly discussed natural philosophy, but whom he also accompanied to the theatre, concerts and firework displays. He later claimed that as a child he was not particularly bright, nor a deep thinker, but that he had an overactive imagination which he struggled to keep in check: 'facts were important to me & saved me. I could trust a fact' (Williams et al., 1971, vol. 2, pp. 913–14).

## 4.2   A CAREER IN SCIENCE

By the end of his apprenticeship in 1812, Faraday had decided that he wished to pursue a scientific career. This was, to put it mildly, an unusual ambition at a time when, outside medicine, there was no career structure for science in England. Those who did hold scientific positions were generally university trained and did not come from the working class. However, it is possible that Faraday had recently acquired a role model. Early in 1812 a customer of Riebau's gave him tickets to attend four lectures by Humphry Davy (1778–1829),

Professor of Chemistry at the Royal Institution. Davy himself had been a poor boy with little education, the son of a woodcarver. Yet he had managed to make a scientific career for himself and was now one of the most respected chemists of the day, whose spectacular demonstration lectures attracted hordes of London's elite.

Davy's early career had relied on **patronage** – the support of wealthy or influential people – and Faraday tried the same route. He wrote to Sir Joseph Banks (1743–1820), Britain's leading scientist and President of the Royal Society, asking for a job, but was rebuffed, leaving him 'almost disconsolate' (memorandum by an unknown author to Peel, 31 March 1835, in James, 1993, vol. 2, p. 775). At Riebau's suggestion, Faraday turned his attention to Davy. He wrote up a neat version of the notes he had taken at Davy's lectures, bound them, and presented them to Davy. This was no simple matter: if he followed the practice he described for the City Philosophical lectures the notes will have gone through four drafts, from rough headings taken down during the lecture itself, to a lucid and connected flow that followed Davy's style of delivery as closely as Faraday could remember it. Davy was sufficiently impressed to interview Faraday, but advised him to stick to bookbinding, adding that he would bear him in mind in the future. Unable to support himself by science and deeply unhappy, Faraday took a job as a journeyman bookbinder with Henri de la Roche when his apprenticeship ended in October 1812.

However, Faraday's luck was soon to turn. In late October 1812 Davy's eyesight was temporarily damaged by an explosion in the laboratory and he employed Faraday part-time to read and write for him. Davy was so satisfied by Faraday's competence that he appointed him as laboratory assistant at the Royal Institution when the position became vacant in February 1813.

**Activity**  Look back at the previous section. In what ways do you think his early private life laid the foundations for Faraday's later reputation as a scientist?

**Discussion**  My first reaction was that Faraday had evidently taught himself quite a bit about science from the books he bound, and had learned even more by attending lectures. He had also made a group of friends with whom he could bounce ideas around. He had been encouraged to experiment and given some facilities for doing so. This experience formed the basis for his scientific discoveries.

Another contribution of his early life to his science might, I think, at first sight be regarded as a negative one. He lacked something that most other natural philosophers had – a university education. So Faraday had not been taught to think in the same ways as his fellow natural philosophers. However, this might in fact be a positive contribution, for it could allow Faraday to view things from a different perspective and 'think outside the box', arriving at new methods and conclusions.

If I look back to the previous activity, and things mentioned by *The Times* obituarist, I can think of other early experiences that might have been important to Faraday's later success. My interpretation is that as a bookbinder he was working in the early nineteenth-century media industry. Even before he started attending scientific lectures he would have been aware of how things were presented to the public, the importance of getting things right for a particular audience, what sold and what did not, and how to represent ideas in words and pictures. He was very well positioned to present his scientific work to the public in the most compelling ways possible.

I have given you my own thoughts about Faraday's early life and how it underlay his later scientific reputation. You may have thought of other experiences and connections. You might like to think about what evidence you could use to justify your interpretation.

Faraday now began what was, in effect, a second apprenticeship, this time in chemistry. His living quarters were a couple of rooms in the attic of the Royal Institution. The laboratory where he worked was in the basement. Here he prepared experiments and assisted in them. He also helped prepare and perform the lecture demonstrations, and became a connoisseur of lecturing technique.

**Activity**    Read the excerpts from letters that Faraday wrote to his friend Benjamin Abbot (1793–1870) soon after going to work at the Royal Institution (Reading 4.2). What do you think they show about Faraday's attitude to lecturing? Did anything surprise you about them?

**Discussion**    Faraday seems to me to take an unusually comprehensive view of lecturing. I was surprised by the number of things he considered – everything from the physical environment and time of day to the appropriate content for lectures. He appears extremely thorough in his approach; to master all these aspects would require a great deal of hard work over an extended period of time on the part of the lecturer.

Above all, I was struck by how aware Faraday was of the needs of his audience. He was concerned with how to get them to the lecture in the first place, how to keep them awake, and how to keep them interested. This seems to provide more evidence of the public awareness that Faraday might have learned while a bookbinder.

Six months later Davy was invited to undertake a scientific tour of the Continent, receiving a special passport from Napoleon. Davy was accompanied by his new wife – a wealthy widow whose fortune allowed Davy to retire from the Royal Institution – her maid and Faraday, acting as his assistant. They visited Paris, Italy, Switzerland and southern Germany. During this tour Faraday met many of the leading European scientists of the day. He witnessed his first piece of original scientific research when Davy confounded the French chemists by demonstrating that iodine was an element and could not be broken down into simpler chemical substances. They returned to Britain in April 1815 when Europe became politically unstable following the escape of Napoleon from Elba.

Back in London, Faraday was reappointed assistant in the Royal Institution and worked with Davy's successor William Brande (1788–1866), and occasionally for Davy who still had some influence in the laboratory. Faraday started to become known to the wider Royal Institution circle, undertaking chemical analyses as part of the Royal Institution's work and assisting in Davy's invention of a miners' safety lamp. He also began publishing short scientific articles in the *Quarterly Journal of Science*, which was edited by Brande.

In 1815, aged twenty-four, Faraday had not only found a job in science, but one in the most publicly visible scientific institution in the country. The Royal Institution had been founded in 1799, prompted by a need to promote science to a wide audience during the wars with France. It was one of a large number of scientific societies and institutions springing up around this time, but it differed from the others in being firmly aimed at the upper classes. Davy had promoted the Royal Institution as the venue for fashionable demonstration lectures, and had established the laboratory as a place of scientific research. From 1815 until his death in 1867 Faraday's life and work revolved around the Royal Institution at 21 Albemarle Street. It was his private home, his laboratory and his public forum.

## 4.3  THE ROYAL INSTITUTION: HOME

The year 1821 was possibly the most important of Faraday's life. On 21 May he was appointed Acting Superintendent of the House at the Royal Institution, responsible for the upkeep of the building and supervision of the servants. The post carried no additional salary, but Faraday was able to negotiate larger living quarters. Three weeks later, on 12 June, he married Sarah Barnard (1800–79), whom he had been courting for the previous year or more. The couple set up home on the top floor of the Institution. The following month Faraday became a full member of the Sandemanian Church when he made his confession of faith on 15 July. On 3–4 September, while working in the basement laboratory, he made his first major scientific discovery, that of electromagnetic rotations.

I have emphasised the locations of Faraday's home and laboratory in the Royal Institution. Number 21 Albemarle Street was not a purpose-built building. Like many other societies, the Royal Institution existed in what was originally a private house. The upper floors and basements were traditionally private spaces in upper-class eighteenth-century British homes. They were the realm of bedrooms and service functions and were certainly not on display. In between, the ground and first floors were the public spaces, and this is where the library and the lecture theatre were located in 21 Albemarle Street.

Thus the arrangement of the building echoed the distinctions made between private life, private and controlled laboratory science, and public forum, while maintaining the close physical proximity of all three: 'living above the shop' was common in the nineteenth century, when there was little public transport. However, for Faraday work and home were more closely connected than the idealised distinctions suggest. His wife left her young niece in his care in the laboratory while she went out shopping. He summoned his family down to the laboratory to view trials of demonstration experiments before risking them in public, and he invited selected visitors upstairs into his home after lectures.

**Activity**    Read Cornelia Crosse's account of her first visit to Faraday's home in 1850 (Reading 4.3). What does she say that gives you an impression of privacy and separation from the public spaces in the Royal Institution? What impression do you get of the attitudes of Michael and Sarah Faraday to their home and private lives?

**Discussion**    Crosse emphasises the long flight of stairs that separates the Faradays' home from the public rooms. At the top of the stairs was another barrier – a front door where you had to knock to be admitted. The use of the word 'homely' also suggests that the rooms beyond the door were private. Even inside the door there was an outer sitting room before reaching Faraday's 'inner sanctum' where he was relaxing in private.

Thus Crosse gives an impression of physical barriers creating a separation between the publicly famous scientist who appeared in the lecture theatre and of whom she was in awe, and the homely private man beyond the doors with whom she could discuss novels.

Sarah Faraday seems to have been very concerned to preserve their home, and Michael's private life, as a place for relaxation, which she equated with not thinking about scientific matters. She was clearly reluctant to let him visit another home that might be more scientifically stimulating. I get the impression that Faraday was probably more relaxed about the overlap between his scientific and home life; he certainly seems to have welcomed the chance for a scientific chat.

In assessing Sarah and Michael Faraday's attitudes to science and relaxation as portrayed here, it is worth noting that Faraday had suffered a severe nervous breakdown during the early 1840s, from which he never fully recovered. Sarah's attempts to prevent him getting over-stimulated may have been an attempt to prevent a recurrence of his illness. Her protective attitude is suggested by her pose in the portrait in Figure 4.2.

Michael and Sarah Faraday lived on the upper floors of the Royal Institution for over forty years. By all accounts it was a very happy marriage, although they never had any children. However, the Faraday and Barnard family circle was a very close one. Sarah and Michael's brothers and sisters were frequent and welcome visitors, and at least two nieces lived with them for a number of years.

Home was where Faraday read popular novels, played games with his young relatives and chatted to friends. Above all, though, Faraday's home was a Sandemanian Christian one. The Sandemanian Church began in eighteenth-century Scotland. Members of the sect lived

Figure 4.2   Michael and Sarah Faraday, *c*. 1840–50, daguerreotype photo. Unknown photographer. Photo: © The Royal Institution, London/The Bridgeman Art Library.

strictly according to their interpretation of the precepts laid down in the Bible and formed a small, close-knit community who supported each other spiritually and practically, and frequently intermarried. Sandemanians were socially more liberal than other dissenting sects, and were allowed moderate drinking and trips to the theatre and concerts. However, they also differed from other sects in adhering rigidly to the dietary laws laid down in the Old Testament book of Leviticus (such as not eating pork), in repeating the Last Supper in all its details on Sundays, and in not attempting to convert others to their faith. Sarah was the daughter of a Sandemanian silversmith and had already committed herself as a full member of the Sandemanian Church before her marriage, and Michael became a full member soon after their wedding.

When he became a full member of the church, Faraday pledged himself to an uncompromising faith and a code of conduct that affected all his lifestyle and career choices. He spent every Sunday, and often other weekdays, with his fellow Sandemanians, frequently returning early from scientific meetings in order to do so.

> He prayed with them, exhorted them, was exhorted by them; they washed each other's feet and broke the communion bread together ... [In] an important sense Faraday was much closer to Thomas Boosey (a publisher and bookseller), George Leighton (a bookbinder) and Mary Straker (a poor but devout member of the congregation) than he was to the numerous scientists who passed through the doors of the Royal Institution.

(Cantor, 1991, pp. 5–6)

Although Faraday was elected a Deacon in the 1830s and an Elder in the 1840s and again in the 1860s, this did not imply any authority or power over the other members. Instead, it was a job to be undertaken in the service of a community, all of whose members were considered spiritually equal. As Deacon, Faraday visited the sick and poor and attended to the running of the meeting house. As an Elder he baptised infants, and visited other meeting houses to support their congregations. In 1863, for example, he visited Dundee to help resolve a dispute, and delivered an exhortation there to an unusually crowded meeting house (Cantor, 1991, pp. 2–4).

Thus, in the Sandemanian Church, Faraday found not only very particular religious beliefs, but a different public role for himself, although not a particularly influential one. More influential was the effect that his Sandemanian beliefs had on his public reputation as a man of science. Sandemanians stressed an ideal of service not only in their church but also in public life. Faraday perceived public position as inevitably tainted by self-serving political power struggles, and inconsistent with his Christian values. Thus, he declined the presidency of the Royal Institution when he was offered it in 1864. He saw himself as the Institution's servant rather than its leader. Similarly, he turned down the presidency of the Royal Society in 1848 and again in 1858.

However, these decisions were not just debated privately, between Faraday and his God, or even with Sarah. Faraday was very conscious of his 'honour', possibly because he was aware that although he was moving in upper-class circles, he had not been born there. By 'honour' he meant not only that he should act in accordance with his moral code, but that he should be publicly accepted as doing so. So his decisions were often debated in the newspapers for all the world to see, as in the many letters he published denying rumours that he had received a knighthood, or would accept one if offered. This stance enhanced his reputation. Although commentators rarely acknowledged his Sandemanian beliefs, uninterest in public position was one of the things that they admired about Faraday. It chimed with the high moral stance that was intrinsic to the Victorian view of a 'gentleman of science'.

Faraday's faith also had a direct impact on his scientific work.

**Activity**

Read Cantor's account of Faraday's reliance on experiments and facts (Reading 4.4). What relationship does Cantor suggest between Faraday's religion and his science? How does Cantor think Faraday's private mental life and psychology affected his approach to science?

Note that in this extract, **empiricism** means relying primarily on experimental results.

**Discussion**

Cantor suggests that Faraday's religion influenced his scientific approach and methodology. Faraday applied the same methods in religion and science. Sandemanians tried to achieve a plain, literal understanding of the Bible. The Bible was the word of God, but nature was also God's work. Faraday referred to it as 'the book of nature' and tried to achieve an equivalent plain, literal understanding of it. This meant relying on experimental facts and results, and trying to understand them simply and clearly without pursuing imaginative theories as many scientists did. To do this required unusually careful investigation and close attention to detail.

Cantor also suggests that Faraday's reliance on facts had a psychological as well as a religious origin. He was afraid of getting carried away by his imagination. He based his own image of himself on his experiments ('without experiments I am nothing'), and clung to facts to save his sanity during a nervous breakdown.

Although we might think of 'nature' as signifying the great outdoors, for Faraday (and other nineteenth-century scientists) the facts were best pinned down in the controlled privacy of the laboratory. This was where Faraday made the discoveries for which he is famous.

## 4.4  THE ROYAL INSTITUTION: LABORATORY

As we have seen, Faraday's first major scientific discovery came in 1821. It was the first of a series of discoveries by which Faraday revolutionised views of what electricity and magnetism were and how they operated. Before Faraday they were thought to be mysterious fluids; by 1836 he had shown that they were forces.

In 1820 the Danish philosopher Hans Christian Oersted (1777–1851) noticed that a magnetic compass needle moved when it was near a wire carrying an electric current. Both electricity and magnetism were very mysterious in the early nineteenth century, and Oersted's discovery that they were somehow connected excited enormous interest throughout Europe. While investigating the new phenomenon on 3–4 September 1821, Faraday found that a wire carrying an electric current would rotate continuously around a magnet. His discovery was extraordinary because it showed that the force that moved the wire did not pull or push it directly towards or away from the magnet. Instead, the force pushed the wire sideways at right angles to the magnet. No other known forces did this. Faraday's rotations later gained immense public and economic significance as the origin of the electric motor, and today the effect has become so familiar that we have ceased to wonder at it, but for Faraday and his contemporaries the sideways force was unprecedented and only added to the excitement of electrical science. Faraday's experiment is summarised below.

### Experiment 1: rotations

Things only move if a force acts on them. In 1821 the only forces known acted in a straight line between two bodies, as in a hand exerciser (see Figure 4.3).

Oersted's experiment was a problem because it seemed to show a twist instead of a push–pull between the wire and the magnet. Faraday tried to find out what was happening by very detailed observation of the experiments.

He suspended a magnet horizontally near a vertical wire. He connected the wire to a battery so a current passed through the wire, as shown in Figure 4.4. (Batteries were invented by Alessandro Volta around 1800. Early batteries were filled with liquid – like a car battery today – and might be any size from a simple glass jar to the 'Great Battery' that Davy had installed at the Royal Institution, which filled an entire room.)

Faraday found that whether the magnet twisted towards the wire or away from it depended on small differences in the position of the wire relative to the magnet. He drew lots of diagrams of these positions. His final set of diagrams looked down from the top on a single magnet and four wire positions, indicating whether the wire would be pushed away from or towards the magnet (see Figure 4.5).

Figure 4.3    Gripmaster hand exerciser. Photo courtesy of PROHANDS www. prohands.net

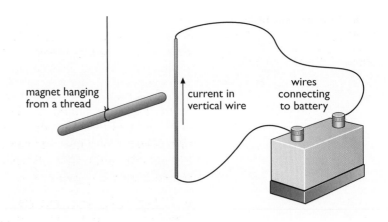

Figure 4.4    Magnet suspended horizontally near a vertical current-carrying wire.

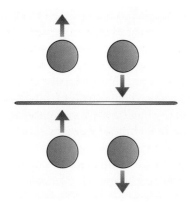

Figure 4.5 Current-carrying wire with arrows showing the direction in which it wants to move, near a magnetised needle. Adapted from Faraday's diary.

This is where Faraday made a leap of imagination to circular motion. He mentally 'joined the dots' in his diagram, imagining the wire moving in circles, as shown in Figure 4.6.

Faraday wrote in his diary: 'These indicate motions in circles round each pole' (quoted in Gooding and James, 1985, p. 117).

To demonstrate what he thought would happen, Faraday supported a wire above the pole of a magnet, and arranged that the bottom end of the wire was free to move. He connected the wire to the battery using mercury (which conducts electricity, but is a liquid so the wire could move), as shown in Figure 4.7. He found that the bottom end of the wire rotated round and round the magnet.

Faraday knew how extraordinary this was: 'there was neither attraction nor repulsion', he wrote in his diary. The force was acting in circles round the magnet. No other known forces did this. This realisation changed the way scientists thought about things, just as Einstein later did when he formulated the theory of relativity.

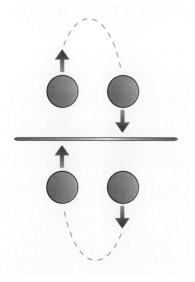

Figure 4.6 Separate movements of a current-carrying wire might join together into circular motion around a magnetised needle. Adapted from Faraday's diary.

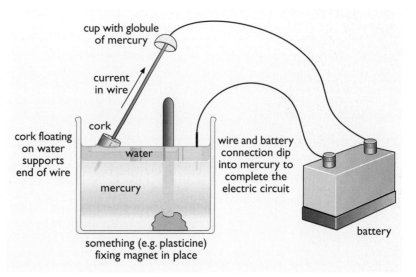

Figure 4.7 Diagram of Faraday's experiment to show that a current-carrying wire moved around a vertical magnet.

This discovery led to the first serious attention being paid to Faraday by the scientific community, and he was elected a **corresponding member** of the Paris Académie des Sciences. By coincidence, the day of his election was his thirty-second birthday. His election to the Royal Society followed in 1824. His potential as a major scientific figure had started to be recognised.

In 1825 Faraday was appointed Director of the Laboratory, after Brande moved to a position and a house at the Royal Mint. Brande remained Professor of Chemistry and technically Faraday's superior, but an increasing amount of Faraday's time was taken up with Royal Institution business. He had little time to spare for further experiments on electricity and magnetism, but when he was able, Faraday looked in particular for evidence of **induction**, where a current in one wire would cause a current in another, nearby wire. He eventually discovered this in 1831 using an iron ring around which he wrapped two coils of wire. His experiment was the basis for two applications that are essential to the use of electricity today: the electric transformer and the electric generator. Without these there would not be electricity in our homes today, powering everything from heating and lighting to computers. The experiment and these industrial applications are described below.

### Experiment 2: induction

Throughout the 1820s Faraday performed occasional experiments to try to detect electromagnetic induction, prompted by two beliefs:

- that all forces, and electric and magnetic forces in particular, are essentially similar
- a principle of symmetry in nature. In this case, if electricity has an effect on magnetism, then magnetism should have an effect on electricity.

In these experiments Faraday was expecting a continuous effect – something that just went on and on, as long as the current in the first circuit was flowing – just as his rotations wire went on rotating round the magnet all the while current flowed through the wire.

But through the earlier part of 1831 he performed a large number of investigations on *transitory* effects, such as the ripples when a stone is dropped in a pond. When he started looking for induction again, in August 1831, he was alert to transitory effects.

Faraday wound two separate coils of insulated wire around an iron ring and connected one of the coils to a battery. He put a magnetic needle to detect a current by the second coil. Because the wires were insulated, electric current could not simply flow out of the right-hand coil and into the ring or into the left-hand coil (see Figure 4.8).

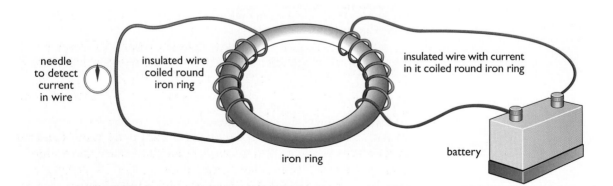

Figure 4.8    Coils of insulated wire around an iron ring.

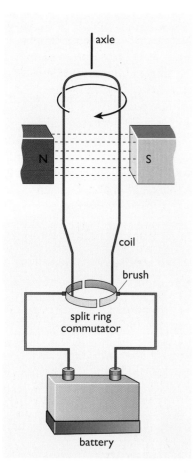

Figure 4.9   Diagram for a simple motor or generator.

When Faraday connected the first coil to the battery so that a current started flowing through it, he noticed that the compass needle flicked, indicating a transitory surge of current in the second wire. He had discovered that *changes* in the current through the first coil caused an electric current in the second coil. This was electric induction.

Over the next two months, Faraday realised that the important thing in inducing a current was to have a changing magnetic force near the second coil. In his induction experiment, the changing current in the first coil produced the changing magnetic force, but he did not need the first coil if he could change the force in some other way: he could just move the second coil around near a magnet to induce a current. This was the converse of the rotations experiment where an electric current caused a magnet to move. Faraday had established a symmetrical relationship of the type he believed ought to exist between forces.

This symmetry is the basis of the electric motor and electric generator. The apparatus in Figure 4.9 can be either a motor or a generator.

It shows a coil of wire between the poles of a magnet (N and S); the dotted lines show the magnetic force. The brush and split ring commutator are just a way of connecting to the battery so that the wires do not get twisted when the coil rotates.

If you connect up the battery, a current flows through the coil and it turns round in the magnetic field – attach an axle to it and you can make it turn wheels or machinery. This motor is based on Faraday's rotation experiment.

If you do not connect the battery, but you turn the coil round and round by a handle, or by a water turbine as in a hydro-electric power station, so that it is moving in the magnetic force, then a current starts flowing in the wire and you have generated electricity. This generator is based on Faraday's induction experiment.

An easier way to get a changing current in Faraday's original, induction ring experiment is to use an alternating current source (e.g. mains electricity) rather than a battery. Then the current keeps reversing, the magnetic force through the ring keeps changing, and you get a continual, but constantly alternating current from the second coil. This is a transformer, as used today in electrical equipment at all scales, from the national grid to televisions and video recorders.

This second clutch of major discoveries consolidated Faraday's position at the Royal Institution and led to his public recognition. In 1833 John Fuller (1757–1834), a member of the Royal Institution, gave money to create the Fullerian Professorship of Chemistry at the Royal Institution especially for Faraday.

Faraday's beliefs – that all forces are essentially similar; and that there is symmetry in nature – were common to many other nineteenth-century scientists. In Faraday's case, however, they paralleled his religious conviction that, like the Bible, the 'book of nature' was written in plain and simple style. Following these precepts Faraday

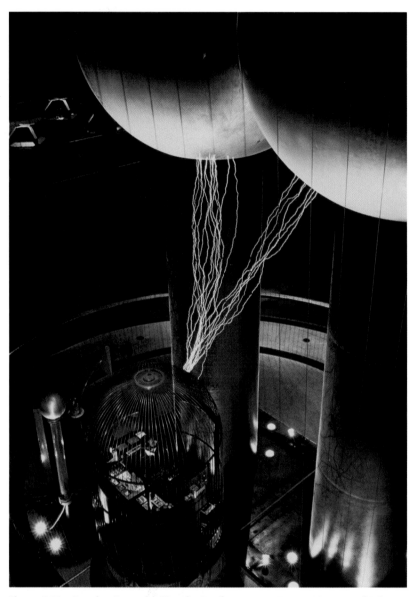

Figure 4.10    Faraday Cage with Van de Graaf generator. Boston Museum of Science, USA. Photo: Peter Menzel/Science Photo Library. Faraday showed that electrical disturbances always remain on the outside of a closed, conducting surface, such as a cage made of copper wire mesh. In this picture the operator controlling the electrical machine from inside the cage is quite safe from the large sparks hitting the cage (the dome-shaped structure at the bottom of the picture). For the same reason, passengers in aeroplanes are safe during lightning strikes, and mobile phones do not work in lifts.

formulated a new theory of the way chemical and electrical actions are related, explaining how electricity passes through chemical solutions. He invented the Faraday Cage which showed that electricity was a force rather than a fluid, as was commonly believed (see Figure 4.10 and Plate 1.4.1), and he developed a theory of how batteries work.

Of particular importance were Faraday's attempts during 1844 and 1845 to show that magnetism is a property of all matter, not just of a few metals such as iron. It would then be like other forces such as gravity. He found the evidence he was looking for in September 1845 when he shone polarised light through a special type of glass in a magnetic field. (In normal light the light waves can vibrate in any direction – up, down, sideways, or at an angle. In polarised light the waves can vibrate in only one direction. Polaroid sunglasses work by letting through only light that is vibrating up–down and cutting out all the other light.) The plane of polarisation of the light changed, depending on the orientation of the glass in the magnetic field. Faraday concluded that the glass was somehow a magnetic substance, although it could not be magnetised in the same way as iron. He showed that more than sixty other substances were similarly affected, and inferred that magnetism was a universal property of matter. He revealed these discoveries at the Friday Evening Discourse described at the start of this chapter.

Through most of these experiments, Faraday used diagrams of 'lines of force' to work out what he thought was happening, and what to try next in the laboratory. The diagrams and their purpose are described in Experiment 3.

### Experiment 3: lines of force

Faraday needed a way of explaining his ideas about electromagnetic forces to other people. To use historians' jargon, he needed a way of *representing* his ideas. An example of a representation is the word 'sun' or the drawing ☼. Neither actually is the sun, but they are both representations that communicate the idea of the sun.

To be useful to Faraday a representation had to do two things:

1  it had to lead to new ideas and help him work out what was happening
2  it had to be understandable by other people.

So, what ways of representing forces were available to Faraday? He could use words, but words are often ambiguous. Many scientists used mathematics to describe forces, but Faraday had never learned enough maths to be able to do this. That left diagrams and pictures, but they would have to be diagrams of a sort that other people were familiar with and could understand.

There were several forms of scientific diagram around at the time, but a large number of them involved lines and curves. For example, Alexander von Humboldt (1769–1859) drew charts of latitude and longitude with curves joining points of equal temperature, such as this one with America on the left, France in the middle and Asia on the right (from *Annals de Chemie et de Physique*, 1817) shown in Figure 4.11.

Lines as a method of representation were very fashionable, particularly among non-mathematical scientists.

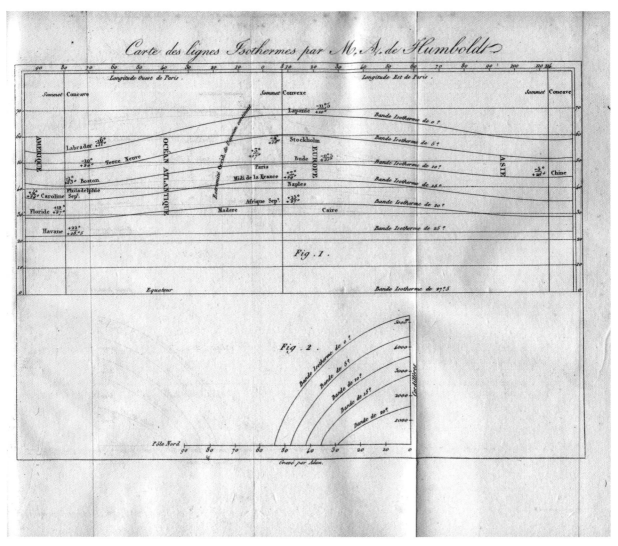

Figure 4.11   Alexander von Humboldt, chart from *Annales de Chimie et de Physique*, 1817, vol. 5. Archives & Special Collections, Bangor University. The chart shows lines joining points of equal temperature (isotherms) at different latitude and longitude.

Faraday represented magnetic forces by drawing imaginary 'lines of force' in the space around a magnet. A line of force showed the direction in which a tiny imaginary magnet would move near a real magnet or current-carrying wire. In his rotations experiment (see Experiment 1), Faraday could imagine circular lines of force around the wire pushing against the fixed magnet and moving the wire round, as in Figure 4.12.

Faraday could see similar lines in the patterns iron filings make when they are scattered on a piece of paper above a magnet (see Figure 4.13). This made the lines more believable to him and his contemporaries.

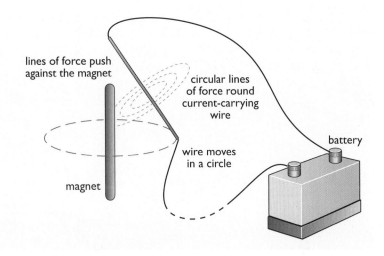

Figure 4.12 Diagram showing the circular lines of force surrounding a current-carrying wire pushing against the fixed magnet and moving the wire round the magnet.

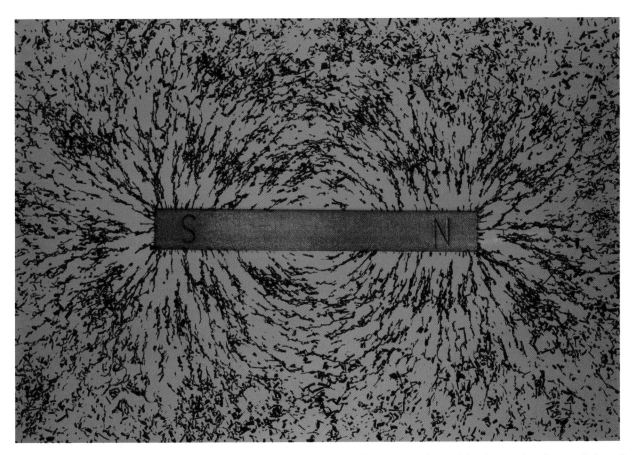

Figure 4.13 Patterns iron filings make when scattered on paper above a bar magnet. Photo: Richard Megna/Fundamental Photos/ Science Photo Library.

Lines of force proved to be an extremely useful way of explaining Faraday's thoughts to other scientists and to the public. He introduced the term 'electromagnetic field' to describe the idea that any point in space had electric and magnetic properties which could be pictured by the lines of force. As he worked at his ideas on the nature of matter and universal forces in the 1840s and 1850s, the field became his central theoretical concept. The idea was taken up by William Thomson (1824–1907) and James Clerk Maxwell (1831–79), who described it mathematically and in doing so predicted that light is an electromagnetic wave. The electromagnetic field became and remains one of the central concepts of physics to this day.

The experiments I have just described, for which Faraday is still remembered, were speculative research, with no specific practical aim. For Faraday, such experiments were 'reading the book of nature'. During the eighteenth century, natural philosophy had changed from a study of the natural world as a whole, conducted in front of an audience and often outdoors, to an investigation of discrete and well-defined phenomena in the private and controlled conditions of the laboratory. Founded right at the end of the eighteenth century, the basement of the Royal Institution provided Faraday with one of the best equipped laboratories in Europe.

Activity    Look at the picture of Faraday in his laboratory (Figure 4.14). What impression does it give of the private world of science and its relation to scientists and/or the public?

Discussion    I am struck by how well ordered everything looks! The bottles are beautifully stacked on the shelves. There is lots of space and very little clutter lying around. The focus is all on the scientific apparatus; even Faraday is over on one side and half-hidden behind the bench. The implication, I think, is that science, or nature, consists of well-ordered facts that will speak for themselves; the personalities of the people making the discoveries are unimportant.

The laboratory also seems a very private space. The entrance looks as though it is through a series of lobbies or passages, and the only window seems to be a skylight. Faraday is the only person in all this space. There is no sign of a lab assistant, although we know that Faraday had one.

Was the laboratory really as private as its location in the basement and this picture suggest? In several ways it was not. For one thing, the doors seem to have been open to anyone who wanted to visit, especially while Brande was in charge. As Faraday's reputation grew he was increasingly sought out in the basement by people wishing to talk to him about all manner of things: 'All the rest of the time has been wasted in nearly useless conversation with callers, there is no end to them in this house', he complained to a friend in 1828 (Williams et al., 1971, vol. 1, p. 91). By the mid 1830s the situation had become so bad that he issued instructions to the porters that he was not to be disturbed on Tuesdays, Thursdays and Saturdays, the strict enforcement of which rule sometimes led to mild embarrassment.

Figure 4.14 Harriet Moore, *Faraday in his Basement Laboratory* (at the Royal Institution, Albemarle Street), 1852, watercolour on paper, 40 x 47 cm. Photo: © The Royal Institution, London/The Bridgeman Art Library.

Second, the Royal Institution was, in effect, Britain's only public research laboratory. In the nineteenth century there was a general belief that understanding nature through science would lead to its control through technology for the betterment of humankind. However, it was very difficult to take scientific knowledge developed in the highly controlled environment of the laboratory and apply it successfully outside. Davy had been very lucky when he developed the miners' safety lamp with Faraday's help, but he became a victim of his own success as he sought to apply science elsewhere. Davy managed to disable the entire Royal Navy in the mid 1820s by the failure of his electro-chemical method to protect the copper sheets coating the wooden hulls of ships. Faraday, at Davy's behest, spent most of the latter part of the 1820s unsuccessfully trying to improve optical glass. This was the work that delayed his investigations into electromagnetic induction until 1831. Faraday learned from these failures and became exceedingly cautious when dealing with the practical application of science.

However, as a Sandemanian Faraday remained committed both to an ideal of public service and to trying to use science to benefit society. These commitments ensured that he did enough practical work to keep both himself and the Royal Institution in the public eye. Although the glass work was a failure, Faraday was appointed as a scientific advisor to the Admiralty and as part-time Professor of Chemistry at the Royal Military Academy, Woolwich. Several generations of Royal Engineer and Royal Artillery officers learned their chemistry from him. Faraday thus became a familiar figure in military and government circles, and one can imagine hearing the cry 'send for Faraday' in Westminster or Whitehall when complex issues required scientific and technical input. He was asked to advise on issues ranging from lightning conductors to how best to attack the Russian naval fortress of Cronstadt. He conducted two government inquiries, including that into the explosion at Haswell Colliery, County Durham, on 28 September 1844 in which 95 men and boys were killed. This was politically highly sensitive and the Prime Minister, Robert Peel (1788–1850), personally asked for Faraday's aid.

By far and away the most extensive practical work Faraday undertook was for the Corporation of Trinity House, the English and Welsh lighthouse authority. Beginning in 1836, this was an important strand in his career for the following thirty years; more than 10 per cent of Faraday's surviving letters deal with lighthouse matters. In the 1840s he invented a new type of lamp which was installed not only in all Trinity House lighthouses, but also in the Athenaeum, the new Houses of Parliament and Buckingham Palace. In the late 1850s and early 1860s Faraday oversaw the testing and installation of electric lighting at the South Foreland and Dungeness lighthouses. This was one of the earliest practical applications of the electric generator, developed from his own discovery of electromagnetic induction in 1831. That Trinity House was willing to consider it is evidence of the confidence they felt in Faraday's advice. However, in the long term the project proved too expensive and was abandoned in 1880. Trinity House did not seek to electrify again until the 1920s.

His public service ensured that Faraday was known as a government scientific advisor. But how did the public get to know about his more esoteric discoveries? Faraday's experiments were highly significant and have influenced physics and chemistry ever since. How did he tell people about them? Faraday was very aware of the public face of science, and of how to present his work effectively.

## 4.5   THE ROYAL INSTITUTION: PUBLIC FORUM

The progress of Faraday's experiments from first private ideas to public demonstration was also a physical journey from the basement laboratory to the grand first-floor lecture theatre of the Royal Institution.

Figure 4.15   Alexander Blaikley, *Faraday delivering a Christmas lecture on gold and silver before Prince Albert, the Prince of Wales (later Edward VII) and Prince Alfred*, engraving from the *Illustrated London News*, 16 February 1856, vol. 28, p. 177. Photo: © The Royal Institution, London/The Bridgeman Art Library.

Activity    Look at the picture of Faraday lecturing in the Royal Institution lecture theatre (Figure 4.15). Compare this with Figure 4.14, of him in the laboratory. How do the spaces differ?

Discussion    Unlike the laboratory, the lecture theatre looks to me like a very public space. It is packed with people, and it is arranged so that all the seats face the lecturer. He is the focus of the audience's attention. Although Faraday is, once again, off-centre, he is in a commanding position from the audience's viewpoint. Even here, though, what is really highlighted by the spotlights is the scientific apparatus on the bench. The scientific facts seem to be what is important rather than the lecturer who is explaining them. Whereas the laboratory picture seemed to emphasise the discovery of scientific facts in private, I think that this lecture picture emphasises their display to the public.

Public lectures were significant occasions in the first half of the nineteenth century. They provided not only education and self-improvement, but also fashionable entertainment. Faraday was very conscious of the commercial value of lectures and acutely aware of all aspects of lecturing success. When he began giving lectures he took great pains to get things right. He took elocution lessons to improve his delivery. He spent hours developing robust demonstrations that would not let him down at the crucial moment and that made the effects he was discussing clearly visible to his audience. He tried to make sure that his language was understandable. Above all, his enthusiasm for his subject was contagious and he rapidly developed a reputation as an unusually charismatic lecturer.

**Activity**     Read Juliet Pollock's account of Faraday's lectures (Reading 4.5), which she attended as a member of the audience. To what does she attribute his success?

**Discussion**     Pollock emphasises that Faraday was in complete command of the situation. His apparatus and experiments were well organised and under his control. To achieve this mastery of the experiments must have taken hours of preparation, although Pollock does not comment on this. Faraday was even in command of his audience, largely through his enthusiasm, conveyed by his eloquence, and his body language, all of which communicated vividly with his listeners.

But the lecture theatre was not just a public space. It was located between two private spaces, and Faraday's private life spilled over into it. On quiet evenings 'we rode round the theatre on a velocipede [an early form of bicycle] which was then a new thing' recorded Sarah's brother, George, who was fourteen when Faraday got married (Jones, 1870, vol. 1, p. 419). His lecture demonstrations had often been tested first on his family. In Faraday's Sandemanian home there were no social divisions. Cantor suggests that it was precisely because Faraday did not feel at home in the hierarchical structure of nineteenth-century society that he took such care to be in control of his lectures (Cantor, 1991, pp. 116–18). Public life was stressful for him, but he learned how to conduct himself within it.

When Faraday was appointed Director of the Laboratory in 1825 the Royal Institution was facing a financial crisis, partially driven by a fall in membership. In response, Faraday initiated the Friday Evening Discourses, where the leading scientists of the day demonstrated their work to members of the Institution and their guests. Lecturers were asked to make sure they were intelligible to non-scientists and to deal with current topics. The Discourses proved highly attractive to the media and Faraday was assiduous in ensuring that journalists were present. This provided very effective publicity for the Royal Institution and also for himself as the most frequent performer. Faraday also established the Christmas lectures, a set of six lectures delivered to children. In the course of his career Faraday delivered nineteen series himself. They became so well known that Prince Albert, Queen Victoria's husband, brought the Prince of Wales and Prince Alfred to hear them – they are shown sitting in the front row of the theatre in Figure 4.15. Both these lecture series continue to the present day, and the Christmas lectures are televised annually.

In the early 1850s, Faraday became involved in a storm of debate over mesmerism, spiritualism and table-turning that was sweeping the country. Many people thought that his discovery of universal magnetism might provide an explanation for these phenomena. Faraday's religious and scientific sensibilities were offended, and he performed some experiments that showed there was no connection. He was appalled by the widespread public ignorance about science that the debate revealed. In response he arranged a course of seven lectures in which eminent scientists discussed their particular speciality in terms of education. His own lecture, 'Observations on mental education', was subsequently published, widely discussed and frequently reprinted.

Aspects of the last ten years of Faraday's career can be interpreted as implementing the views expressed in this lecture. For example, in 1860 and 1861 he allowed his Christmas lectures on the 'Various forces of matter' and the 'Chemical history of a candle' to be published as short books. Previously Faraday had vetoed such proposals, but with his desire to make science more accessible to the public, this change of mind becomes understandable. Faraday's lectures on the candle were an enormous success. They have been continuously in print ever since and have been translated into many languages, including French, Polish and Japanese.

**Activity**

Read the excerpt from the 'Chemical history of a candle' (Reading 4.6). Do you notice anything about Faraday's style that might have contributed to the success of his lectures and the book?

Then read the piece from Faraday's scientific paper on 'Experimental researches in electricity' (Reading 4.7). This piece describes his early experiments on building an electric generator, and contains his first public use of the idea of lines of force. Do not worry about understanding the details of what Faraday is saying, but jot down some notes on how his style differs when writing for a scientific, rather than a popular, audience.

**Discussion**

In the piece from the 'Chemical history of a candle' Faraday uses fairly simple language and tries to relate what he is saying to the everyday experiences of his audience. He illustrates his general point, that the chemical nature of water is the same whether it is found as ice, liquid or steam, with specific examples that would be familiar to his audience. His listeners would all have had vivid memories of the sub-zero temperatures and frozen pipes a few days before the lecture. Faraday calls on these memories to bring his subject to life.

When writing for a scientific audience Faraday is much more willing to use complex language and scientific jargon. Even here, though, he seems concerned with finding clear ways to get his meaning across, as in his introduction of the lines of force. He is not only introducing diagrams to make himself clear, but 'dots the 'i's and crosses the 't's', pinning down the details of the ways the conductor might cut the lines of force.

Faraday's image-consciousness extended beyond his personal reputation in the lecture theatre. He was equally conscious of the image of the Royal Institution. This is particularly evident in his efforts in 1836 and 1837 to add fourteen Corinthian columns to the facade of the building. Faraday was so committed to this project that he paid some of the cost out of his own pocket. This architectural feature is shown in Figure 4.16. It continues to dominate Albemarle Street, and unifies what was probably a very messy frontage. It stated unambiguously to the public that something different happened at Number 21 compared with the hotels, clubs and publishers elsewhere in the street. It perhaps also best symbolises the mutual relationship between Faraday and the Royal Institution; without each other, both man and institution would have had entirely different histories.

Figure 4.16    Thomas Hosmer Shepherd, *The Royal Institution* (showing the facade added in 1837), *c.* 1838, watercolour on paper. Photo: © The Royal Institution, London/The Bridgeman Art Library.

Faraday never retired from the Royal Institution. Although he offered to do so in 1861 when he was seventy, the Royal Institution realised the value of his continuing presence and rejected his resignation. In 1864 Faraday was offered the presidency of the Royal Institution, provoking a serious crisis in his life. Faraday regarded himself as the servant of the Royal Institution, even though it must have been clear to him and was certainly clear to others that he had been the dominant public figure there for nearly four decades. But to become President would have publicly acknowledged his role as master, something that his religious convictions would not let him countenance.

Faraday continued to live in the Royal Institution during the lecture season from January to June, but spent an increasing amount of time in the summer and autumn at Hampton Court, where Queen Victoria had granted him the use of a house. As he declined, Brande's successor, John Tyndall (1820–93), gradually took over running the Royal Institution, but it continued to be a family affair and both Sarah Faraday and their niece, Jane Barnard (1832–1911), helped out. The petty-cash books are written in Jane Barnard's writing.

Faraday died peacefully at Hampton Court on 25 August 1867. The funeral was held five days later, the cortège stopping briefly at the Royal Institution before making its way to Highgate Cemetery. He was buried in one of the plots that had been bought by members of the Sandemanian community when the cemetery was built in the late 1830s. Sarah was later buried beside him when she died in 1879.

**Activity**
*You will need to allow a total of two hours for this activity.*

Now work through the DVD ROM 'Faraday'.

## CONCLUSION

I hope that you now have some idea of the very complex elements that went into making Faraday's reputation.

**Activity**

Look back over the chapter and at the notes you made while watching the DVD and write a few words summarising what you think the most important things were in helping Faraday to achieve fame.

**Discussion**

My summary is that I think that Faraday's major scientific discoveries were a very important basis to his contemporary fame, but no one would have known about them if he had not also been very good at public relations, enhancing both his own reputation and that of the Royal Institution with which he was closely identified. His religion underlay his approach to science. It led him to pay unusually close attention to experimental facts and helped him to see nature in new and productive ways. It also underlay the high moral code for which the Victorians admired him. In this respect Faraday was in the right place at the right time, conforming to Victorian views of what a true scientist should be like.

Your summary may be different. The issue is a very complicated one, relying on the interplay of lots of different factors in Faraday's life and in the society around him. In a summary we choose to emphasise what we consider the most important facts and relationships. You might have highlighted Faraday's public service, his management of the Royal Institution, his lecturing technique, or his upwardly mobile social status. Your choice is likely to depend on what else you know about science or the Victorian period and how Faraday's life fits into this previous knowledge. The essential thing is that your conclusions are justified by evidence.

## REFERENCES

Cantor, G.N. (1991) *Michael Faraday: Sandemanian and Scientist*, Basingstoke and London, Macmillan.

Gooding, D. and James, F.A.J.L. (1985) *Faraday Rediscovered: Essays on the Life and Work of Michael Faraday, 1791–1867*, Basingstoke and New York, Macmillan.

James, F.A.J.L. (1993) *The Correspondence of Michael Faraday*, vol. 2: *1832–40*, London, Institution of Electrical Engineers.

Jones, B. (1870) *The Life and Letters of Faraday*, 2 vols, London, Longmans, Green.

Williams, L.P., Fitzgerald, R. and Stallybrass, O. (eds) (1971) *The Selected Correspondence of Michael Faraday*, 2 vols, Cambridge, Cambridge University Press.

# RESOURCES

Reading 4.1    **The late Professor Faraday**

The world of science lost on Sunday one of its most assiduous and enthusiastic members. The life of Michael Faraday had been spent from early manhood in the single pursuit of scientific discovery, and though his years extended to 73, he preserved to the end the freshness and vivacity of youth in the exposition of his favourite subjects, coupled with a measure of simplicity which youth never attains. His perfect mastery of the branches of physical knowledge he cultivated, and the singular absence of personal display which characterized everything he did, must have made him under any circumstances a lecturer of the highest rank, but as a man of science he was gifted with the rarest felicity of experimenting, so that the illustrations of his subjects seemed to answer with magical ease to his call. It was this peculiar combination which made his lectures attractive to crowded audiences in Albemarle-street for so many years, and which brought Christmas after Christmas, troops of young people to attend his expositions of scientific processes and scientific discovery with as much zest as is usually displayed in following lighter amusements.

Faraday was born in the neighbourhood of London in the year 1794 [correct date is 1791]. He was one of those men who have become distinguished in spite of every disadvantage of origin and of early education, and if the contrast between the circumstances of his birth and of his later worldly distinction be not so dazzling as is sometimes seen in other walks of life, it is also true that his career was free from the vulgar ambition and uneasy strife after place and power which not uncommonly detract from the glory of the highest honours. His father was a smith, and he himself, after a very imperfect elementary education, was apprenticed to a bookbinder named Riebau, in Blandford-street. He was, however, already inspired with the love of natural science. His leisure was spent in the conduct of such chymical experiments as were within his means and he ventured on the construction of an electrifying machine, thus fore-showing the particular sphere of his greatest future discoveries. He was eager to quit trade for the humblest position as a student of physical science, and his tastes becoming known to a gentleman who lived in his master's neighbourhood, he obtained for him admission to the chymical lectures which Sir Humphry Davy [...] was delivering at the Royal Institution. This was in 1812. Faraday not only attended the lectures, but took copious notes of them, which he carefully re-wrote and boldly sent to Sir Humphry, begging his assistance in his desire 'to escape from trade and to enter into the service of science.' [...] Early in 1813 the opportunity came. The post of assistant in the Laboratory in Albemarle-street became vacant, and Sir Humphry offered it to Faraday, who accepted it with a pleasure which can be easily imagined, and thus commenced in March, 1813, the connexion between Faraday and the Royal Institution which only terminated with his life. [...] The only instance of a suspension [...] of his connexion with the Royal Institution occurred from October, 1813, to April, 1815, during which time he accompanied Sir Humphry as his scientific assistant and secretary in his travels on the Continent. [...] In 1821, while assisting Davy in pursuing the investigation of the relations between electricity and magnetism, first started by Oersted, he made the brilliant discovery of the convertible rotation of a magnetic pole and an electric current, which was the prelude to his wonderful series of experimental researches in electricity. These investigations procured him the honour of being elected Corresponding Member of the Academy of Sciences in 1823, and Fellow of the Royal Society in 1825. In 1827 he published his first work, a volume on *Chymical Manipulation*; and in 1829 he was appointed Chymical Lecturer at the Royal Military Academy at Woolwich, a post he held, in conjunction with his duties at the Royal Institution, for many years. In 1831, his first paper appeared in the *Philosophical Transactions* on the subject of electricity, describing his experimental studies of the science, and from that time for many years the *Transactions* annually contained papers by Faraday giving the method and results of his investigations. [...] It is not too much to say that by the experiments thus described Faraday formed the science of electricity. He established the identity of the forces manifested in the phenomena known as electrical, galvanic, and magnetic; he ascertained with exactness the laws of its action; he determined its correlation with the other primal forces of the natural world. While he was still pursuing the brilliant career of investigation which thus proved so successful, the chair of Chymistry was founded at the Royal Institution in 1833, and Faraday was naturally appointed the first Professor. In 1835 he was recommended by Lord Melbourne for a pension of 300*l*. [£300] a year, in recognition of his great distinction as a discoverer. From that time his career has been one of increasing honour. Oxford conferred on him an honorary degree upon the first occasion of the meeting of the British Association at the University. He was raised from the position of Corresponding Member to be one of the eight foreign Associates of the Academy of Sciences. He was an officer of the Legion of Honour, and Prussia and Italy decorated him with the crosses of different orders. The Royal Society conferred on him its own medal and the Romford medal. In 1858 the Queen most graciously allotted to him a residence at Hampton Court, between which and Albemarle-street he spent the last years of his life, and where he peaceably died on Sunday. The belief in the disinterested zeal and lofty purity of life of the students of philosophy, which was one motive for Faraday's petition when a lad to Davy to enable him to become a servant in the humblest walks of science rather than to spend his days in the pursuit of trade, was redeemed by Faraday's whole life. No man was ever more entirely unselfish, or more entirely beloved. Modest, truthful, candid, he had the true spirit of a philosopher and of a Christian, for it may be said of him, in the words of the father of English poetry, –

'Gladly would he learn, and gladly teach.'

The cause of science would meet with fewer enemies, its discoveries would command a more ready assent, were all its votaries imbued with the humility of Michael Faraday.

Source: obituary from *The Times*, 28 August 1867, p. 7, Issue 25901, col. C.

Reading 4.2    **Early observations on lecturing**

[W]hen I found myself pleased, [I] endeavoured to ascertain the particular circumstance that had affected me; also, [...] I observed how the audience were affected, and by what their pleasure and their censure were drawn forth.

[...]

There is another circumstance to be considered with respect to a lecture room of as much importance almost as light itself, and that is ventilation. [...] How have I wished the lecture finished, the lights extinguished and myself away merely to obtain a fresh supply of [air]! The want of it caused the want of attention, of pleasure, and even of comfort [...].

[I]t appears proper next to consider the subject fit for the purposes of a lecture. Science is undeniably the most eminent in its fitness for this purpose. There is no part of it that may not be treated of, illustrated, and explained with profit and pleasure to the hearers in this manner. The facility, too, with which it allows of manual and experimental illustration places it foremost in this class of subjects. [...] The fitness of subjects, however, is connected in an inseparable manner with the kind of audience that is to be present [...]

Polite company expect to be entertained not only by the subject of the lecture, but by the manner of the lecturer; they look for respect, for language consonant to their dignity, and ideas on a level with their own. The vulgar – that is to say in general, those who will take the trouble of thinking, and the bees of business – wish for something that they can comprehend. This may be deep and elaborate for the learned, but for those who are as yet tyros and unacquainted with the subject must be simple and plain. [...]

The hour at which a lecture should be delivered should be considered at the same time with the nature of the audience we expect or wish for. If we would suit a particular class of persons, we must fix it at the hour most convenient for them [...]

I need not point out to the active mind of my friend the astonishing disproportion, or rather difference, in the perceptive powers of the eye and the ear, and the facility and clearness with which the first of these organs conveys ideas to the mind [...].

Apparatus therefore is an essential part of every lecture in which it can be introduced; but to apparatus should be added, at every convenient opportunity, illustrations that may not perhaps deserve the name of apparatus and of experiments, and yet may be introduced with considerable force and effect in proper places. Diagrams, and tables too, are necessary [...]. [T]he whole should be so arranged as to keep one operation from interfering with another. If the lecture table appears crowded, if the lecturer (hid by his apparatus) is invisible, if things appear crooked, or aside, or unequal, or if some are out of sight, and this without any particular reason, the lecturer is considered (and with reason too) as an awkward contriver and a bungler.

[...]

The utterance should not be rapid and hurried, and consequently unintelligible, but slow and deliberate, conveying ideas with ease from the lecturer, and infusing them with clearness and readiness into the minds of the audience. A lecturer should endeavour by all means to obtain a facility of utterance, and the power of clothing his thoughts and ideas in language smooth and harmonious and at the same time simple and easy.

Source: Jones, 1870, vol. 1, pp. 66–72.

### Reading 4.3    Cornelia Crosse visits Faraday, 1850

One of the earliest visits we paid in London, after our marriage in 1850, – was an afternoon call on Mr. and Mrs. Faraday at the Royal Institution. [...]

I had never yet seen Faraday. A feeling of awe overcame me, as we ascended the long flight of stairs leading to the Upper Chambers of that famous house in Albemarle Street. With the knowledge that we were approaching the Arcana of Science, I was in no condition of sympathy with the fools that rush in, but rather felt restrained by the reverent spirits of those who fear to tread, on sacred ground. The very sound of the homely door-knocker, rapped on my heart. [...]

We entered, and were kindly greeted by Mrs. Faraday, who led us through the outer sitting room, into an inner sanctum; there was Faraday himself, half reclining on a sofa – with a heap of circulating library novels round him; he had evidently rejected some, that were thrown carelessly on the floor – but his eyes were glued on the exciting pages of a third volume.

'He reads a great many novels, and it is very good for him to divert his mind,' said Mrs Faraday to us, later on. [...]

[W]e wanted to engage the Faradays to pay us a visit at Fyne Court, in the late summer, when they would be able to get away from London. [...]

The conversation had begun simply enough, about the novels of Lever and Trollope, and the promise of the first Exhibition, which was to be opened ere many months; but science was too near to both these enthusiasts for them to remain long without touching on the subject.

Leaving the eager talkers to their allotropic condition of oxygen in the atmosphere [...] Mrs. Faraday drew me aside, and candidly told me, in much kindness, and with true wifely wisdom, that our house, was of all places, the one where she could not permit her husband to spend his holiday. She was well aware that Fyne Court had its laboratories and foundries, in short had electrical arrangements from garret to basement, and she foresaw that Faraday, instead of resting his brains, would be talking science all day long.

Source: Cornelia Crosse (1891) 'Science and Society in the Fifties', *Temple Bar*, vol. 93, pp. 33–5.

## Reading 4.4     Faraday on scientific method

Faraday did not view the physical world as an inanimate object to be subjected to scientific analysis but instead as the work of God that manifested its divine origin. [...]

In a revealing sentence in his lecture on mental education Faraday vividly portrayed the relationship between God, man and nature in the following terms: 'for the book of nature, which we have to read, is written by the finger of God'. [...] [T]he investigation of nature is like reading a book, and just as the Sandemanians sought to understand every word in the Bible without introducing distortions of human origin, so Faraday aimed to comprehend God's other book with integrity and without giving reign to imagination or prejudice. In pursuing the empirical method great care had therefore to be taken to read correctly the God-made signs that are accessible to the scientist.

In order both to curb his overactive imagination and to read God's work correctly, Faraday nailed his flag firmly to the empiricist mast. He believed that facts, and only facts, are the basic signs of nature and the foundation on which the whole edifice of science has to be constructed. As he told the audience at his lecture on mental education, a 'fundamental fact ... never fails us, its evidence is always true', and he portrayed science as dependent 'upon carefully observed facts'.

[...]

Moreover, [...] his appeal to facts possessed clear psychological overtones. Thus, writing to Whewell in 1835 he admitted that 'I feel that my *safety* consists in facts; and even these I am but too anxious [not] to pervert through the influence of preconceived notions'. [...] His fears of losing control and of being carried away by flights of imagination (or by prejudice) were overcome by the safe shelter that firmly based facts could provide. His persona, and with it his science, could be saved by facts and facts alone. As he wrote to Schoenbein in 1858, 'without experiments [which produce facts] I am nothing'!

A letter to Schoenbein dating from February 1845 indicates a further significance of Faraday's cult of facts. This letter comes from the period when his memory was most treacherous, and he was frequently unable to think constructively or understand the work of other scientists. His thoughts were unstable and tended to evaporate unless 'there is some visible body before my eyes, or some large fact approaching with force to the external senses, and easy to be produced, to sustain, by a sort of material evidence for the existence of a thought'. At this dark period of his life Faraday could stabilise his mind by concentrating on 'some large fact' that also provided assurance that he was still in contact with physical reality. If in his philosophy of science Faraday appears to have adopted a form of empiricism found among many eighteenth- and early nineteenth-century writers, it should be remembered that his emphasis on facts bears not only the marks of his religious beliefs but also possesses psychological significance.

Source: Cantor, 1991, pp. 199–201 (footnotes omitted).

Reading 4.5   **Michael Faraday' lectures**

He should be remembered in his characteristic phases; first, as he stood at the lecture table, with his voltaic batteries, his electro-magnetic helix, his large electrical machine, his glass retorts, and all his experimental apparatus about him [...]. His instruments were never in his way, and his manipulation never interfered with his discourse. He was completely master of the situation; he had his audience at his command, as he had himself and all his belongings; he had nothing to fret him, and he could give his eloquence full sway. It was an irresistible eloquence, which compelled attention and insisted upon sympathy. It waked the young from their visions and the old from their dreams. There was a gleaming in his eyes which no painter could copy and which no poet could describe. [...] His thought was rapid, and made itself a way in new phrases, if it found none ready made, – as the mountaineer cuts steps in the most hazardous ascent with his own axe. His enthusiasm sometimes carried him to the point of ecstasy when he expatiated on the beauty of nature, and when he lifted the veil from her deep mysteries. His body then took motion from his mind; his hair streamed out from his head, his hands were full of nervous action, his light, lithe body seemed to quiver with its eager life. His audience took fire with him, and every face was flushed. Whatever might be the after-thought or the after-pursuit, each hearer for the time shared his zeal and his delight.

Source: Juliet Pollock (1870) 'Michael Farady', *St Paul's Magazine*, vol. 5, pp. 293–4.

Reading 4.6    **Chemical history of a candle**

I must first of all tell you that this water may exist in different conditions [...] water [...] is entirely and absolutely the same thing, whether it is produced from a candle, by combustion, or from the rivers or ocean.

First of all, water, when at the coldest, is ice. Now, we philosophers – I hope that I may class you and myself together in this case – speak of water as water, whether it be in its solid, or liquid, or gaseous state, – we speak of it chemically as water. [...] Water may occur as ice; and you have had most excellent opportunities lately of seeing this. Ice changes back into water – for we had on our last Sabbath a strong instance of this change, by the sad catastrophe which occurred in our own house, as well as in the houses of many of our friends, – ice changes back into water when the temperature is raised: water also changes into steam when it is warmed enough. The water which we have here before us is in its densest state, and although it changes in weight, in condition, in form, and in many other qualities, it still is water.

Source: Michael Faraday (1861) *A Course of Six Lectures on the Chemical History of a Candle, to which is added A Lecture on Platinum*, edited by William Crookes, London, Griffin, Bohn, pp. 73–4 (footnote omitted).

Reading 4.7    **Experimental researches in electricity**

83    Upon obtaining electricity from magnets ... I hoped to ... construct a new electrical machine.

101    It is now evident that the rotating plate is merely another form of the simpler experiment of passing a piece of metal between the magnetic poles in a rectilinear direction, and that in such cases currents of electricity are produced at right angles to the direction of the motion, and crossing it at the place of the magnetic pole or poles. This was sufficiently shown by the following simple experiment: A piece of copper plate one-fifth of an inch thick, one inch and a half wide, and twelve inches long, ... was placed between the magnetic poles, whilst the two conductors from the galvanometer were held in contact with its edges; it was then drawn through between the poles of the conductors in the direction of the arrow, fig.16; immediately the galvanometer needle was deflected, ...

114    ... the law which governs the evolution of electricity by magneto-electric induction, is very simple, although rather difficult to express. If in fig.24. PN represent a horizontal wire passing by a marked magnetic pole, so that the direction of its motion shall coincide with the curved line proceeding from below upwards; ... or if it pass the pole in other directions, but so as to cut the magnetic curves in the same general direction,

or on the same side as they would be cut by the wire if moving along the dotted curved line; – then the current of electricity in the wire is from P to N. If it be carried in the reverse directions, the electric current will be from N to P.

Source: Michael Faraday (1832) 'Experimental researches in electricity', *Philosophical Transactions of the Royal Society of London*, vol. 122, pp. 125–62 (footnote omitted).

# 5 STALIN

*Mark Pittaway*

| | | |
|---|---|---:|
| **INTRODUCTION** | | **125** |
| **5.1** | **SETTING STALIN IN CONTEXT** | **127** |
| | Stalin's rise: the creation of a personal dictatorship, 1924–28 | 130 |
| | Revolution from above, 1928–34 | 130 |
| | The era of the purges, 1934–39 | 131 |
| | The Great Patriotic War (1941–45) and its origins, 1939–45 | 131 |
| | Post-war Stalinism, 1945–53 | 132 |
| **5.2** | **STALIN'S CONTESTED REPUTATION** | **133** |
| **5.3** | **THE MYTH OF STALIN** | **136** |
| **5.4** | **INTERPRETING THE STALIN ERA** | **145** |
| **CONCLUSION** | | **149** |
| **REFERENCES** | | **150** |
| **RESOURCES** | | **151** |
| | Reading 5.1 | 151 |
| | Reading 5.2 | 152 |
| | Reading 5.3 | 153 |
| | Reading 5.4 | 155 |

**MATERIALS YOU WILL NEED**

- Illustration Book

**AIMS**

This chapter will:

- introduce you to the issues involved in setting Stalin in his historical context
- introduce you to issues of historical interpretation
- provide an introduction to some of the issues involved in using historical evidence appropriately
- show how myths are constructed around historical figures, with specific reference to Stalin, and how these are constitutive of reputations
- provide you with the means of distinguishing between myths and historical views of particular figures.

# INTRODUCTION

In this chapter we will look at the issues involved in examining
historically the reputation of Josef Stalin (1878–1953) in order to
prompt you to think about what history is, and what historians do.
Stalin was unquestionably one of the major figures of the twentieth
century. He was one of the most significant leaders of the Soviet
Union – the Union of Soviet Socialist Republics (USSR) – the state
created in 1922 to succeed the Russian empire, which lasted until
1991. Stalin was responsible for shaping the country during the 1930s;
he presided over its victory in the Second World War against
Nazi Germany, and oversaw the start of the state having
superpower status in the post-war years.

**Activity**    I'd like to start by asking you about your prior knowledge or views of Stalin.
Quickly note down some words that you think best describe him. If you don't
feel that you know enough to do this at this stage, don't worry; just refer
to the discussion. Don't spend any more than a few minutes on this task –
it is an 'ideas-storming' exercise, and there are no right or wrong answers.

**Discussion**    You may have said any number of things here, but if I had to identify Stalin
in a word or short phrase I might use 'dictator', 'Soviet leader', 'Communist',
'world leader', 'war leader' or 'mass murderer'.

As we will see below, there are a number of different assessments of Stalin's
reputation. Perhaps the one that is most current is that of a violent,
twentieth-century dictator, whose rule was steeped in murder. If we are
attempting a historical evaluation, issues of Stalin's reputation are more
complex. This is almost always the case with any historical evaluation of a
historical figure.

In this chapter we will examine Stalin's reputation historically. I will:

- introduce you to Stalin and his immediate historical context
- demonstrate that his reputation is contested by different actors –
  that is to say, people or institutions that play significant historical
  roles – in different ways
- show you that certain elements of Stalin's reputation have been
  shaped by what I call the *myth* of Stalin
- point out that historians have a duty to interrogate myths because of
  an obligation to tell the truth as they see it about past events, and to
  show that they do so by constructing *interpretations* of the past,
  based on *evidence*
- show that because of the existence and importance of *myth*, many
  *interpretations* exist in a dialogue with myths (for this reason
  historians are centrally interested in how myths come to be
  constructed)
- and finally show that there are legitimate differences of
  interpretation of evidence, which result in scholarly differences
  between historians.

You will note here that I am introducing you to a range of concepts, some of which will seem relatively new, whereas others may be more familiar. In Chapter 1 you were introduced to the concept of using evidence to assess a historical figure, and Chapter 4 will have further developed your awareness of this issue. Both chapters address the uncertainties involved in discovering 'what happened', and consequently they have introduced you to the concept of *interpretation* – or in other words, how we use evidence to construct an account of past events. So some of the more abstract issues that we will explore in this chapter will build on work that you have done already. However, in this chapter I will introduce a new concept, that of *myth*, and I'd like you to spend a small amount of time thinking about that concept before we move on.

**Activity**   Look up the terms 'history' and 'myth' in a dictionary, and then take some time to reflect on the differences between them.

**Discussion**   I expect that most answers to this activity will point out that, in relation to the past, a myth is a distorted account of events, whereas a historical account is more 'truthful'. This is not inaccurate, but the issue is slightly more complicated than this.

*You can consult the* Oxford English Dictionary *online through the course website.*   I looked up 'myth' in the *Oxford English Dictionary* (*OED*). At first sight it didn't seem that the definition helped very much: 'A purely fictitious narrative usually involving supernatural person, actions, or events, and embodying some popular idea concerning natural or historical phenomena.'

Obviously we can't use a definition of myth that emphasises the purely fictional, but we can work to some extent with a definition that stresses a 'popular idea concerning ... historical phenomena'. We need also to revisit the 'fictional' aspect of the *OED*'s definition, because our definition should look something like 'a popular idea concerning historical phenomena, which distorts the reality of past events, or cannot be fitted with the weight of the available evidence'.

When I looked up 'history' I found a large number of possible definitions and a multitude of examples of their use. There seemed to me to be two definitions given by the *OED* which are relevant to us: 'A written narrative constituting a continuous methodical record, in order of time, of important or public events, esp. those connected with a particular country, people, individual etc'; and 'That branch of knowledge which deals with past events, as recorded in writings or otherwise ascertained; the formal record of the past, esp. of human affairs or actions; the study or formation and growth of communities and nations.'

The question of what history is, of course, is a complex one, and there are many definitions and much academic dispute over them. All we need here is a provisional working definition. 'A written narrative constituting a continuous methodical record', as the *OED* puts it, is often the end result of historical investigation. In order to answer what history is, we need to combine our sense of the end product with the description of history as a field of knowledge contained in the second definition. Let's define history as an account of past events based upon the interpretation of all the available evidence that relates to the particular aspect of the past it is studying.

The key, therefore, to grasping the difference between myth and history is that where myth is a distortion and cannot be fitted with the weight of the available evidence, history is an account that aims at capturing the truth about the past through a careful interpretation of evidence. It is worth noting that the issue is slightly more complex, for myths about the past play important roles in shaping the actions of historical actors. Historical accounts of the past are often constructed as replies to mythical accounts. Therefore, even though they are distinct, in practice the two are locked in continuous dialogue with each other.

I'd like you to put to one side any notes you have made on this activity for now. We will revisit and expand upon some of these themes later in the chapter.

## 5.1 SETTING STALIN IN CONTEXT

Josef Stalin was born Iosif Vissarionovich Dzhugashvii in 1879, in the provincial town of Gori in Georgia, then part of the Russian empire, the son of a none-too-successful cobbler. Little is known of his early life, but by the age of twenty he was already involved in socialist political activism in his native Georgia, following his expulsion from the theological seminary in the Georgian capital, Tblisi, where he had been studying. An activist in the Russian Social Democratic Workers' Party, which sought the outright revolutionary transformation of the Russian empire, Stalin came to the attention of the police. In and out of prison, he associated with the **Bolshevik** faction, which split from the Social Democratic Workers' Party as a consequence of an ideological dispute over strategy. The Bolsheviks argued against their rivals in favour of immediate socialist revolution across the empire.

By the outbreak of the First World War, Stalin already occupied a key position on the Central Committee of the Bolshevik Party, and had gained a formidable reputation as a revolutionary organiser. Arrested and imprisoned by the political police in 1913, he spent most of the First World War in **internal exile** in Siberia. When the monarchy fell during Russia's February 1917 Revolution, Stalin was able to join other leading Bolsheviks, newly returned from exile, at the heart of the revolution in Petrograd, then the capital of the Russian empire. With the Bolsheviks' seizure of power in October, Stalin became one of the leading figures building a new socialist state in the aftermath of the revolution.

Our focus in this chapter is not on his early life, but on the 'Stalin era', a period that is generally understood to begin in the mid 1920s, following the power struggle in the leadership of the Communist – formerly the Bolshevik – Party, that arose after the death of Lenin in 1924, and ended with Stalin's death in 1953. As you read this chapter you will notice that I concentrate on one distinct sub-period of the

Stalin era: that between 1928 and 1941. This is because the controversies that surround the events of this period are central to a discussion of Stalin's reputation.

Before I provide you with a sketch, or 'road map', with which to navigate your way around the Stalin era, it is important to set this period in a larger context. Stalin as a political figure and 'Stalinism' – the political system that bore his name – were products of Russia's October Revolution in 1917. This was the second of the revolutions of that year in which the Bolsheviks, or Communists, seized power, after which they began to impose their vision of the future on the Russian empire. In contrast to many of the groups who had helped to overthrow Tsar Nicholas II in February–March 1917, the Bolsheviks and their leader, Lenin (born Vladimir Illich Ulyanov, 1870–1924), believed in the creation of 'a dictatorship of the proletariat', a dictatorial state which justified itself as ruling in the interests of the working class. According to Lenin's conception of the 'dictatorship of the proletariat', power was held by a small group of committed revolutionaries. They would create a new kind of society – a socialist society – from above.

The Bolsheviks' 'dictatorship of the proletariat' and the extreme violence of the years of the civil war (1918–22), in which those on the losing sides of the events of 1917 attempted unsuccessfully to overturn the revolution, shaped the creation of a repressive state, capable of exerting considerable despotic power in the interests of the defence of the revolution. Russia's revolutionary state was a bold experiment. It was the creation of the world's first socialist revolution, and while political upheaval elsewhere in Europe following the First World War briefly suggested that other states might follow the route of Russia, such expectations were quickly dashed. Consequently, Russia and then the Soviet Union – effectively the socialist successor state of the Russian empire, created in 1922 (see Figure 5.1) – was the world's only socialist state by the early 1920s, and it was ringed by other states which were profoundly hostile.

One problem was that its leaders had little clear strategy for building a socialist state and society. All were disciples of the thinker Karl Marx (1818–83), who believed that a socialist state would only emerge in advanced, industrial societies. Marx's writings left few clues for the practical revolutionary on how a socialist society could be built, and Russia, with its large peasant majority and its peripheral role in the European economy, was far from being an advanced, industrial capitalist society. The Bolsheviks were divided: some argued that the future of the revolution could only be secured by exporting it; others stressed the importance of consolidation – of building a successful Soviet state; that is, a state whose institutional design was based on the principles of the Bolshevik conception of the 'dictatorship of the proletariat' outlined above. There were also differences between those who advocated radical nationalisation (the taking of most private property into state ownership) and rapid industrialisation on the one hand, and those who called for a gradual construction of socialism, which allowed for some private enterprise and for market forces to operate for a considerable period of time. While Lenin remained alive his authority was unquestioned, but from 1922 he fell seriously ill; he died in 1924. Stalin, as General Secretary of the Communist Party, controlled the party's organisation, but at this point he had to share power with other revolutionary leaders who possessed more prestige and power in the party. Of these the most important were Leon Trotsky (1879–1940), who led those on the left of the party and advocated radical domestic policies and as rapid an export of revolution as possible, and Nikolai Bukharin (1888–1938), who represented the position that stressed consolidation.

Figure 5.1   Map of the Soviet Union, 1922.

Having set the scene I'm now going to provide an outline of the Stalin era, which you may need to refer to as you work through later sections of this chapter. The following chronology, with commentary, is divided into five sub-periods – what historians call a **periodisation** of the Stalin era.

## Stalin's rise: the creation of a personal dictatorship, 1924–28

As we saw above, at the time of Lenin's death the party was divided on the question of the strategy it needed to pursue to build a socialist society. The Soviet Union, created from the Russian empire in 1922, was isolated internationally. Following the regime's victory in the civil war, Lenin had – in the interests of consolidating Bolshevik rule – introduced what was termed the New Economic Policy (NEP), which protected private ownership in agriculture and thus brought support from the rural majority. Under the NEP, unemployment was high and market forces played a considerable role in the economy – two factors that caused disquiet in the party.

In 1924 Trotsky, the most charismatic of the revolutionary leaders, was the obvious successor to Lenin. Stalin used his control of the party machine and allied himself to the right of the party by arguing that, in view of the Soviet Union's international isolation, the regime would have to build 'Socialism in One Country' in order to survive. During 1926 and 1927, Stalin used this alliance to remove Trotsky and his allies from all positions of influence in the party, and eventually forced Trotsky into exile in 1928.

## Revolution from above, 1928–34

Having dispensed with the left of the party, Stalin moved to extend his power by attacking the more cautious right. He was instrumental in launching the First Five-Year Plan in 1928. It broke radically with the practices of the NEP by dispensing with market mechanisms. Its aim was to secure the survival of the Soviet state by industrialising as rapidly as circumstances allowed. The plan rested on the construction of a 'command economy' through which economic actors were to respond to central instructions rather than market forces. Stalin combined the introduction of this plan with an attack on the right, which began with the Shakhty Trial in 1928 in which a group of mining engineers were accused of sabotaging the national economy. This trial culminated in the removal of Bukharin and his allies from all positions of influence.

Stalin pressed on with his 'revolution from above' not only by continuing rapid and radical policies of industrialisation, but by destroying market forces and private property along with agriculture in the **collectivisation** campaign begun in 1930. Collectivisation meant that peasants would no longer be able to farm plots that they owned.

Instead their farms would be subsumed into larger units and would be farmed on an industrial scale. This campaign produced a situation close to civil war in the countryside as peasants resisted giving their land to the new agricultural collectives. The problem was resolved through massive repression.

Stalin's 'revolution from above' saw the consolidation of his own personal dictatorship and the beginning of what was later called his 'cult of personality'. This meant that power became highly personalised, and all events inside the country were presented as an extension of the will and wisdom of Stalin himself. These changes also brought massive social upheaval. The collectivisation drive led to famine in Ukraine and parts of European Russia in 1932–33, in which around six million died. It also led to a huge influx from the countryside into overcrowded cities as millions took employment in expanding industries. It was an era of considerable contrasts: upward mobility for some, and hardship for many.

## The era of the purges, 1934–39

This period began with the unexplained assassination of the Leningrad party boss Sergei Kirov (1886–1934) in December 1934. Stalin blamed the assassination on a conspiracy of followers of Trotsky inside the Soviet Union, and this initiated a wave of 'show trials' – politically motivated trials based on fabricated evidence, designed to demonstrate that external enemies were responsible for the assassination – during 1935. The technique of the show trial was not new (indeed, the Shakhty Trial was an earlier example), but the second half of the 1930s saw an explosion in the number of such trials and the extent of repression was unprecedented. A wide range of setbacks was blamed by the authorities on so-called 'conspiracies' of various kinds from an 'external enemy', and a wave of repression gripped the country which affected party members, government officials, economic and cultural leaders, and military commanders, among others. The extent of the purges is demonstrated by the fact that between the years 1930 and 1953, 88 per cent of all executions occurred in the two peak years of the purges, 1937 and 1938 (Overy, 2005, p. 194).

## The Great Patriotic War (1941–45) and its origins, 1939–45

During the 1930s the Soviet Union became fearful of the growing military power of Nazi Germany, with its strongly anti-communist ideas and stated intentions of expanding to the east and, by implication, into Soviet territory. In August 1939 the Soviet Union made an agreement with Germany when its Foreign Minister, Vyacheslav Molotov (1890–1986), signed a treaty with Joachim von Ribbentrop (1893–1946), his German opposite number. Under the terms of this agreement (the so-called Molotov–Ribbentrop Pact, also known as the Nazi–Soviet Pact) the Soviets invaded eastern Poland, overran the formerly independent Baltic states (Estonia, Latvia and Lithuania), and attempted, unsuccessfully, to subjugate Finland. But the truce did not last long and Germany attacked the Soviet Union in June 1941 with the intention of destroying the Soviet state and redrawing the map of eastern Europe and European Russia. It was a vicious war of extermination and although the Soviet state barely survived in late 1941, it was able to turn the tide, defeating the Germans at the battle of Stalingrad in 1942–43. From this point the Red Army (the Soviet Union's army) was able to advance and occupy Berlin, bringing an end to the war in Europe in May 1945. At this point the Soviet Union occupied all of eastern Europe but, though victory brought the Soviet Union superpower status and Stalin tremendous personal prestige, it was achieved at enormous human cost.

## Post-war Stalinism, 1945–53

The post-war period was dominated by the reassertion of ideological control over the Soviet Union. This involved a reversal of the relaxation of repression directed against groups such as the church and intellectuals during the war years in the interests of building a necessary degree of national unity. Thus the post-war period saw the restoration of a highly repressive political system reminiscent of that of the 1930s, even if the excesses of the purges were never repeated on the same breathtaking scale. The period was also shaped by the pressures of reconstructing a country which had suffered catastrophic economic damage and population loss at the same time as it found its status on the international stage enhanced. It saw the extension of both Soviet territory (see Figure 5.2) and influence, with the creation of new communist states, inspired by the Soviet example, in eastern Europe, China and Korea. This, in turn, led to the rise of tension with the other unambiguous victor of the Second World War, the United States, and thus the beginning of the Cold War which would last until 1989. This period ended with the death of Stalin in 1953.

**Activity**    Spend ten to fifteen minutes reviewing the outline of the Stalin era above. Briefly identify three or four themes that strike you as common to the five sub-periods into which I've divided the Stalin era.

**Discussion**    This is my list of some of the themes that run across the five sub-periods:

- Stalin's personal power, and the importance he placed on his own control of the party, and on ideological conformity

- the extent of repression

- concern with the Soviet Union's international position and, indeed, its growth in prestige as an international actor throughout the period

- social change – the transformation of the Soviet Union from a predominantly agricultural, peasant-based society to a 'socialist' industrial society.

Figure 5.2   Map of the Soviet Union, 1945.

## 5.2   STALIN'S CONTESTED REPUTATION

Stalin's reputation has been shaped by the impact of the substantial repression that occurred during his rule and consequently by his responsibility for politically motivated mass murder. There is no question that the period outlined in the previous section was one of unprecedented state-led violence. Statistical counts of state-directed murder are the subject of tremendous historical controversy in a range of different contexts – whether we are talking about the number of victims of Nazi rule in Germany, of Pol Pot's Cambodia or those of Stalin's Soviet Union. Although it is impossible to get a comprehensive and reliable final figure of the number of Stalin's victims, we can gain an idea of the scale of death from the incomplete evidence that is available. For example, we might concentrate on those who came into contact with the repressive agencies, most notably the NKVD (*Narodnõi Komissariat Vnutrennih Del*, or People's Commisariat for Internal Affairs, the main organ responsible for internal security in the Stalin era), during the period of Stalin's rule. According to figures produced by painstaking research in the archives since the fall of the Soviet Union in 1991, a total of 776,074 people were executed by the Soviet state during the period between 1930 and

1953. Over a shorter period – between 1934 and 1947 – a staggering 6,711,037 people were imprisoned in its network of prison camps – known as the Gulag – of whom 980,091 died or were killed while in custody (Overy, 2005, pp. 194, 614). These figures underrate the extent of politically motivated murder. They do not include, for example, the six million people who are estimated to have died during the famine of 1932–33, which is now widely recognised to have been a consequence of state policies designed to collectivise agriculture in the countryside and feed the exploding populations of the major cities during the industrialisation drives of the period. Nor do they include politically motivated acts of violence by the Soviet state against whole ethnic groups: during the Second World War, for example, the state deported members of ethnic minorities from the Crimea and the Caucasus to Kazakhstan, Kirgiztan, Siberia and Uzbezkistan. The 'political unreliability' of these groups was cited as the reason for their removal. Of the 608,749 deported from the Caucasus in 1943–44, 146,892 were dead five years later; of the 228,392 forced from their homes in the Crimea, the equivalent figure was 44,887 (Werth, 1999, p. 223).

Although attempts to produce a precise count of Stalin's victims have been mired in historical controversy and a comprehensive account is unlikely ever to be produced successfully, there can be no doubt of Stalin's direct responsibility for the murder of millions of Soviet citizens and the suffering of countless others during his period of rule. Because of this fact, the scale of death in the Soviet Union under Stalin has been central to the various constructions of his reputation. Not surprisingly, many historical constructions of his reputation have emphasised the bloody nature of his dictatorship, seeing him as a 'Red Tsar', a 'breaker of nations', or as the archetypal 'totalitarian' dictator (Sebag-Montefiore, 2004; Conquest, 1992). These constructions have been reflected in many dominant media representations of both Stalin and the Stalin era current in much of western Europe and North America. Yet, perhaps surprisingly, this coexists with contrasting constructions of his reputation; ones that are widely current in the Russian Federation at the time of writing in early 2006, which are openly nostalgic, which discount or understate the reality of the tremendous violence that marked Stalin's rule, and which attribute to Stalin and his era certain positive traits. One survey of young Russians conducted in late 2004 revealed what the researchers termed 'positive' and 'ambivalent' views of the dictator among the subjects of their investigation. In one opinion, cited as typical, a young man told the researchers that 'Yes, there were repressions and famine under Stalin, but it was with him that we won World War II' (Mendelson and Gerber, 2006, p. 7).

Thus the reputation of Stalin is contested and shaped by factors other than the scale of politically motivated murder for which he was responsible. It has also been affected by his role as a war leader during the **Great Patriotic War**. This bloody conflict, launched by Hitler's invasion in 1941, resulted in the deaths of between 26 and 27 million Soviet citizens (Ellman and Maksudov, 1994) before eventual victory. Both the trauma of a war so bloody and the fact of victory in the midst of such suffering have reflected upon the reputation of Stalin as a war leader, despite heated historical debate about whether his role in the eventual victory was positive or negative.

Similarly, Stalin's reputation has been affected by the enormous social transformation of the Soviet Union during the period of his rule – especially urbanisation, industrialisation and agrarian transformations which were introduced during the years of the First Five-Year Plan, and the parallel collectivisation campaign that accompanied it. On the one hand, as historian Sheila Fitzpatrick has pointed out, this social change brought about enormous material hardship: 'communal apartments, abandoned wives and husbands who failed to pay child support, shortages of food and clothing and endless queuing' (Fitzpatrick, 1999, p. 2). At the same time it also led to enormous upward social mobility, the transformation of the economy, and the development of a distinctively Soviet – and in some ways Stalinist – everyday culture, in which ordinary Soviet citizens became integrated into a more unified society (Kotkin, 1995). For many, because of Stalin's close personal association with these changes, his reputation became closely entangled with the judgements of newly urbanised Soviet citizens about the transformation of their daily lives.

**Activity**

I'd like you to think about some of the different 'reputations' of Stalin extracted from the discussion above, namely:

1   Stalin as dictator, mass-murderer, director of repression, or 'Red Tsar'
2   Stalin as a war leader and 'saviour of the nation'
3   Stalin as the creator of a new society.

These different reputations are affected by various processes that characterised his rule. In order to help you think about the relationship between historical process and reputations, go back to the end of the previous section where I identified four themes that ran through my discussion of the Stalin era. Write down the themes from the history of the era that have played the most prominent role in shaping a particular reputation of Stalin.

**Discussion**

This was my attempt to match reputation to historical theme:

| | |
|---|---|
| 1 Stalin as dictator ... | the extent of repression – the technique of using 'show trials', through which events were blamed on apparent 'external enemies' |
| 2 Stalin as war leader | concern with the Soviet Union's international position and, indeed, its growth in prestige as an international actor throughout the period |
| 3 Stalin as creator of a new society | social change – the transformation of the Soviet Union from a predominantly agrarian to a socialist industrial society. |

To some extent these various versions of Stalin's reputation reflect the fact that different observers and commentators place different weight on the importance of phenomena that characterised his rule. We should bear in mind, though, that this is true only to an extent. The contested nature of Stalin's reputation has also been influenced by myth. Indeed, the 'cult of personality' that surrounded Stalin was a state-constructed myth designed, in part, to legitimate Stalin's leadership. As we will see below, this myth, and the way actors attempted to destroy it after Stalin's death in 1953, have played a central role in the way Stalin has been regarded.

## 5.3    THE MYTH OF STALIN

*Additional images for this section can be found in the Illustration Book.*

Following Stalin's death in March 1953 – just as with Lenin's death a little under thirty years previously – there was no clear successor. Lavrentii Beria (1899–1953), Nikita Khrushchev (1894–1971), Georgi Malenkov (1902–88), and Molotov, Stalin's veteran Foreign Minister, were all contenders for power. Beria was arrested and executed as a traitor within months of Stalin's death at the behest of other leaders, and Malenkov was forced to resign in 1955. By early 1956, Khrushchev had become the most powerful man in the Soviet Union, yet Molotov remained as the most significant representative of the 'old guard' who might mobilise nostalgia among the rank-and-file of the party from the Stalin era. It was in this context that Khrushchev used his speech at the Twentieth Congress of the Communist Party not only to distance himself from Stalin, but to attack his legacy directly. The speech was sensational and had a considerable effect on the communist movement worldwide.

Activity

Reading 5.1 is an excerpt from Khrushchev's speech to the Twentieth Congress in 1956 in which he detailed the crimes of Stalin. Read the excerpt now and take notes, organising them around the following questions:

1    According to Khrushchev, what were the main differences between Stalin and Lenin?

2    What does Khrushchev regard as Stalin's major crimes?

Discussion

1    Khrushchev argues that under Lenin a 'collective leadership' prevailed in which there was considerable discussion of appropriate political strategy at the top of the party. As far as Khrushchev was concerned, Lenin understood the need for the revolution to remain close to the 'people' who had instigated it. Stalin, on the other hand, concentrated power in his own hands, severely repressed those who disagreed with him, isolated himself from the people, and attacked many of those in the party who supported it – using the concept of the 'enemy of the people' to justify his action. We might say, therefore, that Khrushchev regarded Stalin's rule as a deformation of the original revolution.

It ought to be said here that Khrushchev's view of Lenin can be described as a myth. We know, for example, that an apparatus of repression of considerable size was established by Lenin in the immediate aftermath of the revolution, and that it was frequently used in the 1920s by Lenin against those he regarded as his opponents – even against those who supported the goals of the revolution and the construction of a socialist society. This has led some historians to argue that Stalin's crimes were the natural development of Lenin's actions, and of the October Revolution. This interpretation is open to dispute.

2   At the most basic level, Khrushchev sees the deformation of Lenin's heritage and his severe repression of the ranks of the party during the late 1930s as being the greatest of Stalin's crimes. When he describes arrests, executions and the identification of 'enemies of the people', he is referring to events that took place during the sub-period of Stalin's rule which I have called 'the era of the purges'. One of the things that struck me about this speech is that Khrushchev only ever refers to crimes committed against the party, members of party bodies, and party organs. He omits many of Stalin's crimes – for example, he never mentions the famine that followed collectivisation in 1932–33, in which six million died.

From the late 1920s onwards, Stalin shaped a 'cult of personality' around himself, which constituted a state-manufactured myth that associated a single person – himself – with almost every action of the state during a period in which Soviet society was transformed utterly. Thus, as historian Moshe Lewin has put it, starting at the beginning of the 1930s 'Stalin actually became the system' (Lewin, 1997, p. 120). Because of its importance, we need to examine the nature of the myth that Stalin promoted of himself. Figures 5.3 and 5.4 are reproductions of posters that were designed to popularise aspects of Stalin's transformation of the Soviet Union through industrialisation and collectivisation. The first image, produced in 1932, was a call for industrial workers to assist with agricultural work (this is what was meant by 'shock work', in which workers from one enterprise volunteered to work in another during crucial periods in order to help fulfil national economic goals). It exhorted workers to support the new collective farms, and thus ensure the success of the socialist organisation of agriculture introduced by Stalin's regime over the previous two years. The second is a later poster announcing the final completion of the first line of Moscow's new metro in 1934. A key public works project, it was heralded as a sign of the new, modern society the Soviet Union was to become as a result of industrialisation and economic planning.

**Activity**    What image of Stalin is being promoted in these images?

**Discussion**    The message here is clear: Stalin is identified in both of these posters as the leader of the transformation of the country which was underway during the first half of the 1930s. It is possible to imagine his association with the completion of a prestige project such as the Moscow metro as something that would increase his popularity. Given the tremendous hardship for many Soviet citizens that agricultural collectivisation caused, one wonders about the likely impact of the first poster.

Figure 5.3   Gustav Gustaovich Klutsis, 'Shock Workers to the Fields, to the Battle for Socialist Construction,' 1932, poster, colour litho. Deutsches Plakat Museum, Essen, Germany. Photo: Archives Charmet/The Bridgeman Art Library.

The cult that surrounded Stalin was not just to be found in official propaganda – that is, material designed to promote support for the goals of the Soviet state – but had an ever more ubiquitous presence in the daily lives of Soviet citizens during the 1930s. Figures 5.5 and 5.6 concern two aspects of the culture of the workplace during the 1930s. The Soviet Union's employees were expected to work to the production targets that were laid down in the various National Economic Plans. Workers were constantly exhorted to work harder in order to meet their targets, not only by their managements but also by

Figure 5.4    Gustav Gustaovich Klutsis, 'Metro', *c*. 1934, poster. Photo: The David King Collection.

the party, which had a local cell in every workplace in the country. Both of the images in Figures 5.5 and 5.6 concern campaigns that aimed to persuade and coerce workers to work harder. Figure 5.5 is a poster that propagates the First Five-Year Plan. Its message exhorts workers to work harder and faster in order to complete work previously planned for five years in four – the two plus two of its title. Figure 5.6 depicts a vase sent by workers in Leningrad's Lomossov porcelain factory as a gift to Stalin on the occasion of the Soviet Union's victory in the Second World War in 1945. On such important political

Figure 5.5    Yakov Guminer, '2 + 2 = 5', 1931, poster. Photo: The David King Collection.

occasions, factories would often send messages (in this case a gift) to mark their achievements in raising production in honour of the achievements of Soviet leaders in connection with such events.

**Activity**    Again, look at the images in Figures 5.5 and 5.6 and write down what you think they tell us about the nature of Stalin's 'cult'.

**Discussion**    There is a remarkable similarity between Figures 5.5 and 5.3. Just as Figure 5.3 is an exhortation – closely associated with the person of Stalin – to workers to join the collectivisation campaign, Figure 5.5 is an attempt

Figure 5.6    'The Victory Vase'. Photo: SCR Photo Library, London.

to mobilise workers behind the fulfilment of the economic plan – an attempt to make workers work harder in the service of Stalin's regime. You might wonder how connecting demands for more work to the regime's political goals affected the leader's popularity among those expected to work faster and harder in factories, mines and on construction sites across the Soviet Union! Figure 5.6 also raises this question, but does not provide clear answers. Clearly the vase was a celebration of the hard work of workers in the service of the war effort, and was a 'gift' to Stalin that both commemorated that fact and 'thanked' the leader for his leadership. Thus, it might be argued, it can be used as evidence of enthusiasm for the regime and the leader among workers at the moment of victory. But there is an alternative reading. Work campaigns were never voluntary, and the Soviet state exercised considerable coercive power against those who failed to conform to its demands. Therefore, the making and giving of the vase could be read as the product of an orchestrated performance of loyalty to Stalin by workers, obtained under the threat of repression.

The discussion here has raised the question of the *reception* of the cult of Stalin and the power of the Stalin myth. The visual evidence I have presented can be subjected to a number of different interpretations, and does not offer a definitive answer to the question of its reception. In order to interrogate the issue further we would need much more evidence, and many different kinds of evidence, to guide us in presenting an appropriate interpretation. Some historians have attempted the complex task of using archival sources – the internal reports of the party and of the security police in particular – to reconstruct public opinion in the Soviet Union during the 1930s and 1940s. Much of this research suggests that, despite the tensions in Soviet society, the Stalin myth was very powerful. Many accepted the official image of the 'great and wise' leader, and often blamed the incompetence and corruption of local officials for extreme deprivation. As the historian Sarah Davies has pointed out, the Stalin that existed in the minds of ordinary Soviet citizens was not the superhuman Stalin of much visual representation, but one who embodied far more traditional ideas of appropriate leadership. Stalin was seen by many 'as a father-like defender of the people' (Davies, 1997, p. 166).

We should never assume that a society reacts to power in a uniform way unless we have overwhelming evidence of it, but it seems that the partial acceptance of the Stalin myth was considerable during the 1930s. The myth of Stalin cannot be discussed adequately without

Figure 5.7 Certificate of Participation in the Moscow Victory Parade, 24 June 1945. State Historical Museum, Moscow. Inv: GIM OPI. F. 426. Ed. chr. 307-n. 103982/1. Photo: State Historical Museum, Moscow.

making some mention of the role the Second World War played in both consolidating and strengthening it. Stalin's role as a war leader, and his personal association with victory in what had been a struggle for national survival in the face of possible genocide at the hands of Nazi Germany in 1941, increased his personal prestige enormously. Figure 5.7 can be taken as evidence of the way in which victory strengthened the Stalin myth, and the certificate reproduced there demonstrates the association. It was issued to the representatives of the Soviet armed forces who took part in a victory parade in June 1945 in Moscow's Red Square, which formed the main celebration of the end of the Second World War. The parade itself, in which veterans selected from all those involved in the fighting saluted Stalin (see Figure 5.8), further reinforced the association. Despite the considerable tensions in the Soviet Union at the end of the war – not least because armed guerrilla conflict directed against the imposition of communist authority continued across much of the western Soviet Union – in the country Stalin 'was widely regarded as the embodiment of

Figure 5.8   The Victory Parade in Moscow, 24 June 1945. Unknown photographer. Photo: Mary Evans/Alexander Meledin.

Figure 5.9   Victory Day in Tblisi, Georgia, 9 May 1997. Unknown photographer. Photo © Shakh Aivazov/AP/EMPICS.

patriotism and victory. Even many who detested him had come to accord him a basic respect' (Service, 2005, p. 484). Among representatives of a certain generation and across the former Soviet Union, Stalin's role as a war leader played a central role in ensuring that the myth surrounding him proved for some to be more enduring than the Soviet Union itself. This is shown by Figure 5.9, a photograph taken in 1997 in Stalin's native Georgia several years after the collapse of the Soviet Union.

Before we move on from this subject, it is worth noting that the myth of Stalin as a wise leader is not the only myth produced by Stalin's 'cult of personality'.

Activity    Take a moment to review your notes and my discussion of the activity on Khrushchev's speech to the Twentieth Congress at the beginning of this section. In what senses might Khrushchev be creating his own myth of Stalin – in opposition to the positive myth created in the 1930s? What is the content of that myth?

Discussion    You might have noted down the following points:

- In opposition to the positive Stalin myth promoted during the 1930s and 1940s, Khrushchev creates an emphatically negative myth. In fact, you could well make the point that Khrushchev's myth was created in direct opposition to the positive one that has been discussed in this section of the chapter.

- Khrushchev attributes to Stalin direct responsibility for everything he regards as negative about Stalin's era. Although there can be no doubt about Stalin's primary responsibility for the extent of repression and state-directed murder during his rule, the nature of the historical processes that led to it was often much more complicated than Khrushchev's account suggests.

- By drawing a contrast between the behaviour of Lenin and Stalin, Khrushchev argues implicitly that the nature of Stalin's dictatorship ran counter to the principles of 1917. As we saw earlier, this view can be challenged.

## 5.4   INTERPRETING THE STALIN ERA

Myths have, therefore, played a central role in constructing Stalin's reputation, both positive and negative. For this reason, myths are of central interest to historians, for they are something with which historical interpretations and explanations must engage, either to confirm or to challenge. Implicit in the discussion in Section 5.3 of the myths that surrounded Stalin is the notion that myths themselves are important subjects of historical enquiry; that is to say, they are created in particular historical periods, by particular actors, and any understanding of them changes with the passage of time. This last theme is one that will be explored in more depth later in the course in relation to other periods and places. Although the myths that surround figures such as Stalin are of central interest to historians, they do not constitute historical explanations for what happened during the Stalin era. So how would a historian approach the Stalin era?

In the introduction to this chapter I defined history as an account of past events based upon the interpretation of all the available evidence that relates to the particular aspect of the past it is studying. In order to construct this account, we need to interpret the evidence, and this involves asking questions of it. The following are good examples of the kinds of questions historians might ask in order to construct a historical account of the Stalin era, and thus assess Stalin's reputation:

1   What was the nature of Stalin's contribution to the history of the Soviet Union?
2   How far were his policies in the 1930s (for example, industrialisation and collectivisation) determined by his communist ideology, or a reaction to circumstances?
3   To what extent were the crimes of the era, like those committed during the Great Purges, directed personally by Stalin, or shaped by processes that escaped central control?
4   Did the policies Stalin pursued during the 1930s and 1940s help or hinder the Soviet Union in emerging victorious at the end of the Second World War?

Although answers to these questions may have implications for the mythical views of Stalin's reputation, they approach the question of his reputation indirectly, by asking how and why things happened the way they did, and questioning Stalin's role in the events and processes.

The answer to these questions must, of course, fit with the weight of the available evidence. There is considerable dispute between historians over interpretations, and not every opinion or view of the past is valid; indeed, some views are simply not compatible with historical evidence. Here is one example, relevant to the assessment of Stalin's reputation. During the mid 1990s, many sympathisers with Russia's communists asserted that Stalin was responsible for the murders 'of less than a million people' (quoted in Conquest, 1996, p. 143). Although there is disagreement about the precise number of Stalin's victims, such a low figure is simply incompatible with any of the historical evidence available, whether from the archival collections of the Soviet state or from census material now available for the Stalin era. Though you can say – and you would be right – that such statements are morally abhorrent, the crucial test for historians in weighing any contentious statement about the past is whether it fits with the available historical evidence. The one quoted above simply does not.

Therefore, the key to evaluating Stalin's reputation historically is to develop interpretations of his rule based on the weight of the historical evidence. In theory, therefore, all one has to do is to find the correct interpretation, and it should then be possible to produce a definitive historical evaluation of Stalin's reputation. But it is never that simple, and there is considerable room for dispute between historians about the *reliability* of the evidence, as well as how it should be approached, and how it ought to be interpreted.

In order to give you a better appreciation of this point, we will explore an example of a legitimate difference between historians in their interpretation of historical events. What follows is simply by way of an introduction, for some of the issues that are raised here will be taken up again by later chapters in the course.

**Activity**  Go back to my outline of the Stalin era in Section 5.1 and review the section entitled 'The era of the purges'. Then turn to Readings 5.2 and 5.3. These extracts offer differing accounts of the purges of the late 1930s, one written by Robert Conquest, and the other by Ronald Grigor Suny. Earlier in this section I gave you four examples of the sort of questions historians might ask in assessing Stalin's reputation historically. Both these excerpts could be taken as 'answers' to my third question about the extent of Stalin's responsibility for the purges. Each gives a different answer to this question. Compare and contrast their explanations for the events of the late 1930s concerning:

1  the role of Stalin

2  the reason for the purges

3  the extent of the purges

4  the role of society.

You may find it helpful to organise your notes in a grid like the one below (by way of an example I have filled in the first part of the grid):

| | Conquest | Suny |
|---|---|---|
| 1 **The role of Stalin** | Conquest argues that Stalin was in complete control over the purges which were directed in detail from Moscow. | Suny argues that 'the will and ambition of Stalin' was 'the principal catalyst to the Terror'. He directed those trials and purges which affected the ruling elite, but in his last paragraph Suny argues that to some extent they escaped Stalin's control, and spread. |

**Discussion**  This was my attempt to fill the remaining rows of the grid:

| | Conquest | Suny |
|---|---|---|
| 2 **The reason for the purges** | The purges, or 'the terror' as Conquest calls it, was launched as a means of control, to terrorise and subordinate the population to the regime. | Suny underlines the lack of consensus among historians about the causes of the terror, but argues that they were about consolidation of the personal dictatorship of Stalin, and aimed at tightening his control over the party and governmental elite. |

| | | Conquest | Suny |
|---|---|---|---|
| 3 | The extent of the purges | Conquest argues that 'the terror was directed against the population as a whole'. | Suny argues that 'the purges destroyed primarily those in power'. |
| 4 | The role of society | Society, according to Conquest, was completely disorientated by the purges. They broke the will of the population to act independently of the Soviet state. | Suny suggests that social tensions in Soviet society played a role when the purges escaped Stalin's control and spread beyond Moscow to the localities. He also argues that the removal, imprisonment and murder of many in senior positions created unprecedented opportunities for social mobility. |

This exercise should provide you with a sense of how the conclusions historians can draw from the evidence differ considerably. There are many reasons for this, which can include (a) the nature and range of the evidence a particular historian consults, (b) the judgements that a historian makes about a particular piece of evidence, and (c) the way in which a given historian approaches his or her subject.

Such radical differences between historians raise the question: which one, if any, of these is right? In order to help you think about possible answers, I want to introduce you to one kind of evidence that a historian might use to help answer this question. This is an extract from a personal account of life in the central Russian city of Magnitogorsk, constructed at the beginning of the First Five-Year Plan in the early 1930s and centred on a steel plant, which was a showpiece of Stalin's industrialisation. The extract is from a book written by John Scott (1912–76) and published in 1942. Scott was an American citizen sympathetic to the social experiment underway in the Soviet Union, who lived and worked in the city during the 1930s.

**Activity**    Turn to the extract from Scott's memoir, *Behind the Urals: An American Worker in Russia's City of Steel*, reproduced as Reading 5.4. Scott presents an account of the impact of the purges on the local society in Magnitogorsk. How far does this account support or contradict either of the two interpretations in Readings 5.2 and 5.3 (and do say if it doesn't provide many pointers either way)? Divide up the issues in a similar way as in the previous activity:

1   the reason for the purges
2   the extent of the purges
3   the role of society.

There is one significant exception: the section on 'the role of Stalin' is missing. This is because there is nothing in this extract that can help us ascertain Stalin's role. You will almost certainly find it helpful to refer to the discussion in the previous activity.

Discussion    This is what I came up with:

1   Scott cannot present any direct evidence that sheds light on the reason for the purges, but he assumes that Stalin must have been closely involved in them – note at the end of the extract that he attributes to Stalin a role in halting 'the purge'. Clearly, though, his evidence suggests that the purges were essentially about the control of management and administration across the country. If one accepts Scott's account – and one must accept that Scott was far from being in a position to know what the deliberations of NKVD or of politicians in Moscow were – then it seems unlikely that the purges were directed in detail by Stalin, as Conquest suggests, but nor is there sufficient evidence to back Suny's contention that they escaped his control (though this does not seem unlikely from his chaotic description of what happened in Magnitogorsk).

2   While Scott alludes to the climate of fear that gripped Magnitogorsk (and the rest of the Soviet Union) during the peak years of the purges, his account suggests that Suny's account is more likely to be correct than Conquest's. He argues that those in management and administration were more likely to be targeted than manual workers, and hints that workers were able to use the climate of the purges as a weapon against management in the factories, while many gained opportunities for promotion as their superiors were locked up.

3   To some extent both Conquest's and Suny's accounts of the purges are supported by Scott's account of life in Magnitogorsk. He records the climate of disorientation and fear brought about by the purges; he underlines that some arrests created opportunities for social mobility, as identified by Suny. More significantly, Scott shows how the extent of the arrests not only created fear, but could lead to explosive protests, which might in turn destabilise the regime.

This reading of an extract from one source should have given you some sense of the complexities involved in constructing historical interpretations and in reading evidence. These are issues that you will meet again in later chapters of the course.

## CONCLUSION

In using Stalin as a case study, this chapter has introduced you to some of the issues involved in evaluating the reputation of a controversial historical figure using the approaches of the historian. You will be able to explore these further in later chapters of the course as well as acquire new skills that are of relevance to historians. Let me summarise the ground that we have covered in this chapter. We have:

- arrived at a working definition of history
- discussed the differences between myths about the past and history
- explored some of the major historical themes relevant to the study of the Stalin era (*c.* 1926–53)
- used Stalin's 'cult of personality' as a case study to examine how myths about the past are shaped
- explored the relationship between myths and historical interpretations of the past
- seen how historical interpretations, based on the evidence, can differ, and thus why History as an academic discipline is characterised by considerable debate
- begun to explore how evidence can be used to evaluate historical interpretations.

## REFERENCES

Conquest, R. (1993) *Stalin: Breaker of Nations*, London, Weidenfeld & Nicolson.

Conquest, R. (1996) 'Excess deaths in the Soviet Union', *New Left Review*, no. 219, p. 143.

Davies, S. (1997) *Popular Opinion in Stalin's Russia: Terror, Propaganda and Dissent, 1934–1941*, Cambridge and New York, Cambridge University Press.

Ellman, M. and Maksudov, S. (1994) 'Soviet deaths in the Great Patriotic War: a note', *Europe–Asia Studies*, vol. 46, no. 4, July, pp. 671–80.

Fitzpatrick, S. (1999) *Everyday Stalinism. Ordinary Life in Extraordinary Times: Soviet Russia in the 1930s*, New York and Oxford, Oxford University Press.

Kotkin, S. (1995) *Magnetic Mountain: Stalinism as a Civilization*, Berkeley, London and Los Angeles, University of California Press.

Overy, R. (2005) *The Dictators: Hitler's Germany, Stalin's Russia*, Harmonsworth, Penguin.

Lewin, M. (1997) 'Stalin in the mirror of the other' in Kershaw, I. and Lewin, M. (eds) *Stalinism and Nazism. Dictatorships in Comparison*, Cambridge and New York, Cambridge University Press, pp. 107–34.

Mendelson, S.E. and Gerber, T.P. (2006) 'Failing the Stalin test', *Foreign Affairs*, vol. 85, no. 1, January–February, pp. 2–8.

Scott, J. (1989) *Behind the Urals: An American Worker in Russia's City of Steel*, enlarged edition prepared by Stephen Kotkin, Bloomington and Indianapolis, Indiana University Press.

Sebag-Montefiore, S. (2004) *Stalin: The Court of the Red Tsar*, London, Phoenix Press.

Service, R. (2005) *Stalin: A Biography*, London, Pan Books.

Werth, N. (1999) 'A state against its people: violence, repression, and terror in the Soviet Union' in Courtois, S. et al., *The Black Book of Communism: Crimes, Terror, Repression* (trans. J. Murphy and M. Kramer), Cambridge, MA, and London, Harvard University Press, pp. 33–268.

# RESOURCES

## Krushchev on Stalin

**Reading 5.1**

*Excerpts from the Secret Speech delivered by Nikita Khrushchev, First Party Secretary, at the Twentieth Party Congress of the Communist Party of the Soviet Union, 25 February 1956*

During Lenin's life the central committee of the party was a real expression of collective leadership ...

In addition to the great accomplishment of V.I. Lenin for the victory of the working class and of the working peasants, for the victory of our party and for the application of the ideas of scientific communism to life, ... V.I. Lenin made a completely correct characterization of Stalin, pointing out that it was necessary to consider the question of transferring Stalin from the position of Secretary General because of the fact that Stalin is excessively rude, that he does not have a proper attitude toward his comrades, that he is capricious, and abuses his power ...

[...]

When we analyze the practice of Stalin in regard to the direction of the party and of the country, when we pause to consider everything which Stalin perpetrated, we must be convinced that Lenin's fears were justified. The negative characteristics of Stalin, which, in Lenin's time were only incipient, transformed themselves during the last years into a grave abuse of power by Stalin, which caused untold harm to our party ...

Stalin acted not through persuasion, explanation, and patient cooperation with people, but by imposing his concepts and demanding absolute submission to his opinion. Whoever opposed this concept or tried to prove his viewpoint, and the correctness of his position, was doomed to removal from the leading collective and to subsequent moral and physical annihilation. This was especially true during the period following the 17th party congress, when many prominent party leaders and rank-and-file party workers, honest and dedicated to the cause of communism, fell victim to Stalin's despotism ...

Stalin originated the concept 'enemy of the people'. This term automatically rendered it unnecessary that the ideological errors of a man or men engaged in a controversy be proven; this term made possible the usage of the most cruel repression, violating all norms of revolutionary legality, against anyone who in any way disagreed with Stalin, against those who were only suspected of hostile intent, against those who had bad reputations. This concept, enemy of the people, actually eliminated the possibility of any kind of ideological fight or the making of one's views known on this or that issue, even those of a practical character. In the main, and in actuality, the only proof of guilt used, against all norms of current legal science, was the confession of the accused himself, and, as subsequent probing proved, confessions were acquired through physical pressures against the accused ...

Lenin used severe methods only in the most necessary cases, when the exploiting classes were still in existence and were vigorously opposing the revolution, when the struggle for survival was decidedly assuming the sharpest forms, even including a civil war.

Stalin, on the other hand, used extreme methods and mass repressions at a time when the revolution was already victorious, when the Soviet state was strengthened, when the exploiting classes were already liquidated, and Socialist relations were rooted solidly in all phases of national economy, when our party was politically consolidated and had strengthened itself both numerically and ideologically. It is clear that here Stalin showed in a whole series of cases his intolerance, his brutality, and his abuse of power. Instead of proving his political correctness and mobilizing the masses, he often chose the path of repression and physical annihilation, not only against actual enemies, but also against individuals who had not committed any crimes against the party and the Soviet Government. Here we see no wisdom but only a demonstration of the brutal force which had once so alarmed V.I. Lenin ...

[...]

What is the reason that mass repressions against activists increased more and more after the 17th party congress? It was because at that time Stalin had so elevated himself above the party and above the nation that he ceased to consider either the central committee or the party.

Source: from the *Congressional Record: Proceedings and Debates of the 84th Congress, 2nd Session (May 22, 1956–June 11, 1956), C11, Part 7 (June 4, 1956)*, pp. 9389–403, in *Modern History Internet Sourcebook* (http://www.fordham.edu/halsall/mod/1956khrushchev-secret1.html).

Reading 5.2    **Terror**

The terror of 1936–8 was an almost uniquely devastating blow inflicted by a government on its own population, and the charges against the millions of victims were almost without exception entirely false. Stalin personally ordered, inspired and organized the operation. He received weekly reports of, as a recent Soviet article put it, not only steel production and crop figures, but also of the numbers annihilated. He personally examined and signed, it is true, only the top-level death sentences. But slaughter was not left to local authorities. ...

What is sometimes neglected by those of us who never faced such things, is the extreme intensity with which the terror bore down not only upon its victims but upon the population as a whole. Millions lived year after year in an insane world of denunciation and hysteria. As Soviet writers tell us today, people's whole psychology was distorted in unnatural and inhuman ways – to the degree that even now the recovery has not yet been complete.

The massive system of threats and rewards – at least the reward of survival – conditioned the minds of millions into an almost Pavlovian submission to the state's insistences, and not seldom an acceptance, with relief, of the state's false enthusiasms. More independent minds were reduced to despair and apathy. Such are the usual psychological concomitants of life in completely abnormal conditions.

[...]

The terror was directed against the population as a whole, with a million-odd executions of which the mass graves are now being discovered all over the country; millions more were sent to die in the Arctic camps. But it also devastated the party: half its membership was arrested, and over a million died by execution or in camps. Of the Central Committee itself, 70 per cent perished.

It is not clear when Stalin decided to wind up the superterror and revert to what were by comparison normal levels of repression. By the middle of 1938 he had killed, or had in prison ready for execution, the great majority of the Central Committee elected in 1934, and also the great majority of the generals. At a slightly lower level the terror had also reached a certain limit. For instance, on the Byelorussian railway system it was plain that any further arrests would lead to total breakdown. The big factories had lost almost all of their properly qualified engineers. The economy was heading downhill. The mere number of the population was sixteen or seventeen million fewer than the Plan had projected. The NKVDs of the republics were simply being ordered to shoot tens of thousands for no reason but to keep the terror going.

Source: Conquest, 1993, pp. 206–8.

**Reading 5.3    Terror and autocracy**

The unlimited despotism of Stalinism was the product of the Great Purges, which simultaneously eliminated all possible resistance and created a new and more loyal elite with which the tyrant could rule.

There is no consensus among scholars as to the motivations behind the Purges. Interpretations range from the idea that purging was a permanent and necessary component of totalitarianism in lieu of elections (Zbigniew Brzezinski) to seeing the Great Terror as an extreme form of political infighting (J. Arch Getty). Dissatisfaction with Stalin's rule and with the harsh material conditions was palpable in the mid-1930s, and the regime was faced with the difficulties of controlling the family circles and local feudatories (particularly in the union republics). One of the effects of the Purges was the replacement of an older political and economic elite with a younger, potentially more loyal one. The largest number were promoted workers and party rank-and-file, young technicians, who would make up the Soviet elite through the post-Stalin period until the early 1980s. 'Stalin – and, for that matter, the majority of Soviet citizens', writes Sheila Fitzpatrick,

> saw the cadres of the mid-1930s less in their old role as revolutionaries than in the current role as bosses. There is even some evidence that Stalin saw them as Soviet boyars (feudal lords) and himself as a latter-day Ivan the Terrible, who had to destroy the boyars to build a modern nation state and a new service nobility.

Yet neither arguments from social context nor functionalist deductions from effects to causes have successfully eliminated the principal catalyst to the Terror, the will and ambition of Stalin. The Great Purges have been seen traditionally as an effort 'to achieve an unrestricted personal dictatorship with a totality of power that [Stalin] did not yet possess in 1934.' Stalin guided and prodded the arrests, show trials, and executions forward, aided by the closest members of his entourage: Molotov, Kaganovich, Zhdanov, Malenkov, Mikoyan, and Ezhov. Here personality and politics merged, and the degree of excess repression was dictated by the peculiar demands of Stalin himself, who could not tolerate limits on his will set by the very ruling elite that he had brought to power.

[...]

The Purges destroyed primarily those in power. 'It is one of the mysteries of Stalinism', Lewin summarises,

> that it turned much of the fury of its bloody purges against this very real mainstay of the regime. There were among the *apparaty* [members of the government or party apparatus], probably, still too many former members of other parties or of the original Leninist party, too many participants and victors of the civil war who remembered who had done what during those days of glory. Too many thus could feel the right to be considered founders of the regime and base on it part of the claims to a say in decisions and to security in their positions. Probably, also letting the new and sprawling administration settle and get encrusted in their chairs and habits could also encourage them to try and curtail the power of the very top and the personalised ruling style of the chief of the state – and this was probably a real prospect the paranoid leader did not relish.

Stalin's initiation and personal direction of the Purges was the catalyst to thousands of smaller settlings of scores. In the context of deep and recurring social tensions the state gave the green light to resentments against the privileged, the intelligentsia, other ethnicities, outsiders. The requirement to find enemies, to blame and punish, worked together with self-protection and self-promotion (and plain sadism) to expand the Purges into a political holocaust. At the end the Soviet Union resembled a ruined landscape, seriously weakened economically, intellectually, and militarily, but at the same time dominated by a towering state apparatus made up of new loyal *apparatchiki*, disciplined by the police, and presided over by a single will.

Source: Ronald Grigor Suny, 'Stalin and his Stalinism: power and authority in the Soviet Union, 1930–53' in Ian Kershaw and Moshe Lewin (eds) *Stalinism and Nazism: Dictatorships in Comparison*, Cambridge, Cambridge University Press, 1997, pp. 26–51 (footnotes omitted).

**Reading 5.4**    # Administration and the Purge

Soviet purge technique was highly developed. All arrests were made at night. Surprise was always sought for; people were arrested when they least expected it, and left alone for weeks when they expected every night to be taken. The arrests were made by agents having no idea of the accusations against the person being arrested. They arrived, usually a sergeant in uniform and two plain-clothesmen, in an automobile, knocked at the door, politely presented an order signed by the prosecuting attorney or by the head of the city NKVD, authorizing them to search the apartment and arrest a certain person. The door was then locked; no one could come or go during the search. A civilian witness was taken at random from an adjacent apartment. He or she watched the search going on, then was requested to sign a paper stating that the authorities had not abused their power; that is, beaten anybody up or stolen anything. Everything confiscated was listed and a receipt given. The search finished, the polite and completely uncommunicative agents departed with the arrested person. Probably no one in the house except the witness was aware until the next morning that anything had taken place.

After someone's arrest, the family was usually left completely in the dark for several weeks, while the 'arrested' was put in the Magnitogorsk prison to cool off and think things over prior to the first interrogation. This jail was very crowded. Cells meant for twenty people were occupied by fifty. (The crowding naturally put pressure on the authorities to speed up the investigations and get people shipped out.) Several weeks after the arrest, the family usually received a formal notice that the husband or brother had been arrested, and that the family could come at such-and-such a time with a package. They suggested that the package should contain warm clothes, clean underwear, sugar, onions, and garlic. The latter were to combat scurvy which became rather common in the prison owing to the predominantly bread-and-water diet and the lack of fresh air.

[...]

The interrogations usually took place at night and were nerve-wracking ordeals, sometimes lasting weeks, and often pursued between long intervals of cooling off in the prison. The words 'wrecking' and 'counter-revolutionary activity,' as used in the Soviet

Union, mean much more than they would in America. The criminal code of the R.S.F.S.R., Article 58–1, reads:

> Any action is counter-revolutionary which is directed toward the overthrow, undermining, or weakening of the power of the workers and peasants ... or directed toward the weakening of the external security of the Soviet Union, or the administrative, or national gains of the proletarian revolution.

For a definition of wrecking, we turn to Article 58–7 of the same code, which reads in part:

> Undermining of state industry, transport, commerce, monetary circulation, or credit system, as well as of the cooperative systems, committed for counter-revolutionary purposes by counter-revolutionary use of state institutions or factories ... or interference with their normal activity, as well as use of state institutions and factories in the interests of their former owners ... involves ... supreme measure of social protection – shooting ...

Article 58–12 was the article on which many wives were indicted. It reads in part:

> Failure to report definite knowledge of preparation or commitment of a counter-revolutionary crime, involves ... deprivation of freedom for not less than six months.

June 6, 1927

In almost no case did the accused see a defense lawyer during the interrogations. He was pitted alone against one or more experienced, smooth, literal-minded NKVD investigators. Though, according to the code of procedure, the investigation should not last more than two months, the accused sometimes languished for months and years in the prison occupied by men and women under investigation. This, obviously, gave the investigator a very potent whiphandle, '... if you don't want to confess ... go back and think it over; if you do confess, you will get a quick trial – a couple of years in Siberia, where you will have a good job, receive wages, live at home, have the comparative freedom of the town, and perhaps see your family...'.

The denunciation of one accused by another or of both by a third party still free formed the basis for a great many indictments and convictions. A denounces B as having said that Stalin is a son-of-a-bitch and should be shot. B, arrested, finally admits making the statement, and further asserts that C was present, and agreed with the opinion expressed. C, arrested, denies everything; then, confronted with B, admits that there was some such conversation, but insists that A was the initiator. A is arrested, like the others for terrorist intentions against the leaders of the party and government, but begs off on the ground that he did it all in order to expose to the authorities the counter-revolutionary activities of B and C. After six months of bantering and badgering, A, B, and C are sent for ten years to the Kamchatka.

During the rush years of 1937 and 1938 the methods used in the investigations were indefensible according to most civilised standards. Even physical coercion was employed in obtaining a confession from the accused. Promises were made to the accused that if he confessed, his wife would be let alone and permitted to keep her job. The confession signed, the wife was likewise arrested and shown the confession, and told that if she confessed connivance both would get light sentences. She confessed, and both got the limit, and went to Angarstroy to work on construction. Such methods are, of course, taken for granted in criminal proceedings almost all over the world. In the Soviet Union, however, the situation was somewhat different in that the NKVD made a play for, and to a large extent received, the support and cooperation of the population, in their work of defending the country against the inroads of foreign agents and attacks of the old bourgeoisie. Cases like the above cited shook the confidence of many Russians in the NKVD.

The trials were almost always *in camera*, and usually *in absentia*. There were almost no acquittals in Magnitogorsk in 1937, nor were there more than half a dozen death sentences. After the trial, the operative department of the NKVD turned the convicts over to the ULAG (criminal camp administration), whose job it was to get certain construction work done, using the labor of the convicts, and also to carry on re-educational work. The ULAG was a completely separate and independent part of the NKVD organization. They received a prisoner accompanied by a frayed document stating that he had been convicted on such-and-such an article. Beyond this they knew nothing. Their job was to build dams and railroads, and in the interest of high productivity, if for no other reason, they treated the prisoners as well as possible.

[...]

In Magnitogorsk in 1937 the activities of the NKVD were often characterized by great confusion. Prisoners were lost or their identity mistaken. The NKVD came around one night to arrest the former occupant of the apartment over ours who had left Magnitogorsk months before. There were cases where notices were sent to wives, informing them that their husbands had been arrested and requesting them to bring packages, when the husbands were living at home and working normally and continued to do so. These things bespoke the muscle-bound and inefficient organization of the NKVD apparatus.

[...]

The immediate effects of the purge were diverse and sometimes paradoxical. In cases where numbers of responsible workers and functionaries had been arrested at the same time, or within a few days of each other, production suffered heavily for a while. After Shevchenko's removal and arrest, for example, the coke and chemical output went down sharply for several weeks. During the first few days, chaos reigned in the plant. A foreman would come to work in the morning and say to his men, 'Now today we must do this and that.' The workers would sneer at him and say: 'Go on. You're a wrecker yourself. Tomorrow they'll come and arrest you. All you engineers and technicians are wreckers.'

Then things straightened out; a new chief was appointed and Syemichkin became assistant chief engineer. All through the plant young workers and foremen were pushed up a notch or two into the positions evacuated by those arrested. Often the new men were inexperienced, but, in some cases, within a few weeks they were working as well as their predecessors.

In some departments, as for instance on the blast furnaces, production suffered a prolonged setback after the beginning of the purge. Daily pig-iron production in the fall of 1936, for example, averaged around twelve hundred to thirteen hundred tons per furnace. By the end of 1937 it was in the neighborhood of eleven hundred tons per furnace, and in January, 1940, as nearly as could be judged from fragmentary reports, the average figure had fallen to below one thousand tons.

During the course of the purge hundreds of thousands of bureaucrats shook in their boots. Officials and administrators who had formerly come to work at ten, gone home at four-thirty, and shrugged their shoulders at complaints, difficulties, and failures, began to stay at work from dawn till dark, to worry about the success or failure of their units, and to fight in a very real and earnest fashion for plan fulfilment, for economy, and for the well-being of their workers and employees, about whom they had previously lost not a wink of sleep.

On the other hand, the repeated nocturnal arrests, the fear and worry, and the terrorization of an organization which worked in secret, with the power to do what it wanted with anybody, and to whom there was no appeal, had their effects on a considerable section of the population, which read with a sneer and a groan Stalin's slogan, 'Life has become better; life has become more joyful.'

A maxim currently used by vigilant Communists and others was: 'In every backward department there is a wrecker.' The results of the application of such an affirmation are obvious. They played into the hands of the growing apparatus of the NKVD (whose local and national leaders at that time appear now to have been wreckers themselves). Many people reacted by shunning all responsibility. Another maxim became known: 'Seichas khorosho buit telegrafnim stolbom – Nowadays it is a good thing to be a telegraph pole.'

Still other people became exasperated and bitter. It is said that in Sverdlovsk one day several hundred women had come to the NKVD building with packages of food and clothing to be given to their arrested husbands. After standing for several hours awaiting the arrival of some functionary, they were told bluntly that no packages would be accepted that day. The worried women, some with babies in their arms, some who had left their jobs at the risk of being fired in order to give a little sugar and some clean clothes to their beloved ones, became incensed. Someone started a commotion. Someone was pushed against a window. Within five minutes every pane of glass on the first floor of the building was shattered. The authorities could find no leader to arrest. They couldn't run in five hundred women, the jails were already full.

Incidents of this kind, more or less serious, occurred in various parts of the Soviet Union, and reports of them in one form or another probably reached Stalin and the other leaders of the government. They were signals of warning that the purge, if carried too far, could have disastrous results, particularly in case of war. This was a major factor in determining the change in internal policy that took place in the end of 1938 and the beginning of 1939.

Source: John Scott (1989 [1942]) *Behind the Urals: An American Worker in Russia's City of Steel* (enlarged edition prepared by S. Kotkin), Bloomington and Indianapolis, Indiana University Press, pp. 190–7.

# 6 THE DIVA

*Elaine Moohan with contributions by Nick Jones and Robert Philip*

| | | |
|---|---|--:|
| **INTRODUCTION** | | **163** |
| **6.1** | **WHAT IS A DIVA?** | **163** |
| **6.2** | **MADONNA** | **165** |
| | Madonna as pop diva | 165 |
| | 'Like a Prayer' | 168 |
| **6.3** | **SOME BASIC MUSICAL LANGUAGE** | **171** |
| **6.4** | **TRAINING TO BECOME A DIVA** | **173** |
| **6.5** | **MARIA CALLAS AND THE AUTHORITY OF THE HISTORIC RECORDING** | **174** |
| | Biography | 174 |
| | Callas as a singer: Puccini's *Tosca* | 175 |
| | The music of the scene | 178 |
| | Prestige and the opera house | 180 |
| **6.6** | **THE CONCERTO DELLE DONNE OF FERRARA** | **182** |
| | Luzzaschi, court composer | 182 |
| | Concerto delle donne | 184 |
| | The Ferrarese madrigals | 186 |
| | Historical voices | 188 |
| **CONCLUSION** | | **188** |
| **REFERENCES** | | **189** |
| **RESOURCES** | | **190** |
| | Reading 6.1 | 190 |
| | Reading 6.2 | 190 |
| | Reading 6.3 | 191 |
| | Reading 6.4 | 192 |
| | Reading 6.5 | 193 |
| | Reading 6.6 | 195 |
| | Reading 6.7 | 195 |
| | Reading 6.8 | 196 |
| | Reading 6.9 | 196 |

**MATERIALS YOU WILL NEED**
- Audio CD: The Diva
- DVD Video: The Diva

**AIMS**

This chapter will:
- give you an understanding of the concept of 'the diva'
- encourage you to develop close listening skills
- introduce some technical language used to describe and discuss music
- help you to appreciate some of the complexities of musical composition and the demands these make on performers
- demonstrate what is involved in the training of opera singers.

## INTRODUCTION

The main aim of this chapter is to give you an understanding of the concept of 'the diva' and what it means to describe a singer as 'a diva' (*diva* is Italian for goddess). We will consider the specific characteristics that lead to a performer gaining a reputation as a diva, and discuss whether this label can be applied to singers from various musical backgrounds and in different historical periods. Unlike other chapters in this book which focus on a single historical figure, in this chapter you will study several figures and their different singing styles. This chapter will also help you to develop close listening skills so that you will be able to appreciate some of the complexities of musical composition and the demands these make on the singer, and will provide you with some technical language to describe and discuss music.

## 6.1 WHAT IS A DIVA?
### Elaine Moohan

*Throughout this chapter you will be given CD timing references to locate specific points in the recordings.*

The stereotypical diva in the classical music world is someone of supreme talent, with great vocal facility and an ability to convey the emotional nuances of the music to her audience. To this artistic reputation is often added a particular personality – someone who is almost larger than life, with an identifiable public persona. The term 'diva' also carries the more negative connotations of one who is unreasonably demanding and difficult to work with, who storms off in rehearsals and refuses to communicate with colleagues. In an interview, the conductor Sir Charles Mackerras describes the diva thus:

> I think it is an aura that some of them [singers] exude ... Something which many good, even excellent singers may not necessarily possess. There has to be something unusual as well as competent about a diva, something compelling about her personality, whether you like it or not, whether it be charming or repellent ... or both at the same time.

> (quoted in Matheopoulos, 1998, p. xix)

Although diva is generally used in its feminine form – and tends to be applied to female singers of **opera** – it has a male equivalent, divo. In recent times the term diva has been applied more broadly to female singers working in a variety of musical styles and genres. Such modern-day divas include Judy Garland, Marlene Dietrich, Edith Piaf, Ella Fitzgerald, Aretha Franklin, Barbra Streisand and Madonna.

There are four case studies in this chapter (Madonna, a young **soprano** in training, Maria Callas, and the Ferrarese ladies' vocal ensemble), presented in reverse chronological order, and starting with modern **pop music** before moving back in musical history to the operatic world of the mid twentieth century, and from there back to the late sixteenth century. We will study how the reputation of the singers in the case studies is established and transmitted, and consider whether they are deserving of the name diva. As we travel backwards we will see that the means by which a performer's reputation has been established and maintained noticeably changes. In the modern pop world a keen knowledge of the media can be used to present a desired image to the general public, but in the mid twentieth century opera singers were not well versed in the ways of the media. On the contrary, their every move could be reported without much control from them. We will consider some written documents as well as audio recordings to assess whether performers such as Maria Callas are indeed worthy of being called divas. The reputation of singers in the late sixteenth century can be established only from the written word, and in this case study we need to examine printed music instead of audio recordings.

Our first case study is of the media-savvy pop singer Madonna, whose reputation has been built as much on her ability to reinvent herself as on her artistic merits. Her manipulation of the media and personal publicity machine to control her public image is certainly one characteristic of the diva. We will then study a short DVD film that follows a young soprano in training at the Opera School of the Royal Scottish Academy of Music and Drama. We will watch her in various stages of rehearsal as she tackles the challenges of learning major roles and bringing two of these to performance. This short film will give you some understanding of the artistic, mental and physical demands required to reach the peak of the profession.

The next case study, taken from the world of mid twentieth-century opera, considers Maria Callas, much of whose life was lived in the public eye, where she seemed to live out the tragedy of the roles that she performed. This is indeed the tragic side of the diva, yet it is balanced by Callas's consummate artistic talent, which earned her the pet name among opera lovers of 'La Divina'.

Finally, we will investigate the reputation of the female singing ensemble at the northern Italian court of Ferrara in the final decades of the sixteenth century. Unlike Madonna and Callas, the musical reputation of these ladies was fuelled by their lack of public appearances and the restrictions imposed on the number of people permitted to listen to them perform. We can come closer to an understanding of their true vocal ability by reading contemporary descriptions of their singing and making a close study of the printed music and modern recordings.

You may find that you do not like all of the recorded examples in this chapter, and you may decide that not all of the singers are worthy of the name diva, but the guided listening activities will help you to appreciate particular aspects of each musical style and performance, and enable you to offer an opinion on which characteristics are typical of the diva in the broadest sense.

## 6.2   MADONNA
Nick Jones

### Madonna as pop diva

Madonna Louise Veronica Ciccone (b. 1958) was possibly the biggest female pop star of the 1980s and early 1990s, and continues to this day to fascinate and attract close attention – and not just from the media and her enormous legion of fans, but from academics too. This attention is understandable: she has had more Number Ones and consecutive hits than any other woman; she has received and been nominated for a plethora of music awards; and she has sold over 300 million records (100 million singles, 200 million albums) worldwide – more than any other female artist. Madonna's position in the music industry was further cemented in 1992 when she signed a $60 million contract with Time-Warner, giving her full control over her own production company, Maverick.

But is Madonna's reputation based merely on her musical talents, as the above suggests, or do other factors play their part? You might already have your own thoughts on this, but here is my response, starting with purely musical considerations.

### Voice

As mentioned above, divas are usually renowned for their vocal prowess. It is somewhat ironic, then, that Madonna's voice is often criticised as being the weakest aspect of her performance. But is this criticism justified? In this case study we are going to look at two of Madonna's songs from the 1980s: 'Material Girl', taken from her second album *Like a Virgin* (1984), and 'Like a Prayer', taken from her fourth album of the same name (1989). This decade was phenomenally successful for Madonna, both artistically and commercially, yet discussions of her and her music generally fail to engage with one important issue: the extent to which this success was due to her merits as a singer.

**Activity**   I want you to listen to 'Material Girl' – you'll find the song on track 1 of the Audio CD 'The Diva'. As you listen, jot down a few words to describe Madonna's vocal style.

I find Madonna's voice to be quite thin and reedy, and lacking in power and resonance. In many respects, her voice does not display any of the vocal qualities typically associated with the diva. But in making such a judgement, are we not being somewhat unfair to Madonna? After all, she is a pop diva rather than an opera diva. Clearly, then, we will need to broaden our investigation to understand fully what 'pop diva' means in this specific context. There will be an opportunity for us to trace the development of Madonna as a singer through the 1980s in the second half of this case study.

Figure 6.1    Image of Madonna in concert, Live Aid, 13 July 1985. Photographed by Ebet Roberts. Photo: © EBET ROBERTS/Redferns.

## Author-producer-entrepreneur

Many commentators have highlighted the significant degree to which Madonna exerts influence and creative control over her product. One of the most important ways she achieves this is by overseeing the music's authorship and production. Susan McClary, a leading feminist musicologist, discusses this in an article dating from 1991.

**Activity**    Turn to Reading 6.1 and read the extract from McClary's article. Do you agree with her argument?

I find McClary's argument persuasive, and the point regarding Madonna's creative control over her songs is effectively made. However, I think that one aspect of her argument is contestable. Her

Figure 6.2  ... and twenty years later, at Live 8, 2 July 2005. Photographed by Mick Hutson. Photo: © MICK HUTSON/Redferns.

assertion that 'It is quite rare for women singers to contribute so much to the composition of their materials' struck me as being rather odd. Bearing in mind the article's date (1991), I'm sure you can think of other examples of female singer-songwriters that can be used to challenge this statement – Joni Mitchell, Kate Bush or Tracy Chapman may have come to mind. One thing is for certain, though: the notion of Madonna as a powerful woman, being in command of her own destiny and successful in the roles of author, **producer** and entrepreneur, makes for a highly appealing role model.

## Image/persona

There has been much interest in Madonna's image, often at the expense of any serious discussion of her music. There is no doubting that she has star appeal and succeeds in attracting fans from diverse social, cultural and racial backgrounds. Madonna has always exercised control over her public persona – a characteristic common to many divas – but one can argue that she has taken it to an extreme; that her obsession with commercial success and fame has led her to change continually and manipulate her image to stay in the public eye. As Roy Shuker has pointed out: 'Madonna represents a bankable image, carefully and continually constructed in an era of media globalization' (2002, p. 283).

## Mass media

**Activity**   Now turn to Reading 6.2, and read the extract from an article by musicologist Stan Hawkins. What is the main thrust of his argument?

Hawkins describes the importance of music video in relation to Madonna's career. He suggests that Madonna's fame and reputation are partly due to the way that she has exploited video for promotional purposes. The point he makes in the final sentence is also extremely important. Indeed, the rapid development in methods of mass communication over the last twenty to thirty years, and the technological change that has accompanied it, has meant that many different types of media – audio, video, television, film, newspaper, magazine and the internet – now filter through to the remotest areas on earth. Many celebrities, especially pop stars, are subjected to an unprecedented degree of global exposure. Madonna, then, is unquestionably one of the most famous women on the planet.

## 'Like a Prayer'

I now want to explore Madonna's 'Like a Prayer'. A number of Madonna's songs exist in several different versions – such as extended dance remixes – and 'Like a Prayer' is no exception. In this section we will be discussing the version taken from the album *Like a Prayer*. I have chosen this song mainly because it contains plenty of interesting and diverse musical elements.

### 'I hear you call my name' – the lyrics

**Activity**   What I'd like you to do first is to listen to the first part of the song on track 2 of the Audio CD, up to time index 1'46". As you do so, listen closely to the lyrics. You may wish to jot down some of the most prominent words as you listen. As Chapter 1 has made you aware, poems can be intentionally ambiguous – they can have a number of meanings. Song lyrics too can have multiple meanings, chiefly depending on how they are received and understood. So what do you think this song is about?

Unlike many of Madonna's songs, the lyrics for 'Like a Prayer' do not outline a clear narrative. How are we, then, to interpret the words? There is plenty of religious imagery here – praying, angels, heaven, God. Madonna, though, is apparently addressing an earthly being, promising metaphorically to take them 'there'. But where precisely is 'there'? A higher *spiritual* plane? A higher *sexual* plane? Perhaps this song is to be understood as an innocent love song – or not. Listen to the first part of the song again, still focusing on the words, and, if it helps, write down a few thoughts before moving on.

### 'Now I'm dancing' – the music

Although Madonna's style of pop music has always been dance-oriented, her songs – moving in tandem with musical fashion – have embraced a wide variety of genres, including **disco**, **rap** and **electronica**.

Activity    In 'Like a Prayer' Madonna skilfully blends with her usual style of pop a very well-known style of music. Now listen to the complete song on track 2 of the Audio CD and see if you can identify this other style.

Madonna appropriates black Gospel music. This is a form of African-American religious music, featuring large church choirs and **virtuoso** soloists, whose vocal style is characterised by a fervent energy and spiritual ecstasy. A Gospel choir and female soloist (a Gospel diva, perhaps) are prominent throughout 'Like a Prayer', especially so in the section from 3'38" to 4'12", where joyous vocal exclamations from the choir are overlaid with soulful improvising from the soloist – a form of 'call and response' that is characteristic of traditional African-American Gospel music.

Activity    Now I want you to listen to the song again. This time concentrate on Madonna's vocal style, as you did with 'Material Girl'. How does it compare with the earlier track?

Madonna's vocal style is strikingly different from that on 'Material Girl'. Far from being thin and lacking in power, Madonna's voice is strong and rich; in fact it complements the Gospel style very well. By comparing the two tracks you can appreciate how Madonna's voice developed and matured within a relatively short space of time. In fact, maturity is one of the overriding characteristics of *Like a Prayer*, and the album undoubtedly helped establish Madonna as a serious artist.

I now want to look at the song's musical material in more detail. To do this, we're going to concentrate on the first three minutes. This part of the song has a fairly conventional verse–chorus (or verse–refrain) structure. But what's unusual here is that the music for the verses is entirely different from that for the chorus: each has its own distinctive musical character. Turn now to Table 6.1. You'll see that, using two categories, I've identified the main musical materials for the verses. They evoke an aural religious imagery in the music itself, which reflects the religious imagery in the lyrics. If it helps, listen to the song again from the start to 2'55", following my commentary.

*Table 6.1    The verses*

| Instrumentation and voices | • church organ |
| --- | --- |
| | • gentle 'tinkling' percussion |
| | • Gospel choir (wordless 'oohs') forming a 'halo' of sound above Madonna's voice |
| | • Madonna's singing is sustained, yet subdued |
| General character and other points of interest | • very serene |
| | • spiritual, religious |
| | • a thinness to the music, although the organ and choir give a certain amount of body to the overall sound |

Activity    Using my commentary as a guide, identify the main musical materials for the chorus, again using the categories 'Instrumentation and voices' and 'General character and other points of interest'. Then compare your comments with my commentary in Table 6.2.

Here is how my commentary looks:

*Table 6.2    The chorus*

| Instrumentation and voices | • lively drums |
| --- | --- |
| | • animated and joyous Gospel choir (singing words) |
| | • active guitar strumming |
| | • mobile bass line |
| | • Madonna's singing is more lively and has greater strength |
| General character and other points of interest | • very active and upbeat |
| | • a sexual physicality to the music |
| | • much thicker – a fullness to the sound |

Activity    To conclude our work in this section, I want you to listen to the complete song again. While listening, think of all of the aspects of the music that you've worked on, especially the instrumentation, the vocal characteristics of both Madonna and the Gospel choir, and how the music relates to the lyrics. I also want you to listen out for some of the tensions inherent in the song – pop/Gospel, calm/movement, spiritual/sexual. These provide a somewhat unsettled undercurrent to the music. This turbulence is brought prominently to the surface in the music video.

### 'I wanna take you there' – the music video

As Hawkins (Reading 6.2) highlighted, Madonna was one of the first pop artists to recognise the importance of music video. She also learned that it could liberate her songs from a purely sonic experience, and could extend and enhance their narrative possibilities. Arguably, some of her most interesting videos are those that are narrative-driven. These often contain controversial themes, such as teenage pregnancy ('Papa Don't Preach'), pornographic exploitation ('Open Your Heart') and, in 'Like a Prayer', religion and racism.

Unfortunately we don't have the time or space to discuss the video for 'Like a Prayer' in any detail here, but it is well worth watching it if you get the opportunity in order to develop your study of Madonna as the archetypical pop diva. If you've seen it, then you'll already know that the video contains a number of controversial images, including burning crosses, a statue of a black Jesus behind bars, stigmata (wounds of Christ) on Madonna's hands, and an interracial kiss. Although the song itself is undoubtedly a self-sufficient textual and musical structure, the video opens up a variety of new meanings. Of course, you may think that the images are there to foreground and sell the music, as well as to promote the singer. There is always plenty of room for cynicism where Madonna is concerned!

Clearly, then, Madonna's success and reputation extend well beyond her musical and vocal talents, although these in themselves are significant. Her status as a pop diva is also due to other factors, including her chameleon-like image, the notion of her as a powerful female and controversial figure, and the ways in which her work is disseminated.

## 6.3   SOME BASIC MUSICAL LANGUAGE
### Elaine Moohan

Now that you have had the opportunity to do some close listening activities, and have got a feel for how a song can be structured using the lyrics as a skeleton, it is time to introduce you to some technical language. This will help you to describe what you listen to more accurately. I will use an operatic **aria** as an example here, but the musical terms I define can be applied to any kind of music.

**Activity**   Listen to track 3 on the Audio CD while following the lyrics in Reading 6.3. This is the first section of the aria 'Una voce poco fa' from the opera *The Barber of Seville* (first performed in 1816) by Rossini (1792–1868), sung by the legendary soprano Maria Callas, whom you will study in more depth in Section 6.5. As you listen, try to describe the vocal melody using everyday words. Listen as many times as necessary, using the printed lyrics to help you follow the music until you are happy with your description.

I would describe the performance of the vocal line as smooth (the technical term for 'smooth' is **legato**), even though the rhythm is not so smooth. There are several high notes, in the upper part of the voice between 1'04" and 1'45", which Callas seems to produce effortlessly, and the section ends with a final flourish, or **ornament**, crafted to display her vocal agility – and perhaps improvising skills: the composer wrote only four notes here (2'31"). All this technical vocal control is typical of the opera diva, but it amounts to nothing if there is not also the musicality to convey the sentiments of the text. It is the combination of both that creates a true star of the opera house.

Activity    Listen to track 3 again, this time concentrating on the orchestra. How does its music relate to the vocal line? Is it similar in character? Try to describe the sound of the orchestra when it accompanies the voice.

The orchestral music is notably different from that of the singer, although it also uses uneven rhythms. These uneven rhythms give the opening **phrases** an almost fanfare quality, and there is nothing here that relates to the first vocal phrase. Indeed, it is difficult to guess from this introduction what the first vocal entry will be like. When the voice enters at 0'37", the orchestra plays very little in the **accompaniment**. If you tried to describe the **texture** at this point, you could use words such as 'thin' or 'light' – the kind of words that we generally use to describe texture. This lightness is achieved not only by writing very little for the orchestra to play, but by asking the string instruments to play **pizzicato**, or plucked.

Finally, we should mention the different volumes used in this section, the musical term for which is **dynamics**. Dynamics are written on the music by the composer and indicate the loudness of one section relative to another. In this extract, the opening few seconds are marked to be played 'very loudly', becoming 'very soft', then 'very loud' again immediately before the voice enters 'softly'. The Italian terms used are **piano** (soft) and **forte** (loud), which become **pianissimo** (very softly) and **fortissimo** (very loudly). These are abbreviated on printed music to *p*, *f*, *pp*, and *ff*.

Activity    Now listen to the second part of this aria, track 4 of the Audio CD, and try to describe the constituent elements using some of the technical language introduced above. In this section you will hear more of the vocal agility required of any soprano who wishes to perform this aria, particularly from 5'05" to the end.

Here is my description of this section:

| CD time reference | Lyrics | Comments |
|---|---|---|
| 0'00" | | A legato melody played by the flutes and clarinets with a light accompaniment in the rest of the orchestra, played pianissimo. The music becomes fortissimo briefly at 0'20". |
| 0'31" | Io sono docile, son rispettosa, sono ubbidiente, dolce, amorosa. Mi lascio reggere, mi fo guidar. | Vocal entry where, unlike the first section of this aria, the singer takes up the melody played by the flutes and clarinets at the start of this section. |
| 1'08" | Ma se mi toccano dov'è il mio debole, sarò uno vipera, e cento trappole prima di cedere farò giocar. Io sono docile ... | Many shorter-duration notes are introduced into the vocal line, and the strings play a pizzicato accompaniment. |
| 2'13" | Ma se mi toccano ... | The singing becomes much more virtuosic, using the full soprano range. |

You should now feel able to use some technical language to describe certain aspects of a piece of music. The terms introduced here are common to all forms of music, so you can practise applying these to each piece you listen to this week, both in this chapter and in your private listening. Before moving on, listen to this track again. If you found this exercise difficult, use my description to consolidate your study.

## 6.4 TRAINING TO BECOME A DIVA
Elaine Moohan

*You will need to allow half an hour to watch the DVD Video 'The Diva'. It will take longer to make notes, and you will need to allocate a further hour if you want to watch the additional material.*

For this part of your study of 'the diva' you should watch the short film shot at the Opera School of the Royal Scottish Academy of Music and Drama in Glasgow (DVD Video 'The Diva'). In this, you will follow a young soprano, Catharine Rogers, through several stages of rehearsal in preparation for a public performance, ending with her own critical analysis of her achievements. Although opera students are required to study many subjects – for example, languages, stagecraft and movement – in addition to singing, and tackle several operatic roles suited to their voice type and particular stage of development, our film follows Catharine working on just two contrasting roles: namely, the Countess in Wolfgang Amadeus Mozart's (1756–91) *The*

*Marriage of Figaro* (first performed 1786), and Romilda in Serse (first performed 1738) by Georg Friedrich Handel (1685–1759). All of the preparation in her individual singing lesson, ensemble rehearsal and staging rehearsals culminates in a public performance of a selection of operatic scenes that forms part of the formal examination process.

As you watch this film you will be introduced to some more technical language – in particular, those terms that are used to describe how a trained voice should be produced, as well as terms that refer to different styles of operatic music. Two important terms to understand from this film are 'aria' and '**recitative**'. These terms not only suggest a particular style of music, but give some indication of the composer's approach to setting the text and how this impacts on the advancement of the plot. Listen to how these terms, and others, are used and defined as a basis for supplementing and refining the entries in your glossary.

You will also hear descriptions of the voice types most suited to the roles of the Countess and Romilda. Make a note of the vocal qualities required to be successful in each role. You may wish to include any physical and/or emotional challenges that each presents.

## 6.5   MARIA CALLAS AND THE AUTHORITY OF THE HISTORIC RECORDING
Robert Philip

### Biography

Maria Callas was probably the most famous opera star of the mid-twentieth century. There is nothing unusual about an opera singer becoming famous. From the castrati (male sopranos) of the eighteenth century, to the 'Three Tenors' (an ensemble comprising the **tenors** José Carreras, Placido Domingo and Luciano Pavarotti, brought together initially to sing at the World Cup finals held in Italy in 1990), to the present day, the top opera singers have always attracted attention beyond their roles in the theatre. Callas is, however, regarded as a special case, partly for musical reasons, and partly for reasons that go beyond music. In this case study, I'll attempt to tease out some of the reasons why she was, and continues to be, so famous.

A chronology of her life is given in Reading 6.4. This is, of course, only a very brief summary of some of the important milestones. There have been many articles and several books written about Callas, and it would be easy to fill out a chronology over several pages, but the summary will give you some idea of the mixture of musical and non-musical ingredients in the pattern of her life.

Activity   Apart from the fact of having sung particular operas in various places, what other events in the chronology in Reading 6.4 strike you as possibly having contributed to Callas's fame?

Here are some things that strike me:

1   Her international career was short. It was only in the late 1940s that she made her breakthrough, and ten years later she stopped appearing regularly on the opera stage. She was only 42 when she finally retired from the stage, and she died at the age of just 54.

2   Her spectacular weight loss in 1954 was, unsurprisingly, much reported and debated in the press. She became a glamorous figure and was subjected to intense public scrutiny.

3   When she retired, she did not fall from public view. The decline in her opera appearances coincided with the ending of her marriage and the start of her very public relationship with the most prominent Greek shipping magnate, Aristotle Onassis, who was to leave her to marry Jacqueline Kennedy (he had never married Callas). This was all covered extensively in the press. Callas came to be seen as a somewhat tragic figure, a view heightened by reports of her last years spent as a recluse in Paris and her solitary death.

These events, and the perceptions that arose from them, have obvious parallels in the lives of many famous people. One might say that there is a particular variety of fame associated with personal and professional difficulty, a short career, opportunities missed or squandered, public unhappiness, broken relationships, illness and early death. There is a long list of people whose fame was, in some ways, enhanced by such factors: Elvis Presley, Tony Hancock, Marilyn Monroe, Diana Princess of Wales, George Best, and so on. You will have no difficulty in supplying other names.

In the case of an opera singer, and particularly one who is a woman, there is a perception of added poignancy. When a female opera singer is revealed as personally vulnerable, she can easily be seen as mirroring in her life aspects of the roles that she has played on the stage. This may seem fanciful (and there is no shortage of fanciful coverage of famous women's lives in the news media), but the fact is that the great nineteenth- and early twentieth-century female roles in opera are mostly tragic. Almost all of the characters die, on stage or just off it, through illness, suicide or murder, or they go mad. The great tragic roles were Callas's forte, and it was all too easy for the public to see this reflected in her personal life. Of course, none of the events of Callas's life would have been of much interest to a wider public if she had not been an outstandingly gifted opera singer.

## Callas as a singer: Puccini's *Tosca*

Now is the moment for you to hear Callas in one of her most famous roles, Puccini's *Tosca*. Giacomo Puccini (1858–1924) wrote the opera in 1897–99, and it was premiered in Rome in January 1900. It is set in Rome in 1800, at the time of the Napoleonic Wars. Tosca (the role

Figure 6.3   Maria Callas as Tosca at Covent Garden, 1964. Unknown photographer.
Photo: Theatre Museum/V&A Images/Victoria and Albert Museum.

sung by Callas) is herself a famous singer. Her lover, Cavaradossi, is a
republican sympathiser who has helped an escaped political prisoner,
Angelotti, to go into hiding. In the second act the Chief of Police,
Scarpia, has arrested and questioned Cavaradossi, who denies all
knowledge of the escape. Scarpia summons Tosca and questions her
too. In the adjacent room, her lover Cavaradossi is being tortured as
Scarpia tries to extract information about the hiding place of the
prisoner from Tosca. In the end, unable to bear the screams of
Cavaradossi, Tosca gives in. Scarpia then presents her with a choice:
either Cavaradossi will be executed, or Tosca can save him by

becoming Scarpia's mistress. She agrees to that, but at the end of the act she kills Scarpia by stabbing him with a knife from his table. As you can imagine, this is a scene that can seem crude and lurid if not performed with absolute conviction.

**Activity**    Listen now to an extract in which Callas sings Tosca, and Tito Gobbi sings Scarpia (Gobbi was as fine a singer as Callas but, being male and a **baritone**, not subjected to such media coverage). You will also hear brief contributions from Cavaradossi and Spoletta (the police investigator who has arrested Cavaradossi). The extract is on track 5 of the Audio CD, and the Italian words and their translation are given as Reading 6.5. You'll notice that occasional phrases are repeated in the music, but you should nevertheless find it possible to follow the libretto. Even if you have never heard this opera or Callas before, attempt to describe the impression that she makes in this scene. Try to put into words how she sings, how she acts, how she responds to the meaning of words. Does she bring the character of Tosca to life?

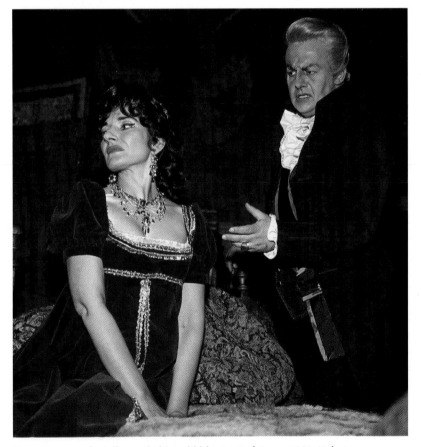

Figure 6.4    Maria Callas and Tito Gobbi in Act 2 of *Tosca*, 1964. Unknown photographer. Photo: "MPTV/LFI".

You may love opera, or you may dislike the very sound of operatic voices. For me, the most important thing in a role like Tosca is not just the quality of the voice, but whether the singer manages to make the character and her situation seem real. There are singers who sound more beautiful than Callas in this music, whose tone is more even from the bottom to the top of the voice, and who have more pleasing high notes. Callas sometimes struggles to control a rather aggressive wobble in her top register, particularly when she is singing loudly (an affliction of many opera singers). She battled throughout her career against vocal problems (real and imaginary, according to some commentators).

What Callas has – which nobody else has in quite the same way – is an extraordinarily powerful and sensitive way of acting the words as she sings them. You don't need to see her in the theatre to sense the force of this. When she sings quietly, her voice has a slightly husky, veiled quality, which can sound tender or vulnerable. The emotional range of her singing is very wide. In this passage she conveys violent anguish and anger, rising to a powerful climax and then subsiding into broken tearfulness. This is enhanced by the contrasting impression of implacable power and determination given by Gobbi as Scarpia. The two play off each other magnificently. Of course, it is not just the singers who achieve this. The conductor, Victor de Sabata, paces the scene with great power, drawing out the menace and drive of the music from the very fine orchestra. Reports of the recording sessions reveal that de Sabata was meticulous in his attention to every dramatic, as well as musical, detail of the score, making the singers repeat some passages many times.

## The music of the scene

It is worth looking at the music and the words that are sung in this scene in order to understand something of how they make such a powerful effect. This will also help you to understand just what the raw material is, out of which Callas and Gobbi and the other musicians construct such compelling performances.

**Activity**    First of all, try to put out of your mind the music you have just heard, and read through the words of the extract reproduced in Reading 6.5. This libretto was adapted by Giuseppe Giacosa and Luigi Illica from a play by the French dramatist Victorien Sardou. How would you describe the impression these words make, just as a script without music?

The lines are very short, and the conversation is abrupt and disjointed. The words do not flow, and there is little that is obviously poetical or 'musical' about them. They are blunt, realistic. Acted on their own, without music, they would need great care and dramatic effort in order to make them come alive on the stage.

**Activity**    Now listen to the CD performance of this extract again. Make a note of any points in the music that strike you. If something seems particularly effective, try to identify what makes it sound like that. Don't worry if you are not accustomed to musical analysis of this kind; just try to describe your impressions of how the music of the scene goes. How is the music paced?

How does it change in volume (dynamics)? Is there a striking effect in the orchestra? Do you notice repetitions of musical phrases?

I described the emotional range of Callas's singing as very wide. The same is true of Puccini's music. The passage begins and ends quietly, with the voices low, both in pitch and in dynamic (pianissimo), but between these points there are two great climaxes, with each singer singing at the top of his and her register, and very loudly (fortissimo). Puccini's writing for the orchestra is very cleverly calculated: the general effect is of great power, but the orchestra only plays very loudly when the singers are singing very high, so that they can still be heard; and the full power of the orchestra is only used when the singers are not singing.

Another striking feature of this scene is how Puccini has taken the disjointed, short-winded text, and used the music to glue it together into a coherent whole. He does this partly by careful dramatic pacing. The scene starts quite slowly, then suddenly increases in pace (at 0'13"), driving forward to the first climax (which is reached at 0'56"). Then, after Cavaradossi's offstage shout, the orchestra becomes quiet again, and starts a second build-up to a climax. This time the character of the orchestral writing is quite different. It consists of short, repeated phrases, building higher and higher, with a menacing character added by the snarling of muted trumpets (at 1'03" and 1'18").

Repetition is an important key to how this scene is built. There is quite a subtle example of this right at the beginning. The rhythm of the opening two musical phrases – 'Orsù, Tosca, parlate./Non so nulla' – is subjected to repetition. First, the orchestra repeats the second of those phrases on its own. Then, after Scarpia has shouted for the torture to continue, the brass instruments play a phrase in the same rhythm as the opening phrase, but faster and much louder. This makes its character so different that you might not have spotted that the rhythm is identical. Tosca then repeats the second of the opening phrases twice ('No ... mostro! Lo strazi ...') This leads on to a climax, where Tosca repeats her final, highest phrase ('Lo strazi l'uccidi!'), and Scarpia answers by repeating his final phrase also ('vostro silenzio assai più'). These repetitions give a sense that the music is developing emotional intensity as the encounter goes on.

As the scene continues, the repetitions become more obvious and more insistent. Scarpia shouts for the door to be left open (0'51", over a tense, held, high note in the violins), and then there is a long build-up to the final climax of this passage, starting with Scarpia's 'Più forte! Più forte!' Throughout this build-up, many phrases are repeated as the music gets gradually higher and louder. What is less obvious is that, underneath, the lower instruments of the orchestra sustain an unchanging bass note throughout this passage. So although the music of the singers and the upper instruments of the orchestra are highly agitated, the whole passage is rooted on a foundation of one sustained note. This adds to the impression of implacable power, and helps to convey the iron will of Scarpia against which Tosca has to battle. As the music subsides, there are more repetitions in the orchestra. Beginning at 2'00", a sorrowful falling phrase is repeated several times, first by the cellos, then by flute, clarinet, and flute again, followed by piccolo with cello, and then taken up by Tosca herself.

The more one becomes aware of these details, the more one can appreciate the skill with which Puccini has created a scene of great dramatic force. So it is worth playing this extract several times in order to get to know how it works.

## Prestige and the opera house

Let us now consider the setting within which Maria Callas became famous. Opera began as a sophisticated court entertainment in Italy at the beginning of the seventeenth century, with the intention of recreating the principles of ancient Greek drama for an elite audience; you will learn about these principles in Book 3 when you study Seamus Heaney's play *The Burial at Thebes*. Now in the twenty-first century, opera and opera houses have become symbols of prestige across the world, the music widely disseminated by recordings and on television. In Italy, where opera began and where the language of many opera libretti is the language of the country, opera has been, since the nineteenth century, a genre that appeals to a wide social spectrum. If you go to a grand opera production in one of the open-air arenas in Italy, such as the famous Roman arena in Verona (see Figure 6.5), you will find yourself among a crowd which, apart from foreign tourists, ranges from immaculately dressed business people in the expensive seats, to casually dressed working-class people in the cheap seats at the back. They all know the familiar operas, including *Tosca*, and they will applaud or cheer at any point where they think the singers are doing well, and boo if they are disappointed. It is a national sport with a high emotional charge, a little like football. There is nothing inherently elitist about opera in Italy, anymore than there is about wine in France. There are opera-snobs and wine-snobs to be found everywhere, but in Italy everyone has a view on opera, and in France everyone has a view on wine. It is woven into the national culture from the top to the bottom.

In other countries, the position of opera is rather different, and each country has its own relationship with Italian opera. What is observable worldwide is the role of opera houses as places symbolising national success and prestige. Countries in every corner of the world that wish to demonstrate that they are, or aspire to be, in the top league of successful nations build opera houses in their major cities. Traditional opera houses are often extravagantly baroque in style, with grand staircases, glittering chandeliers, and seats and curtains of red velvet with gold decoration. The new opera houses around the world vary in

Figure 6.5   Verona's Roman Amphitheatre. Production of Puccini's *La Bohème*, 1994. Photographed by Gianfranco Fainello.
Photo: Gianfranco Fainello/ArenaPAL.

style (see Figure 6.6), and the building materials may be glass, steel and concrete, but the same basic principle applies – that an opera house should look grand, exciting and expensive, more so than an ordinary theatre.

Inhabiting such an environment, a singer such as Callas has much more to contend with than music. Glamour is at the heart of the opera establishment, whatever the social range of those who buy the tickets. The personalities who succeed in it must be huge, both to command the stage over the sound of a large orchestra, and to withstand the pressure and publicity of the world outside the opera house. Part of the appeal of Maria Callas was her combination of strength and vulnerability in the face of all this. In her struggle to succeed, people could all too easily think of her as the incarnation of an opera character like Tosca. In the second act of the opera, Tosca has the courage to kill the evil Scarpia; but at the end of the opera, Tosca herself is tricked, her lover is dead and, as she is cornered, she flings herself to her death over the battlements of the Castel San Angelo in Rome. In art and in life – the Callas fan might like to think – she was a tragic heroine.

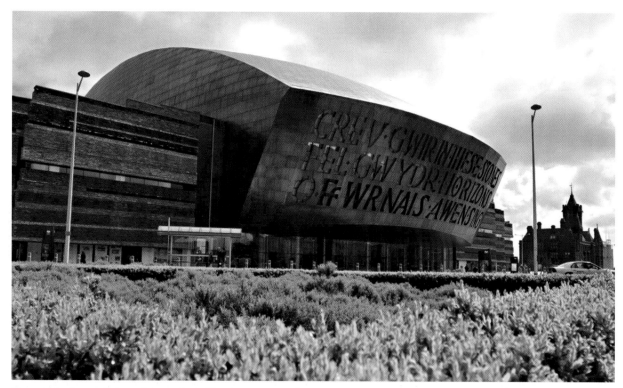

Figure 6.6    External view of the Wales Millennium Centre. Photographed by Neil Bennett. Photo: © Neil Bennett.

## 6.6    THE CONCERTO DELLE DONNE OF FERRARA
Elaine Moohan

We now move from the very public figure of Maria Callas to a singing ensemble that was renowned in its day for private concerts at the ducal court of Ferrara. The northern Italian town of Ferrara was established as a centre for the cultivation of the fine arts, particularly music, from the fifteenth century, when Duke Ercole I d'Este (reigned 1471–1505) was able to attract some of the finest foreign composers to his court. Its final flourish came during the reign of Duke Alfonso II d'Este (reigned 1559–97; see Figure 6.7), when the courtly music was provided by home-grown performers.

### Luzzaschi, court composer

The most celebrated composer/performer at Alfonso's court was Luzzasco Luzzaschi (*c.* 1545–1607), who was associated with the duke's *musica segreta*, or private concerts, from about 1570. Luzzaschi's main contribution to the court repertoire was several sets of **madrigals**, secular songs setting Italian texts, although he is also noted for his **harpsichord** music, being a proficient keyboard performer himself. Many of his madrigals were written for a group of virtuosic female singers – the *Concerto delle donne*. These ladies were famous throughout Italy, and many poets and composers became

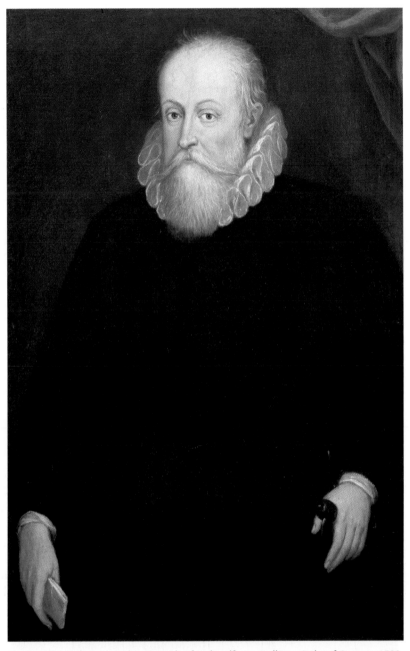

Figure 6.7   Unknown artist, *Portrait of Duke Alfonso II d'Este, Duke of Ferrara*, 1589, oil on canvas. Museo d'Arte Antica, Pinacoteca, Castello Sforzesco. Photo: akg-images/ Electa.

infatuated with them. This infatuation can only have been heightened by the private nature of the concerts and the restrictions on the persons admitted to them. Alfonso not only jealously guarded his singing ladies from public spectacle, but he also guarded his secret repertoire, with the result that Luzzaschi's madrigals were only published in 1601, four years after the Duke's death.

## Concerto delle donne

Although Alfonso created several singing and instrumental ensembles at court, it is the ladies' vocal ensemble formed in 1580 that attracted most attention from contemporary musicians and court commentators, as well as from modern-day scholars. In February 1579, the forty-five-year old duke married his third wife, Margherita Gonzaga, the fifteen-year-old daughter of the Duke of Mantua (see Figure 6.8). Mantua was another renowned music centre of this period, often related to Ferrara through marriage, and possibly because of this Alfonso gathered four ladies who were accomplished singers to act as ladies-in-waiting to his new wife. They were Laura Peverara, Anna Guarini, Tarquinia Molza and Livia d'Arco, and they all came from a social background that would not have automatically allowed them to become courtiers. They were made courtiers by virtue of their musical ability.

The life of Laura Peverara (c. 1545–1601) is the best documented of the four. She was the daughter of a wealthy merchant in Mantua and, like the other ladies in this ensemble, attracted the poetic attentions of the well-known Italian poet Torquato Tasso (1544–95). However, unlike the others, she was the one-time object of Tasso's affections, receiving seventy-five poems from him between 1563 and 1567. Eventually she married Count Annibale Turco in 1583, an occasion that Tasso marked by presenting her with a madrigal collection, *Il lauro verde*, containing settings of poems by himself and other poets of the Ferrarese court by some of the foremost composers of the day. This is one of three such collections that he dedicated to Laura, bearing witness to his affections towards her and reflecting her singing talent. In one of these collections, the texts praise Laura's beauty, ask her to sing, and describe the birds stopping to listen to her. Duke Alfonso clearly held her in high regard, accepting her husband as a gentleman of the court and providing the couple with the palace apartments that once belonged to his sister Leonora.

Little is known of Anna Guarini (d. 1598) except that she was the daughter of the poet and Ferrarese diplomat Giovanni Battista Guarini. In the mid 1580s she married a gentleman of the court, Ercole Trotti, who, driven by jealousy and suspicion, killed her. Tarquinia Molza (1542–1617) was also the daughter of a poet, Francesco Maria Molza. Tarquinia was married in 1560 and widowed in 1569 at the age of twenty-seven. She conducted an affair with Giaches Wert, court composer at Mantua, after the death of his wife in 1583, which resulted in her being banished from court in 1589. Livia d'Arco (d. 1611) was the daughter of Conte d'Arco, a minor noble of Mantua. She too married a courtier at Ferrara, one Alfonso Bevilacqua, a close friend of the Duke. The Duke demonstrated his regard for Livia by taking part in a joust in her honour.

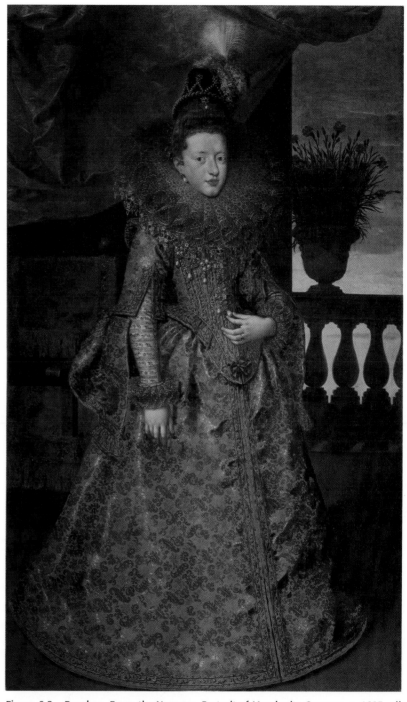

Figure 6.8    Pourbus, Frans the Younger, *Portrait of Margherita Gonzaga*, *c*. 1605, oil on canvas, Galleria Palatina, Florence. Photo: © 1990, Scala, Florence – courtesy of the Ministero Beni e Att. Culturali.

Activity    Turn to the extracts in Readings 6.6–6.8. What do these tell us about the singing of the ladies in this ensemble? Try to note four points.

Here is my summary of what these documents tell us about this ensemble.

1    Although it was clearly a great honour to be invited to listen to this group singing, the style of music was not to everyone's taste. Urbani, who tells us of the honour associated with such an invitation, and who had himself been kept waiting for some months, tells us that the music was not to his liking. Cavalier Grana, on the other hand, seems to appreciate the skill involved in singing the more difficult pieces.

2    The ladies sang in different combinations – solo, duet and trio – and were accompanied on the harpsichord.

3    Professional musicians, such as the composer Striggio, were impressed by the skill of these ladies in being able to sing all the music placed before them, no matter the difficulty.

4    This form of courtly entertainment most commonly took place before a small audience after dining. Urbani indicates that possibly as few as four people were present, while Cavalier Grana and Lombardini suggest that two male guests were invited to the musical evening in the Duchess's apartments.

## The Ferrarese madrigals

The madrigal is a short vocal work generally light-hearted in nature, and so is ideal as after-dinner entertainment. There are two main compositional techniques associated with the madrigal, **imitation** and **word painting**, both of which will become familiar to you as we work through this section. The cultivation of the madrigal is particularly associated with the courts of Ferrara and Mantua throughout the sixteenth century, and it is no wonder that the ducal library at Ferrara contained a significant number of madrigal collections. The purchasing and commissioning of madrigals was closely linked with the success of court musicians: the better the musicians, the more music that was required; providing more music encouraged the musicians to develop their performing skills, and so the cycle continued.

Activity    'I'mi son giovinetta', which you will find on track 6 of the Audio CD, was composed by Luzzaschi and published in 1601 in a volume that contains some of the works that he wrote specifically for the virtuosic singing group in Ferrara. It is written for two sopranos with a harpsichord accompaniment, though it can be difficult to hear the harpsichord in performance and on recordings. This is partly due to the quiet nature of the instrument, and partly because its music doubles with the voices: that is, it plays the same notes that are being sung, making it difficult to hear the instrument clearly when more than one voice is singing. Listen to this madrigal now, following the lyrics provided in Reading 6.9.

Imitation pervades this madrigal. You can hear it in, for example, line 3 (0'24"), where the music sung by one voice is immediately repeated by the second voice. This is illustrated in the musical example below. Even if you cannot read music, I hope that you are able to see that the outline is the same for both voices.

Music example 1

This technique is used at the start of most new lines of text.

Activity    Listen to part of this madrigal again up to the end of line 6 (1'10"), paying particular attention to the imitation between the two sopranos in lines 3 to 6.

Another technique associated with madrigals is word painting. This is where a composer writes a musical shape or sound to reflect the word being sung. There are many examples in 'I'mi son giovinetta', so I shall highlight only a few: you may wish to find some others yourself.

The first noticeable example of word painting comes in line 2 on the words 'rido e canto' ('I laugh and sing') (0'06") where the melodic outline on 'rido' sounds like a laugh, whereas that on 'canto' is a typical vocal flourish. Both voices 'laugh' together in line 6 (0'58") in a lengthy ornament at the end of the line.

A favourite madrigalian word for imitative treatment is 'fuggi' (flee), used in this madrigal in line 12 (2'15"). Luzzaschi draws our attention to this word by changing the rhythmic speed either side of 'fuggi'. At the end of line 11, 'Et ella' (2'11"), the second soprano sings longer note values before 'fuggi', and afterwards both voices sing longer note values, drawing our attention to the running, shorter notes used to set 'fuggi'.

Activity    This passage returns at 2'52". What is different about this return? Listen in particular to the music for the word 'l'ardore' at the end of line 12.

At the return of this passage Luzzaschi writes a more florid vocal line, containing more ornamentation on, for example, 'l'ardore' (3'12"). Look at the musical example below for a visual representation of the ornamentation used. You should be able to see – and hear – the difference even if you cannot read music.

It is this type of ornamentation that gives these madrigals their virtuosic quality because the singers need to be able to synchronise the sounding of very short note values. Luzzaschi, knowing the vocal ability of his singers, could write to their strengths.

Music example 2

## Historical voices

One of the challenges for music scholars today is to understand the sound and musical ability of performers before the age of recording. Our two main sources of information are contemporary accounts of performances and the music itself. Readings 6.6, 6.7 and 6.8 give some sketchy contemporary accounts of performances at the court in Ferrara, but these place more emphasis on the private nature of the concerts than on the virtuosic ability of the singers. Although some writers praise the beauty of the ladies' singing, it is not clear from their writings if this is a true reflection of what they heard, or whether their words were written to please the Duke and further advertise the artistic endeavours of his court. However, the report of Striggio's experience (Reading 6.8) surely indicates the high standards of singing that could be heard in Ferrara since, as a composer and renowned singer himself, he was well placed to appreciate the accomplishments of fellow performers. Further testament to the vocal abilities of these ladies is given in the printed music. This is music that could only have been performed by the most accomplished singers, and is comparable with the vocal acrobatics of later operatic arias, such as that studied in Section 6.3 above. We know that Luzzaschi as court composer was writing for voices that were well known to him, which gives us the confidence to take his madrigals as a clear indication of the abilities of the *Concerto delle donne*.

## CONCLUSION

Now that you have studied performers from three different historical periods, and listened to the music associated with each performer, do you think that each is worthy of the name diva? Do they all embody the qualities expressed by Mackerras in the quote given at the start of this chapter?

> There has to be something unusual as well as competent about a diva, something compelling about her personality, whether you like it or not, whether it be charming or repellent ...

> (Matheopolous, 1998, p. xix)

You will have your own views on this based on what you have read and, to a certain extent, on whether or not you liked the music associated with each historical period. They are all certainly 'competent' in their own field – Madonna, Callas, and the *Concerto delle donne*. There is something in the personality of each that draws admiration and scorn (Mackerras's 'charming or repellent') – equal bedfellows where reputation in music is concerned. Certainly Madonna and Callas display the almost stereotypical behaviour associated with the worlds of pop and opera. The Ferrarese ladies must have displayed a certain amount of charm to be retained as courtiers in an age when they could be dismissed on a whim, as was Molza when her affair with Wert was uncovered.

What about their musical accomplishments? Do they all meet the standards set by their peers to be considered a diva? I would say yes, based on the historical documents and audio recordings available to us, but you may disagree. It is clear from court records and Luzzaschi's printed madrigals that the ladies at Ferrara were among the most skilled performers of their day. To this day, Callas is admired by opera lovers as one of the greatest voices of the twentieth century. As for Madonna, although her voice may not be considered as her strongest asset, her complex self-presentation certainly places her in the category of diva.

## REFERENCES

Luzzaschi, L. (1965 [1601]) *Madrigali per cantare e sonare a uno, due e tre soprano (1601)* ed. Adriano Cavicchi (Monumenti di musica Italiano, Serie II Polifonia vol II), Kassel, Bärenreiter.

Matheopoulos, H. (1998) *Diva: the New Generation: the Sopranos and Mezzos of the Decade Discuss their Roles*, London, Little Brown.

Shuker, R. (2002) *Popular Music: The Key Concepts*, London and New York, Routledge.

## RESOURCES

Reading 6.1

## Living to tell: Madonna's resurrection of the fleshly

[T]he products ascribed to Madonna are the result of complex collaborative processes involving the input of co-writers, co-producers, studio musicians, video directors, technicians, marketing specialists, and so forth. As is the case in most pop, there is no single originary genius for this music.

Yet the testimonies of co-workers and interviewers indicate that Madonna is very much in control of almost every dimension of her media persona and her career. Even though certain components of songs or videos are contributed by other artists, she has won and fiercely maintains the right to decide finally what will be released under her name. [...]

Madonna writes or co-writes most of her own material. Her first album [*Madonna*, 1983] was made up principally of her tunes. She surrendered some of the writing responsibility on *Like a Virgin* [1984] (interestingly, two of the songs that earned her so much notoriety – 'Material Girl' and 'Like a Virgin' – were written by men). But in her third album, *True Blue* [1986], she is credited (along with her principal collaborators, Stephen Bray and Patrick Leonard) with co-production and with the co-writing of everything except 'Papa Don't Preach'. She co-wrote and co-produced (with Bray, Leonard, and Prince) all of the songs on her [fourth] album, *Like a Prayer* [1989]. It is quite rare for women singers to contribute so much to the composition of their materials, and it is almost unheard of for them to acquire the skills required for production. Indeed, very few performers of either sex attain sufficient prestige and power within the recording business to be able to demand that kind of artistic control.

Source: Susan McClary (1991) *Feminine Endings: Music, Gender, and Sexuality*, Minnesota, University of Minnesota Press, Chapter 7, 'Living to tell: Madonna's resurrection of the fleshly', pp. 149, 153–4.

Reading 6.2

## 'I'll Never Be an Angel': stories of deception in Madonna's music

For many pop musicians, the struggle to stardom in the early 1980s occurred within an industry that was undergoing enormous change, especially with the advent of the pop video and the launch of MTV [Music Television] in 1981. It is to this phenomenon of televisual development that Madonna owes her fame. By the mid-1980s, a rapid increase in star celebrities [...] emerged that depended on high visibility through the music video [...]. Within just fourteen weeks of its release, the album *Like a Virgin* had sold over 3.5 million copies. Before Madonna had even started touring, this album became a triple platinum, and by 1985 was the first album by a female artist to be certified by the Recording Industry Association of America (RIAA) for sales of five million units.

Capitalising on the power of this visual medium for commercial promotion, the majority of pop artists in the 1980s started to gain control of their image alongside their music in new and exciting ways. Most significantly, the female musician's traditional relegation to vocalist could now be turned around into a powerful vantage point in videos where the soundtrack could 'operate like a narrator's omnipotent voice-over to guide the visual action' (Lewis 1993, 131). In short, video iconography provided a new dimension to performance – a form of exposure never seen before. Close-up shots of facial expressions, bodily response, costume details could be more adventurous and manipulative on video, with pop stars taking advantage of this intimate mode of expression to control all aspects of their performance. [...]

There can be little doubt that music television asserted definite shifts in the ways in which music could be disseminated and received in the 1980s [...]. Characterised by a very distinctive style, Madonna's authorship surfaced during a period when male-oriented rock and pop styles had also started to change. Rapidly she influenced a generation of fans growing up in the 1980s who began imitating her style in their quest for recognition and empowerment. Against this historical backdrop, Madonna's identity and eventual rise to corporate power can be read as a testament to the development of media culture in the late twentieth century.

Source: Stan Hawkins (2002) *Settling the Pop Score: Pop Texts and Identity Politics*, Aldershot, Ashgate, Chapter 2, "'I'll Never Be an Angel": stories of deception in Madonna's music', pp. 36–7 (footnote omitted).

**Reading 6.3**    **'Una voce poco fa' from *The Barber of Seville* by Rossini**

| | |
|---|---|
| Una voce poco fa | A voice, just now, |
| qui nel cor mi risuonò, | found an echo in my heart, |
| il mio cor ferito è già, | my heart is wounded already |
| e Lindor fu che il piagò. | and Lindor is the one who hurt it. |
| Sì, Lindoro mio sarà, | Yes, Lindoro will be mine, |
| lo giurai, la vincerò. | I have sworn it, I shall succeed. |
| Il tutor ricuserò, | I shall refuse my guardian, |
| io l'ingegno aguzzerò, | my wits I shall sharpen, |
| alla fin s'accheterà, | in the end he'll be appeased, |
| e contenta io resterò. | and I will be content. |
| Sì, Lindoro mio sarà, | Yes, Lindoro will be mine, |
| lo giurai, la vincerò. | I have sworn it, I shall succeed. |
| | |
| Io sono docile, | I am submissive, |
| son rispettosa, | I am respectful, |

| | |
|---|---|
| sono ubbidiente, | I am obedient, |
| dolce, amorosa. | gentle, affectionate. |
| Mi lascio reggere, | I let myself be governed |
| mi fo guidar. | I let myself be guided. |
| Ma se mi toccano | But if they touch me |
| dov'è il mio debole, | where I have my weak point, |
| sarò uno vipera, | I become a viper, |
| e cento trappole | and I'll put in play |
| prima di cedere | a hundred traps |
| farò giocar. | before giving in. |
| lo sono docile ... | I am submissive ... |

Source: Martial Singher (1983) *An Interpretive Guide to Operatic Arias: A Handbook for Singers, Coaches, Teachers, and Students*, Pennsylvania, The Pennsylvania State University Press, pp. 221–2.

**Reading 6.4**   ## Outline of events in Maria Callas's life

| | |
|---|---|
| 1923 | Born of Greek parents in New York (family name Kalogeropoulou). |
| 1937 | Moves to Greece with her mother and sister, after her parents have separated. |
| 1938 | Enrols at the National Conservatory in Athens at age fifteen (the normal minimum age for entry is sixteen). |
| 1941 | Professional opera debut in Athens. |
| 1942 | Sings Puccini's *Tosca* for the first time, in Athens. |
| 1945 | Returns to New York, but fails an audition to the Metropolitan Opera. |
| 1947–9 | Sings various roles in Italy, culminating in a 'stunning' performance in 1949 in Bellini's *I Puritani* at La Fenice Theatre, Venice, standing in for the part at short notice. This makes her name. |
| 1949 | Marries Giovanni Battista Meneghini, a wealthy Italian industrialist and opera lover. |
| 1951–8 | A run of triumphant appearances at La Scala, Milan. |
| 1952 | Signs recording contract with EMI. |
| 1953 | Series of complete opera recordings begins, including Bellini's *I Puritani* and Puccini's *Tosca*. |
| 1954 | Loses 30 kilos in weight. |
| 1956 | First appearance at the Metropolitan Opera, New York, in Bellini's *Norma* and Puccini's *Tosca*. |
| 1957 | Meets Aristotle Onassis, a Greek shipping magnate, at a party in Venice. |
| 1959 | Callas and Meneghini split up, and Callas stops regular stage appearances to spend her time with Onassis. |

| 1964–5 | Further performances of *Tosca* at Covent Garden, London, and the Metropolitan Opera, New York. Retires from the operatic stage because of ill health. |
|---|---|
| 1968 | Onassis marries Jacqueline Kennedy, widow of the assassinated US president John F. Kennedy. |
| 1969–77 | Occasional masterclasses, a 'farewell' recital tour with tenor Giovanni di Stefano. Dies alone in her apartment in Paris, 16 September 1977. |

**Reading 6.5**    ## Extract from libretto for Puccini's *Tosca*

| | | |
|---|---|---|
| SCARPIA | Orsù, Tosca, parlate. | Now, Tosca, talk. |
| TOSCA | Non so nulla. | I know nothing. |
| SCARPIA | Non vale quella prova? Roberti, ripigliamo! | Wasn't that enough for you? Roberti, again! |
| TOSCA | No! Fermate! | No! Stop! |
| SCARPIA | Voi parlerete? | You'll talk? |
| TOSCA | No ... mostro! Lo strazi l'uccidi! | No ... monster! Your torture is killing him! |
| SCARPIA | Lo strazia quel vostro silenzio assai più. | It's your silence that's torturing him. |
| TOSCA | Tu ridi all'orrida pena? | How can you laugh at such pain? |
| SCARPIA | Mai Tosca alla scena più tragica fu! Aprite le porte che n'oda i lamenti! | Tosca on the stage never gave a more tragic performance! Open the door so that she can hear his groans! |
| The voice of CAVARADOSSI | Vi sfido! | I defy you! |
| SCARPIA | Più forte! Più forte! | Harder! Harder! |
| The voice of CAVARADOSSI | Vi sfido! | I defy you! |
| SCARPIA (*to Tosca*) | Parlate! | Talk! |
| TOSCA | Che dire? | And say what? |
| SCARPIA | Su, via! | Come on! |
| TOSCA | Ah! non so nulla! dovrei mentir? | I know nothing! Must I lie to you? |
| SCARPIA | Dite dov'è Angelotti? parlate su, via, dove celato sta? | Where is Angelotti? Just tell me where he's hidden. |

| TOSCA | No! Ah! Più non posso! Che orror! Cessate il martîr! È troppo il soffrir! | No! I can't stand it! The horror! Stop the torture! It's too much to bear! |
| The voice of CAVARADOSSI | Ahimè! | Ah! |
| TOSCA | Mario, consenti ch'io parli? | Mario, will you let me talk? |
| The voice of CAVARADOSSI | No, no. | No, no. |
| TOSCA | Ascolta, non posso più ... | Listen, I can't stand any more ... |
| The voice of CAVARADOSSI | Stolta, che sai? ... Che puoi dir? | Fool, what do you know? ... What can you say? |
| SCARPIA | Ma fatelo tacere! | Make him be silent! |
| TOSCA | Che v'ho fatto in vita mia? Son io che così torturate ... torturate l'anima. Sì, l'anima mi torturate! | What have I ever done to you? It's me you are torturing ... torturing my soul. Yes, you are torturing my soul! |
| SPOLETTA (*muttering words from the Requiem Mass*) | Judex ergo, cum sedebit, Quidquid latet apparebit, Nil inultum remanebit. | At the last judgement Whatever is hidden shall be revealed Nothing shall remain unpunished. |
| TOSCA | Nel pozzo ... nel giardino ... | In the well ... in the garden ... |
| SCARPIA | Là è Angelotti? ... | Angelotti is there? |
| TOSCA | Sì. | Yes. |
| SCARPIA | Basta, Roberti. | Enough, Roberti. |
| SCIARRONE | E svenuto! | He's fainted! |
| TOSCA | Assassino! Voglio vederlo. | Murderer! I want to see him. |
| SCARPIA | Portatelo qui. | Bring him here. |

Reading 6.6     **Orazio Urbani visits Ferrara, 1581**

[Orazio Urbani, a visitor to the Ferrarese court from Florence, writes in February 1581 that an Englishman, who he names as Tomaso Rondelli, was 'greatly honoured by the Duke, particularly in gaining admission to the *musica segreta*'. Urbani himself was permitted to hear the ladies in August of the same year and describes the experience thus:]

Immediately after dining, a game of *primiera* [a card game] was begun in which the Duke, the Duchess [of Ferrara], Donna Marfisa, the wife of Signor Cornelio, and myself took part. ... At the same time music was begun, so that it was necessary for me simultaneously to play cards, to listen, to admire, and to praise the *passaggi*, the *cadenze*, the *tirate*, and such things – all of which matters I understand little and enjoy less! This party did not last one minute less than four hours ...

[Another visitor, Cavalier Grana, who heard the ensemble a few days later, comments on a similar event:]

His Highness was kind enough to seem glad to see me, and after dinner in the rooms of the Duchess [of Ferrara] he had those two ladies sing. At the end they sang a very beautiful new piece, and at that time His Highness was kind enough to call me to listen to it closely, for in truth besides being very beautiful it was decorated with such lovely and diverse *passaggi* that one could not [hope to] hear better.

Source: Anthony Newcomb (1980) *The Madrigal at Ferrara 1579–1597*, 2 vols, vol. 1: *Text*, Princeton, Princeton University Press, p. 25 (footnotes omitted).

Reading 6.7     **Visit of Duc de Joyeuse to Ferrara in 1583**

[Alessandro Lombardini's description of the visit to Ferrara of the Duc de Joyeuse in a letter to Luigi d'Este, dated 23 July 1583:]

In the morning the Duke went to find His Highness at his rooms, and they remained there together for a while. They heard mass in the small chapel and then went to eat, with music as usual by trombones, cornetts, and other instruments. After dining they retired [to their chambers] with great ceremony as usual, the one wanting to accompany the other, and they stayed there until about 3 p.m. Then the Duke [of Ferrara] took him [the Duc de Joyeuse] to the room of the Duchesses, who were together, and, after a few ceremonies and without sitting down, they went into the first room where Luzzaschi was with the harpsichord. La Turcha [Peverara], La Guarina, and the other one, d'Arca, came in as well, and all three sang very nicely, alone, in duets, in trios all together; they sang Echo diologues and many other beautiful and delicious madrigals. His Highness had put in the hands of His Excellency a book with all the things that the ladies were singing, whence they were greatly praised by that Prince and by the other gentlemen.

Source: Anthony Newcomb (1980) *The Madrigal at Ferrara 1579–1597*, 2 vols, vol. 1: *Text*, Princeton, Princeton University Press, pp. 25–6 (footnote omitted).

Reading 6.8    **The composer Striggio visits Ferrara, 1584**

[The composer Striggio visited the court in 1584, when one observer records the following on the standard of music:]

Striggio and another singer [Striggio's son?] are here, and some stupendous singing and playing is going on. They are astounded by the singing of these ladies and by their knowledge, for the ladies sing without rehearsal every motet and every composition that they give them, however difficult these pieces may be.

Source: Anthony Newcomb (1980) *The Madrigal at Ferrara 1579–1597*, 2 vols, vol. 1: *Text*, Princeton, Princeton University Press, p. 68.

Reading 6.9    **Luzzasco Luzzaschi, 'I'mi son giovinetta' ('I am a young maiden')**

| | | |
|---|---|---|
| line 1 | I'mi son giovinetta | 'I am a young maiden |
| line 2 | E rido e canto alla stagion novella – | And smile [laugh] and sing in the new season', |
| line 3 | Cantava la mia dolce pastorella, | Sang my sweet shepherdess, |
| line 4 | Quando l'ali il cor mio | When my heart's wings |
| line 5 | Spiegò come augellin subitamente. | Suddenly spread wide like a little bird's. |
| line 6 | Tutto lieto e ridente | All joyous and smiling [laughing], |
| line 7 | Cantava in sua favella: | It sang in its own tongue, |
| line 8 | Son giovinetto anch'io | 'I too am young, |
| line 9 | E rido e canto a più beata e bella | And I smile and I sing at the most blessed and lovely |
| line 10 | Primavera d'Amore | Springtime of Love, |
| line 11 | Che ne begli occhi suoi fiorisce. Et ella: | Which blossoms in her eyes.' And she: |
| line 12 | – Fuggi se saggio sei, disse, l'ardore, | 'Flee if you are wise, flee from this flame, |
| line 13 | Fuggi, ch'in questi rai | Flee, for in its beams |
| line 14 | Primavera per te non sarà mai – | There will never be a Spring for you.' |

Source: CD booklet accompanying the Harmonia mundi recording of Luzzasco Luzzaschi, 'Concerto delle Dame di Ferrara' performed by Helena Afonso, Cristina Miatello, Marinella Pennichi, Sergio Vartolo. Four translators are named: F.-X. Binnendijk, G. Löhr, M. Roffi and D. Yeld.

# 7 THE DALAI LAMA

*Helen Waterhouse*

| INTRODUCTION | 199 |
|---|---|
| **7.1** **THE DALAI LAMA AND THE WEST** | **201** |
| The western love affair with Buddhism | 204 |
| **7.2** **THE TRADITION OF THE DALAI LAMAS** | **206** |
| The Dalai Lama as Chenresig | 208 |
| The Dalai Lama as a 'god-king' | 211 |
| **7.3** **THE DALAI LAMA'S REPUTATION IN CHINA** | **216** |
| CONCLUSION | 222 |
| REFERENCES | 223 |
| RESOURCES | 224 |
| Reading 7.1 | 224 |
| Reading 7.2 | 224 |
| Reading 7.3 | 226 |
| Reading 7.4 | 228 |
| Reading 7.5 | 228 |

**MATERIALS YOU WILL NEED**
- DVD Video: Dalai Lama

**AIMS**

This chapter will enable you to:

- explore the development of competing reputations
- consider the role and reputation of the Dalai Lama
- study the past in the light of a religious worldview
- engage with the beliefs and practices of a non-western religious system
- use visual and documentary evidence.

# INTRODUCTION

This chapter is your introduction to the discipline of Religious Studies. Our particular focus here is on the reputation of the fourteenth Dalai Lama of Tibet, Tenzin Gyatso (b. 1935). The Dalai Lama is famous across the world, but he comes from a unique culture which (unless you are Tibetan) is different from your own. In choosing him for inclusion in this book we are providing you with a chance to encounter a distinctive view of the world, and one that may well seem strange. Within the academic study of religion we are concerned with understanding views about the world which we may not share, and we often have to put aside our own preconceptions about how people *should* act and think in order to come to an understanding of how they *do* act and think.

In Chapter 5 Mark Pittaway introduced you to a distinction between myth and history by considering the ways in which the reputation of Stalin has been interpreted. He argued that myth is a distortion that cannot be supported by evidence, whereas history is an account of the past that is based on a careful interpretation of evidence. Both myth and history represent attempts to bring order to the world and to supply meaning to circumstances that can otherwise seem chaotic or dangerous. In contemporary western societies history may be preferred to myth, but even in the developed West a historical account of events cannot always provide the kind of meaning for which individuals and human societies search. In relation to questions of ultimate meaning – such as those concerning death and the reasons why people suffer – people often look to myths for answers. We might, then, see myth not as a distortion of evidence, but as an explanation for things that seem to be beyond rational thought or experience.

Like the concept 'history', 'religion' is very difficult to define. You probably have a sense of what *you* think it means, and you will have another chance to consider this question in Book 2, *Traditions and Dissent*, Chapter 3. For now, I would like you to accept that one way of defining religion is as a system of practices, institutions and beliefs that provides meaning to life and death. Religions attempt to answer the really big questions, and they often do that through myths which, no matter whether they are 'true' or 'false' in a historical or scientific sense, are nonetheless powerful. Religious Studies is concerned with history and with claims about truth, but also with the nature and power of the myths that shape cultures.

In this chapter we will consider the reputation of the Dalai Lama and look at some of the different roles he plays. In order to understand his reputation we must rely as much on myth as we do on history. As the chapter develops you will find that there is no single answer to the question 'who is the Dalai Lama?', so we will start with a range of answers to that question. According to where you look, the Dalai Lama is:

- a Tibetan Buddhist monk. This is the way he prefers to describe himself and the reason why we always see him dressed in maroon and yellow robes (see Figure 7.1). He has been a monk all his life.

- the spiritual and political leader of the Tibetan people. This may have been true before the 1950s when the Chinese encroached on – or, alternatively, liberated – the areas where the majority of Tibetans live but, as we shall see, the Dalai Lama's role has been forced to change.

- a living **Buddha**. The Buddha of India, who started the religion we call Buddhism, lived in the fifth century BCE. A Buddha is someone who is enlightened. According to Buddhism, enlightened beings understand the way things really are, and are not subject to the suffering, greed and hatred that characterise the lives of non-enlightened beings. The Dalai Lama recognises that he is sometimes given this status and we will consider what it means in due course.

- a Nobel Peace Prize winner. The Dalai Lama, an admirer of the pacifist policies of Mahatma Gandhi (1869–1948), received the Nobel Peace Prize in 1989.

- an ecological activist. The Dalai Lama has been outspoken on the degradation of the natural environment (which is not directly addressed in traditional Buddhist texts, all of which predate the ecological problems that the world now faces).

- an enemy of the People's Republic of China. Accused by the Chinese of hypocrisy and a lack of wisdom, the Dalai Lama, though loved by the great majority of his own people and respected across much of the western world, is regarded by the Chinese in a much more negative way.

These contrasting accounts show that the Dalai Lama means different things to different people. In the West he is usually presented in largely positive terms, often as a wise follower of peaceful resistance, but the regime of the People's Republic of China (PRC) sees him as an enemy and accuses him of hypocrisy. This contrast comes about as a result of a clash between cultures. (This is a theme you will return to in Book 3, *Cultural Encounters*.) By the time you reach the end of this chapter you should have a clearer understanding of how one man can have such diverse reputations in different parts of the world.

If you think that religion should be – or can be – only a private, personal affair, you may be surprised at the range of issues we need to consider in order to understand the reputation of a single religious leader. Religion elicits responses that range from the intensely positive to negative, and includes complete indifference. Regardless

Figure 7.1    Fourteenth Dalai Lama in Dharamsala, India on 6 July 2005, during celebrations to mark his seventieth birthday. Photographed by Emmanuel Dunand. Photo: © Emmanuel Dunand/AFP/Getty Images.

of how you feel personally about religion in general or about one religion in particular, there is no denying that religion has an impact both on the lives of individuals and on relationships between nations. This is one of the reasons why it makes a fascinating focus for study.

## 7.1    THE DALAI LAMA AND THE WEST

Known for embracing Gandhi's pacifist policies in relation to the Chinese invasion of Tibet and for his pronouncements on human rights and ecological preservation, the Dalai Lama provokes a response from diverse western institutions and political and business concerns. He holds numerous honorary degrees from western universities. He has held talks with world leaders from the realms of politics and religion, and is much in demand from western converts to, or sympathisers with, Buddhism. He is the author of well over a hundred books available in English and other European languages. He also makes appearances on BBC travel programmes, has been used in the USA to

Figure 7.2   Apple Computer billboard, Los Angeles, California, 31 March 1998. Photographed by Gilles Mingasson. Photo: Gilles Mingasson/Getty Images. The Dalai Lama appears in an advertising campaign for Apple Computers that will only be seen in Boston, Los Angeles, New York, Chicago and San Francisco.

advertise Apple computers (see Figure 7.2), and been profiled in *Hello* magazine.

As I write, in 2007, the Dalai Lama is certainly the most readily identifiable Buddhist and one of the most recognisable religious figures in the world.

**Activity**

In 1989 the Dalai Lama was the recipient of the Nobel Peace Prize. Read the citation and his acceptance speech in the Resources section (Readings 7.1 and 7.2). The Dalai Lama's opposition to violence – for which he was awarded the prize – relates specifically to the activities of the PRC in Tibetan areas. He refers to this in the speech and to the plan the Tibetan government in exile put to the PRC in 1987. However, much of the speech emphasises universalism: the idea that all human beings, wherever they are located in space and time, are subject to the same experiences and responsibilities. How does he emphasise common human experience and why do you think he does this?

**Discussion**

First the Dalai Lama accepts the prize on behalf of the oppressed everywhere and for all those who are working for peace and freedom. At the very beginning of his speech he makes clear that although he accepts the prize on behalf of his own people, the Tibetans, he also wants to include others who are in similar circumstances.

He then goes on to argue that all beings are basically the same, with the same concerns, and you may have noticed that he includes the people of China within that. Nearer the end of the speech, after he has made reference to the specific situation between Tibet and China, he returns again to the theme of universality. The idea that suffering is caused by ignorance is central to Buddhist doctrine, but the Dalai Lama uses language that is

accessible to non-Buddhists, and he goes so far as to say that universal responsibility for humanity and for the planet is not dependent on a religious perspective. You will notice that he also refers to scientific advance and emphasises that science and religion are not at odds, especially in relation to the natural environment. (This should remind you of Chapter 4 on Faraday in this book.)

As for why the Dalai Lama has constructed his speech in this way, I think it is clear that he sees the way forward for humanity to lie in cooperative action, and in order for that to happen it is necessary to emphasise common human experience rather than specific ethnic or cultural differences.

Figure 7.3   The Dalai Lama doll made by Schildkröt, Thüringen, Germany. Photo courtesy of Schildkröt Puppen und Spielwaren GmbH, Rauhenstein/Thüringen.

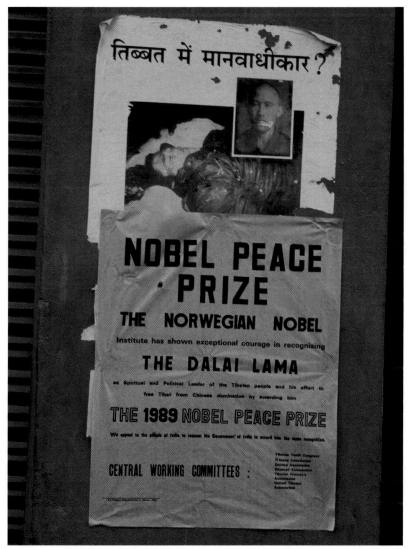

Figure 7.4   Poster announcing the Dalai Lama's Nobel Prize on a wall in Dharamsala, the seat of the Tibetan government in exile in 1989. Photographed by Galen Rowell. Photo: © Galen Rowell/CORBIS.

## The western love affair with Buddhism

The Dalai Lama represents a distinctive subset of a major world religion – Tibetan Buddhism – but he repeatedly makes it clear that his positive view of the future does not entail mass conversion to Buddhism. You have seen in his Nobel Prize acceptance speech that he accepts that not everyone will hold religious views, and elsewhere he emphasises that it is not necessary for people to change their religion:

> In general I am in favor of people continuing to follow the religion of their own culture and inheritance. Of course, individuals have every right to change *if* they find that a new religion is more effective or suitable for their spiritual needs. But, generally speaking, it is better to experience the value of one's own religious tradition. [...] If you are a Christian, it is better to develop spiritually within your religion and be a genuine, good Christian. If you are a Buddhist, be a genuine Buddhist. Not something half-and-half!

(Dalai Lama, 1996, pp. 45–6)

You might be surprised to learn that, in spite of the Dalai Lama's accepting attitude, Buddhism is and always has been a missionary religion. Ever since the time of the Buddha in India, Buddhists have believed that they follow the best possible religious teaching and there are structures within the tradition for the instruction of others. It is a diverse and adaptable tradition, spread across contrasting Asian cultures, and it has many different schools which have developed over its long history and now teach contrasting versions of doctrine and practice. All these versions of Buddhism have the same broad aims, which can be summarised as happiness and understanding.

The Dalai Lama's reputation in the West is based partly on the kinds of qualities that won him the Nobel Prize, but it is enhanced by the fact that Buddhism is enjoying a high profile. It is associated in many people's minds with the allure of the Orient and linked with a positive – if rather vague – notion of 'spirituality'. Without knowing too much about it, western people often assume that Buddhism is a model for peacefulness and wisdom.

Aspects of Buddhist teaching and practice have become absorbed by western culture. In the material sphere, Buddha statues have become home, restaurant and garden furnishing items. Buddhist techniques for training the mind have been adopted and adapted for therapeutic purposes on all levels of counselling and psychology. But it is difficult to pinpoint simple reasons for the appeal of Buddhism, partly because Buddhism itself is diverse, coming to the West as it does from diverse Asian roots.

There have undoubtedly been both 'push' and 'pull' factors at work. Westerners have looked East for wisdom and understanding and at the same time, in an era in which travel is easy, Buddhist teachers from across the Buddhist world (not just Tibet) have been keen to enter new areas. In the case of the Tibetans, this has coincided with the migration of large numbers from their traditional homelands into India and beyond. The West has become a new mission field. Since Buddhism has always seen its message as relevant for everyone, not just for a clearly defined ethnic population, this portable and adaptable religion has moved readily and been welcomed in places where traditional religious positions – for example, belief in a personal, all-powerful God – have waned. Buddhism offers an explanation for suffering and evil which is very different from that offered by **monotheistic** traditions (which believe in one God) and many find eastern ideas more acceptable than traditional, western, religious or non-religious ideologies.

Another reason why some westerners find Buddhism attractive is that it teaches that faith, though important, is not the way to salvation, as it is in Christianity. Instead, Buddhism emphasises practice built on questioning and experience, and this has caught the spirit of the time. Its promoters argue that Buddhism offers practical ways to improve the experience of life. These methods, such as meditation, can be embraced on different levels so that even active Christians and Jews, as well as those who identify with no religion, can and do incorporate techniques derived from Buddhism into their lives. However, comparatively few westerners have been so convinced by the teachings and practices of the religion that they now identify themselves as Buddhists. Buddhists were active in the West throughout the twentieth century, but a 'qualitative shift' (Batchelor, 1994, p. 93) occurred with the counter-culture of the 1960s which enthusiastically embraced eastern ideas. Since that time there have been high-profile 'celebrity' Buddhists who may have added to its appeal. The reputation of the Dalai Lama has been enhanced by his position as a representative of an important form of this tradition.

It is unclear how the Dalai Lama will be remembered in the future. In order to get a more enduring understanding of his reputation than the current western view allows, we need to turn to the Tibetan view of who the Dalai Lama is, for it is difficult to comprehend his status without an understanding of what a Dalai Lama is according to the culture from which he comes. I will therefore turn now to consider a cultural and religious system that is very different from that of the western world.

Figure 7.5    The Dalai Lama lecturing in Central Park, New York City, as part of a sixteen-day tour of the United States, 21 September 2003. Photographed by Keith Bedford. Photo: © Keith Bedford/Reuters/Corbis.

## 7.2    THE TRADITION OF THE DALAI LAMAS

What is a Dalai Lama according to the tradition to which he belongs? Who do the Tibetan people believe the Dalai Lama to be? Who does the present Dalai Lama think he is? In order to address these questions I shall refer, briefly, to Tibetan historical accounts, for the most effective and illuminating way of understanding the Dalai Lama's reputation among Tibetans is through a consideration of the way in which Tibetans think about the world.

Activity    Now read the following paragraph, taken from the Dalai Lama's autobiography, *Freedom in Exile*. Here he acknowledges that his reputation is complex and he tells us how he views himself. Again, don't worry if some of the concepts mentioned here are unfamiliar: it is part of the role of this chapter to explain them to you. This paragraph falls into three sections, which I will call religious status, political role and self-identity. Can you identify these?

> Dalai Lama means different things to different people. To some it means that I am a living Buddha, the earthly manifestation of Avalokiteshvara, Bodhisattva of Compassion. To others it means that I am a 'god-king'. During the late 1950s it meant that I was a Vice-President of the Standing

Committee of the National People's Congress of the People's Republic of China. Then when I escaped into exile, I was called a counter-revolutionary and a parasite. But none of these are my ideas. To me 'Dalai Lama' is a title that signifies the office I hold. I myself am just a human being, and incidentally a Tibetan, who chooses to be a monk.

(Dalai Lama, 1990, p. ix)

**Discussion**   The first section is about the Dalai Lama's religious status. This is the section that is likely to seem most strange and unfamiliar. The Dalai Lama acknowledges here that he is regarded as a Buddha, as the Bodhisattva Avalokiteshvara, and as a god-king.

The second section is about his political power: the king half of god-king is a political role, and the Dalai Lama tells us that he has been a member of a committee of the PRC but is now regarded by the government of the PRC as a counter-revolutionary.

Third, the Dalai Lama tells us how he thinks of himself.

The Dalai Lama claims that he is just a human being who happens to be a Tibetan and chooses to be a monk. This resonates with his claim in his Nobel Prize acceptance speech that he is 'a simple monk from Tibet' and 'no one special'. Even so, he also fulfils his designated role as Dalai Lama in a conscientious manner. In order to do that he subscribes to a Tibetan, Buddhist worldview. This Tibetan view of how the world operates was developed from classical Indian Buddhism. Several centuries after his death, the teachings of the Buddha of India (fifth century BCE) were written down and developed into a complex system incorporating religious practices and doctrines. It is this system that we call Buddhism. There is no space here to give you a thorough introduction to Buddhism, but in this section we will consider the office of the Dalai Lama and some of the reasons why, in spite of his modest claims, Tibetans regard the present Dalai Lama as much more than an ordinary being. We will consider the nature of the relationship between the present Dalai Lama and his predecessors, and the reasons why Tibetans regard this self-confessed simple monk as a living Buddha. This is not built on his personal qualities and attitudes, however commendable or lamentable they may be, but on a distinctive hereditary system.

Buddhism became the official religion of Tibet in the second half of the eighth century CE and there has been a Dalai Lama in Tibet since the sixteenth century. Then the title was applied to a prominent teacher by the Mongol king, Altan Khan, and applied retrospectively to two of that teacher's predecessors. Translated literally, Dalai Lama means something like 'Ocean of Wisdom', but this does not tell us very much about his significance. More helpful is that the Tibetan word **lama** corresponds to the Indian word **guru**. A guru is a religious teacher who deserves the respect and devotion of his followers. In Tibetan, lama is also closely related to the word for mother, which gives a nurturing dimension to the role of a religious teacher.

The present Dalai Lama is, in many ways, a modern man with an interest in science and technology. He regards his title as referring to the office he holds, but he accepts that the series of Dalai Lamas are linked with each other and with enlightened Buddhas in a special way. The Dalai Lama is the most important lama for the Tibetans. He has religious status of the very highest kind, and because religion and politics were integrated in traditional Tibetan society he is also the head of the Tibetan state. In order to understand the Dalai Lama's reputation among Tibetans we need to consider the two interconnected aspects of his role, which for practical purposes I'll call its Buddhist meaning and its socio-political meaning – the 'god-king' part of his reputation.

## The Dalai Lama as Chenresig

Buddhists believe that all sentient beings (beings who perceive through the power of the senses, whether they be humans, animals, gods or ghosts) age, die and are reborn again and again in a tiresome cycle called **samsara**. According to Buddhist doctrine, birth, life, ageing, illness and death are intrinsically unsatisfactory and painful but, even so, beings cling on to existence and continually crave for things: for sensual pleasures of all kinds, for life, or for the end of life. It is this longing or desire, whatever its focus, that keeps them trudging from life to life, and they experience birth, ageing, illness and death over and over again. Beings in samsara suffer: they are not at ease. They experience feelings such as anger and hatred and they fail to understand the nature of life and their place within it. Buddhists call this dis-ease, or unsatisfactoriness, **dukkha**. Dukkha is difficult to translate into English and I have already used a range of possible alternatives. Another way of thinking about it is as 'incapable of satisfying'. The Buddha of fifth century BCE India, who pointed out the truth of dukkha and showed that dukkha is caused by craving, did not deny that good things happen and that beings can experience transient happiness, but he claimed that these good things and this happiness are ultimately unsatisfactory because they are impermanent: even as something good happens, it is tainted by the thought that it cannot last.

The aim of Buddhist practice is real happiness, and the end of pain and suffering. This can only come about when all longings and desires have ended, breaking the cycle of samsara. This is what Buddhists call enlightenment and it occurs when ignorance ends and beings understand the way things really are. When they die, all unenlightened beings are reborn into a new life. The nature of this new life is automatically determined by past actions and intentions. Human beings have a distinct advantage over animals and other categories of being because they can control their actions and intentions in this life, and can choose to act in skilful ways which may lead towards rather than away from wisdom and ethical conduct. The benefit of this, from a Buddhist perspective, is that skilful intentions and actions automatically and inevitably lead towards happiness and an advantageous rebirth. Conversely, unskilful actions lead automatically and inevitably towards unhappiness and a disadvantageous rebirth. The precise nature of rebirth – where one is reborn and in what circumstances – is not controlled by God or gods. Instead, the law of karma – cause and effect – which operates naturally and automatically will determine where and how a being is reborn. Actions that people perform, and the intentions that lie behind them, lead inexorably to results in this life and the next, including the nature of future rebirths.

Buddhism teaches that those who take this seriously and assiduously examine these doctrines in order to understand and apply them can end their experience of suffering. Relevant for our purposes here is that, along the way, they can also acquire certain skills. One such skill is the ability to determine the specific nature and place of their future rebirths. According to Tibetan tradition, the Dalai Lamas have this skill and for them, as for other lineages of special teachers, this ability is of an advanced nature. The Dalai Lamas and other high-status lamas are part of distinctive lineages of human beings who have designated roles within Tibetan Buddhism, such as being the abbot of a monastery or being the Dalai Lama. It is believed that when they die, such lamas can choose where they are reborn and they may leave coded instructions for their followers so that they can be found. The current Dalai Lama was identified when not quite three years old, by a party of senior lamas sent to search for him as the rebirth of the thirteenth Dalai Lama, and therefore the rebirth of the complete series of Dalai Lamas back to the fifteenth century. The recognition process is complex and takes different forms. For example, at the child's birth there may be abnormal weather signs or wildlife behaviour, the searchers may have dreams, or the new incarnation may be asked to pick out artefacts belonging to his predecessor from a tray of similar objects.

**Activity**
*You will need to allow twenty minutes to watch 'Searching for a Reincarnated Lama'. It will take longer to make notes, and you may need to allocate further time if you want to watch the film again.*

The film 'Searching for a Reincarnated Lama', on the DVD Video 'Dalai Lama', tells the story of how the reincarnation of Khensur Rinpoche, the abbot of Drepung monastery, was found. Khensur Rinpoche died in exile in southern India in 1986 and we see his attendants as they near the end of their search for his successor. By the time we join them the Dalai Lama has already performed a divination which has identified a child in Tibet. Similar procedures were used when the Dalai Lama himself was identified. I want you to watch this process because Tibetan Buddhism is a highly visual tradition in the sense that it is ritually active and colourful, and it will help to bring the written account alive for you. As you watch the film, please examine your reactions to it – does it worry or concern you in some way? Are you moved by it? Does it make you angry or sceptical? You may like to discuss your reactions with others on the student forum or record them in your learning journal. As you observe your own reaction, try to remember it is not the only one that is reasonable or possible.

**Discussion**  I suspect that we all react in slightly different ways to this material. When I watch it I am always conscious that I am the mother of sons and I worry about Tashi Tsering and his mother. But I am also consoled by the child's smile, which suggests that he is not unhappy. These reactions do not necessarily help me in my study of religious practices, but it is as well to recognise that they are there. On the other hand, the Buddhist rituals shown in the film, for example the trance state of the Nechung Oracle's medium, do not surprise or upset me because I have become used to such practices, and my training and disposition mean that I accept that people apply values and act in ways that some people living, like me, in the western world may see as superstitious or even dangerous. You will react in your own way on all kinds of levels, depending on your personal life history and experience. You may also consider how you react to the concept of ritual more generally. Do you find religious ritual valuable, incomprehensible, ridiculous, a barrier to something you may regard as 'true' religion, or as dangerous superstition? It is useful to be aware of the kinds of underlying assumptions we bring to the study of religion.

In keeping with tradition, after the thirteenth Dalai Lama died in 1933, his aides went in search of the boy who was his reincarnation, following certain signs and visions. The fourteenth Dalai Lama was discovered in Amdo in the north-eastern province of Tibet, very close to China. The child was groomed and educated for his role from that time in much the same way that Tashi Tsering, now renamed Tenzin Khentse, is being prepared for his role as the abbot of Drepung monastery.

This process may seem extraordinary to secular westerners or to people from other religious traditions (who may accept other extraordinary processes and ideas), but it is taken for granted among Tibetans and represents just a part of the way in which they view the Dalai Lamas. Buddhas (like the Buddha of fifth-century BCE India), and associated beings called **Bodhisattvas**, have come by their own efforts to understand the nature of life in samsara, and they are free from the unsatisfactoriness, anger, hatred and ignorance that characterise it. Instead of blundering along within samsara they have the understanding to escape from it. Rather than escaping, however, they may stay in samsara to help other suffering beings. The Dalai Lamas are closely associated with a particular Bodhisattva, the popular Bodhisattva of compassion called in Sanskrit Avalokiteshvara. (If you say this name slowly and give equal weight to each of the syllables you will get a good approximation to the correct pronunciation – A va lo ki tesh va ra). The same being is known in Tibetan as Chenresig (pronounced Chen ré zee). In some sense the Dalai Lamas are considered to *be* Chenresig. This is part of the reason why Tibetans believe that the Dalai Lama is a living Buddha. The current Dalai Lama, who has been educated in western ways of thinking as well as in traditional Tibetan ideas, has indicated that this is not a straightforward issue, but he also understands that this is how his people have regarded him and his predecessors and he accepts that the idea is compatible with Buddhist thought. In his autobiography he writes:

> I am held to be the reincarnation of each of the previous thirteen Dalai Lamas of Tibet (the first having been born in Tibet in 1351 AD [CE]), who are in turn considered to be manifestations of Avalokiteshvara, or Chenresig, Bodhisattva of Compassion ... Thus I am believed also to be a manifestation of Chenresig ... I am often asked whether I truly believe this. The answer is not simple to give. As a fifty-six year old, when I consider my experiences during this present life and given my Buddhist beliefs, I have no difficulty accepting that I am spiritually connected both to the thirteen previous Dalai Lamas, to Chenresig and to the Buddha himself.

(Dalai Lama, 1990, p. 12)

For the Tibetan people, therefore, the fourteenth Dalai Lama, Tenzin Gyatso, has a status and reputation which are embedded in the entire Tibetan religious and cultural worldview. The Dalai Lama is apparently a wise and compassionate man, but for the Tibetans that is a valuable bonus; he would still be the Dalai Lama if he did not have these personal qualities, and he would still attract their devotion and respect because he *is* the Dalai Lama. I shall shortly introduce you to a problem Dalai Lama, which will illustrate what I mean.

## The Dalai Lama as a 'god-king'

We turn next to the Dalai Lama's reputation as a 'god-king'. From the time of the fifth Dalai Lama, the Dalai Lamas have been the heads of the Tibetan state. Not all the Dalai Lamas have reached adulthood and there have been extended periods when regents have ruled instead. A new Dalai Lama cannot be born until his predecessor has died, so there is always a gap of many years while the new holder of the office is born, grows to maturity, and is trained in Buddhist practice and statehood. The thirteenth Dalai Lama died in 1933. The education and training of the fourteenth Dalai Lama was accelerated for political reasons, and he became head of state in 1950 when only fifteen.

The term 'god-king' portrays something of the political role of the Dalai Lamas. Before recent events in Tibet, the Dalai Lamas did fulfil a kingly role, and although they are not considered to be gods but Bodhisattvas, it is easy to see how the combination of political power and extraordinary religious status led to this reputation.

The Dalai Lamas were the most powerful figures in Tibet before the Chinese incursions, but the powers they exercised were limited. Their primary concern, at least in theory, was the propagation of Buddhism and they had little involvement in the everyday lives of their people. The Tibetan people already recognised the importance of Buddhism and the special relationship between Chenresig and the Tibetan people.

Figure 7.6    The Dalai Lama and his mother during their rest at Birla House, Mussorie, after their escape from Tibet, May 1959. Photographed by Marilyn Silverstone. Photo: © Marilyn Silverstone / Magnum Photos.

The Dalai Lamas spent long periods of every day engaged in religious practices, leaving limited time for other concerns. The current Dalai Lama limits his sleep so that he can find time for Buddhist practice as well as his public duties.

The practical power of the Dalai Lamas in Tibet was also weakened by the fact that the central government in the capital city of Lhasa had little influence over people's lives. Tibet is high in the Himalayan mountain range: the terrain and climate are inhospitable, making a livelihood as well as travel difficult. The people viewed the Dalai Lamas as human incarnations of Chenresig and therefore thought they could be trusted to rule effectively so, in general, they saw no need to take an interest in government. People in rural areas were left to get on with their lives largely undisturbed. This does not mean that Tibetans have always lived peacefully together, in spite of the romantic notion of Tibet that many westerners hold. The elite monasteries and families were economically powerful but although that power has been contested from time to time, Tibetan structures of authority at local as well as at state level were not based on commands issued from the top. Instead, power to make decisions was negotiated between households and the monasteries as more or less equal partners (Samuel, 1993, p. 151).

In the words of the UK scholar of Tibetan Buddhism Paul Williams, among the Dalai Lamas there have been 'great scholars, powerful politicians or simply Buddhist monks that died young before they could make much impact' (Williams, 2004, p. 1). The Great Fifth Dalai Lama (1617–82) has a reputation as having been a highly successful politician who was able to unify the country. The seventh and eighth were uninterested in politics, and the ninth to the twelfth all died young. The thirteenth Dalai Lama, Thupten Gyatso (1876–1933), the immediate predecessor of the current Dalai Lama, living at a time when foreign powers, the British among them, took a close interest in Tibet, was forced to become a political strategist. Williams has made a study of a Dalai Lama who distinguished himself in a distinctive way, and it is worth our while to digress from our study of the reputation of the fourteenth Dalai Lama to consider the reputation of the sixth. This illustrates that the reputation of the Dalai Lamas does not rest on their personal qualities or proclivities, but instead on their traditional status. The sixth Dalai Lama, Tsangyang Gyatso (1683–1706), is not remembered for his political strategy or for skill in study, but for his love poems. Below are two examples from a collection of sixty-six verses which have been attributed to him.

**Verse 17**

Before a great lama,
I asked for holy help.
No good – though thoughts delayed,
They slipped back to my love.

**Verse 53**

I sought my love at dusk;
Snow had fallen at dawn.
Why bother with secrets?
– Footprints left in the snow!

(Williams, 2004, pp. 77, 113)

These poems give some indication of the character of the sixth Dalai Lama. In the first of the two we read of the tension he felt between what he knew he should be thinking about – his studies – and what he was actually thinking about – his mistress. In the second he knows that it is useless to pretend that he did not spend the night with her because his footprints tell a different story.

Tsangyang Gyatso was identified as the sixth Dalai Lama in his teens, rather later than the usual pattern. When taken together, his sixty-six verses suggest that his primary interest was in young women and sex, and not in learning about Tibetan tradition. As far as we can tell, the fact that the sixth Dalai Lama acted like a normal teenager was not regarded as a particular problem at the time, even though, as a monk, he was supposed to be celibate. It *was* a problem that he refused to take full monastic vows and rejected even the novice vows he had taken when young; the Dalai Lamas are supposed to be monks and teachers as well as politicians. Tsangyang Gyatso died at only nineteen and there has always been the suspicion that he was murdered. In 1717, not long after his death, China declared Tibet to be a Chinese protectorate.

The sixth Dalai Lama was identified as the reincarnation of the Great Fifth and few Tibetans have seriously questioned that he was, in their terms, the authentic reincarnation, despite his behaviour and his rebellion against the monastic lifestyle. The current Dalai Lama admits that, politically, the sixth was a disaster, but he does not question his status (cited in Williams, 2004, p. 45). To understand this we need to take account of the way in which the authority of the Dalai Lamas is legitimised, and to help with that we will consider the word 'charisma'. This is not a Tibetan word or concept, but in order to understand the Tibetan system we have to draw upon our own cultural resources, one of which is the English language.

**Activity**

1   Use the course website to access the online version of the *Oxford English Dictionary* (*OED*). (If you cannot use the internet at the moment, you could come back to this exercise later.) The dictionary gives two related explanations of the word 'charisma'. Can you work out the main differences between them? What is the difference between the charisma ascribed to Nelson and Hitler, and the charisma of sense (a)?

2   When I put the word 'charisma' into an internet search engine, I was offered a number of sites that promised to help me increase my own charisma (you might like to try a similar search)! Which of the two kinds of charisma referred to in the dictionary are they promising?

To help you with these questions here is the definition offered in the *Concise Oxford English Dictionary*:

**charisma** /kə'rizmə/ *n.* **1** compelling attractiveness or charm that can inspire devotion. **2** (*pl.* **charismata** / kə'rizmətə/) a divinely conferred power or talent.
ORIGIN C17: via eccles. L. from Gk *kharisma*, from *kharis* 'favour, grace'.

**Discussion**

The abstract noun 'charisma' is used in two different but related ways. Depending on your background you may find one, both, or neither of these familiar. The important thing is that you can see the distinction between them.

1   The first sense of the word that the *OED* refers to, (a), is its theological or religious meaning. Did you notice that this is sense 2 in *The Concise Oxford Dictionary* version? Here it applies to someone who has received a particular blessing from God or gods. Charisma is 'a gift of grace'. All the examples for this meaning given in the *OED* relate to Christian figures or ideas, but the concept is equally useful for other religious traditions. It refers to religious authority – the authority that comes from religious blessing and status within a tradition. The Dalai Lamas have significant charismatic status because they are all said to be linked in the lineage of Dalai Lamas and have a special relationship with Chenresig. In sense (b), however, charisma comes from the ability to lead because of personal characteristics. As well as being charismatic in sense (a), the fourteenth Dalai Lama is also viewed as charismatic in sense (b). For westerners, who know little of his traditional status, it is often the personal aspect of his charisma that is important and attractive. For Tibetans, however, his personal qualities are less important than his status as the Dalai Lama. This is why the sixth Dalai Lama can still be revered as a Dalai Lama even though he caused problems by his personal rebellion.

2   The websites are offering us opportunities to increase our personal charisma: to make us more charming, enthusiastic or inspirational. Individuals use these attractive qualities in all kinds of settings, including religious ones.

Before we leave this discussion of the Dalai Lama's reputation within Tibetan tradition I would like you to glimpse the contrasting ways in which he is treated by his own people and by westerners.

**Activity**
*The film 'Dalai Lama in India' lasts about five minutes.*

Now watch the film 'Dalai Lama in India' on the DVD Video. Here you see short clips of the Dalai Lama with his own people and also with various westerners. What contrasts can you see here?

**Discussion**

This series begins with a young Dalai Lama blessing his people in 1959, soon after he had escaped to India from Chinese-occupied Tibet. The second clip is an extract from the BBC series *Himalaya* presented by Michael Palin, who was clearly struck by the contrasting ways in which westerners and Tibetans react when they meet the Dalai Lama. The awe and devotion in which he is held by Tibetans is also clearly evident in the third clip, as the Dalai Lama talks to a refugee who has recently arrived in India from Tibet. I was also struck by the conversation between the Dalai Lama and the British actor John Cleese. So far as I know Cleese does not identify himself as a Buddhist, and yet here we see him telling the Dalai Lama what Buddhism is all about! His suggestion that the Dalai Lama might try using a public relations company provokes an interesting response. The Dalai Lama sees the Tibetan position in black-and-white terms. For him it is obvious that right is on their side and he sees no need for a particular media presentation.

Of course, we would expect westerners and Tibetans to relate differently to the Dalai Lama but these contrasts point to the very different ways in which the Dalai Lama's reputation is constructed.

## 7.3   THE DALAI LAMA'S REPUTATION IN CHINA

We turn finally to a context in which the Dalai Lama has a very different reputation. Chinese incursions into Tibetan territory in the 1950s were made against a background of periodic tension and cooperation between the two states which had extended back through many centuries. Buddhism has had a major impact on Chinese society and been an influential presence there for much longer than its history in Tibet. It was introduced in China around the first century BCE and has undergone periods of decline and revival since then. The forms of Buddhism that became popular in China were mostly not the same as the type of Buddhism practised in Tibet, but the Manchu emperors were patrons of Tibetan Buddhism, and during the Ching dynasty (1644–1911) the emperors routinely confirmed each newly discovered Dalai Lama. In their turn, it is a source of national pride for Tibetans that the Dalai Lamas instructed the Chinese emperors in Buddhist doctrine and practice. The Dalai Lama referred to the constructive relationship between the two neighbours in his Nobel Prize acceptance speech.

In 1904 the British, fearing influence from tsarist Russia, invaded Tibetan territory from India. The dispute between Tibet and Britain was resolved by diplomatic means, but the British action prompted the Chinese to intervene and they attempted to bring all the regions occupied by Tibetans under their direct control.

You can see from the map (Figure 7.7) that Tibet is divided into two sections. The first is what is now called the Tibet Autonomous Region (TAR) and the second is usually called ethnographic Tibet. Ethnographic Tibet, which includes Amdo, the fourteenth Dalai Lama's birthplace, is the name given to the areas in which, historically, the majority of inhabitants have been Tibetan. Only the TAR areas came under the direct jurisdiction of the Dalai Lama's government.

Following the coming to power of the Chinese communists in 1949, the Chinese People's Liberation Army entered central Tibet and the capital Lhasa itself in 1951. From this time the Tibetans were hopelessly outnumbered. At first the Chinese allowed life to continue pretty much as before and did not interfere with the relationship between the Dalai Lama and his people, but their superior strength meant that there was never any doubt that they could have done so had they wished. By the mid 1950s ethnographic Tibet had been pushed to reform, resulting in individual farmers and the monasteries losing their lands to new collectives in much the same way that individual citizens lost their land in the Soviet Union under Stalin. This sparked violent and bloody clashes between the monks and the Chinese authorities in these areas. By 1959 the uprising of the Tibetans in the outer regions had reached Lhasa, eventually resulting in the secret and perilous exodus of the Dalai Lama and his entourage to India; they had to use

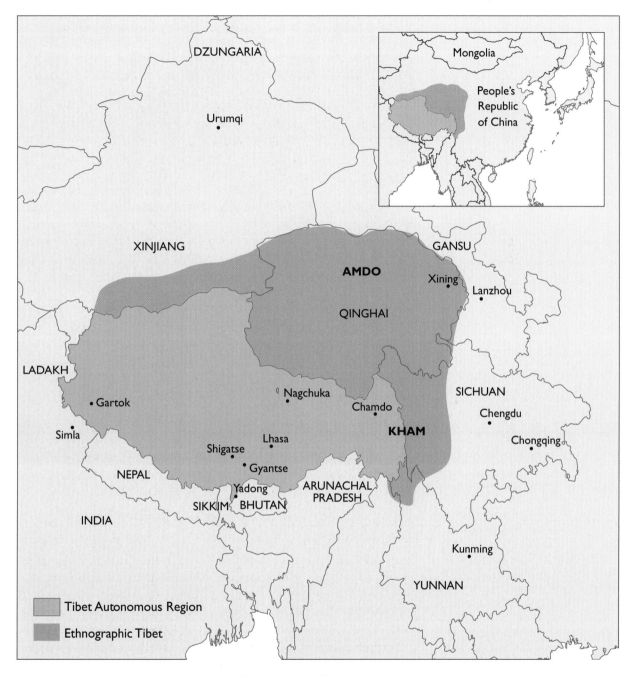

Figure 7.7    Map of 'Tibet' showing the TAR and ethnographic Tibet.

dangerous Himalayan passes without alerting the Chinese to their escape plans. The Dalai Lama was given sanctuary within northern India, although his arrival there was something of an embarrassment to the Indian government which was reluctant to jeopardise its own relationship with the Chinese regime. The Dalai Lama and his government in exile are now settled at Dharamsala in northern India, where they do their best to represent Tibetan interests. Other Tibetan

Figure 7.8    Mao Zedong (centre) with the Dalai Lama (right) and Panchen Lama on 8 June 1956. Unknown photographer. Photo: © Bettmann/CORBIS.

communities are settled in the south and north of the Indian subcontinent.

*The film 'Chinese Incursion' lasts less than five minutes.*

Now read the Tibetan view of this period in Reading 7.3. This extract gives you the very barest bones of what happened. As these events progressed, in addition to the loss of life in the Tibetan army, a large proportion of the Tibetan monastic communities of monks and nuns was tortured and killed along with thousands of lay people. Many historic monasteries were destroyed and stripped of their treasures. These were atrocious acts which have been well documented and there is no doubt that the cruelty of members of the People's Liberation Army was extreme. You can watch visual evidence of this in the film 'Chinese Incursion' on the DVD Video.

After the Dalai Lama had left Tibet, and with the onset of the Chinese Cultural Revolution in 1966, the suppression of religion became the main focus of Chinese Red Guard activity. Religious practice was forbidden and much of what remained of the monasteries was destroyed. Under new leadership in 1978, however, Beijing eased this policy and reinstated freedom of religious belief within certain guidelines.

**Activity**

Now read the Chinese statement on religious freedom made in 1951 and reproduced in Reading 7.4. Why do you think this form of religious freedom is a potential problem for the Tibetans?

**Discussion**

The model of religion that this policy offers is one that is thoroughly subordinate to China's New Democracy. It reduces religion to an optional add-on to life within a political system that does not accept the Tibetan view of the world. This poses a fundamental problem as soon as we start to think about the authority and reputation of the Dalai Lama. As we have seen, the traditional Tibetan view understands the Dalai Lama as Chenresig, and the idea that his authority should be subordinated to a human socio-political system runs counter to Tibetan religion and culture. The Dalai Lama has long been in favour of a democratic system, but it is in the interests of the Chinese regime to present him in a way that appears to justify its own role in Tibet. China is a secular state with its own ultimate values, and it rejects the meaning structures and sense of ultimate good that religions promote.

**Activity**

Reading 7.5 tells us what the Chinese regime has to say about the Dalai Lama himself. Summarise the Chinese perspective based on this source. What do the Chinese think Tibetans have been saved from? Who according to the Chinese must decide the future of the Tibetan people? And how do they understand the role of the Dalai Lama in this process?

**Discussion**

The Chinese refer to the Dalai Lama's rule as **feudal** serfdom under **theocracy**. The term 'feudal serfdom' is used here to present traditional Tibetan society as anachronistic and based on inequality: the privilege of the few based on the hard work of the majority. Theocracy is government by God or gods or by those deemed to be God's representatives. The identity of Tibet as a theocracy reflects the fact that politics was intimately intertwined with religion.

The Chinese claim that the future of Tibet must be decided by *all* the Chinese people. This would, of course, include the Tibetans themselves, but also the majority Han Chinese and members of the other minority groups (of which there are about fifty). This is not a Tibetan view. The Tibetans do not see themselves as part of the Chinese people.

For the Chinese government, the Dalai Lama is hampering the progress of China with unrealistic claims to Tibetan autonomy.

Since 1978 there has been a revival of religious practice within Tibet, where new ways have developed to deal with new circumstances (Goldstein and Kapstein, 1998). During all this activity the Dalai Lama has remained in exile in India. If you look at a recent atlas you will find that Tibet is no longer delineated as a separate state. There has been sympathy for the Tibetan cause but insufficient international, political will to provide practical support, largely because China has enormous military and economic power. The Dalai Lama might have done more to gain international help, including financial support, than he has done by using public platforms to give his backing to popular causes: for example, he could have condemned communism in the 1960s and 1970s and attracted support in the USA. However, he did not do so and, instead, apparently speaks according to his principles rather than for political advantage. In spite of his absence, the Dalai Lama retains the devotion of his people and his reputation remains intact.

The Tibetans refuse to negotiate with China about the Tibet Autonomous Region unless the negotiations also include the ethnographic areas. These outer areas of Tibet have long been settled by the Chinese majority Han people, but also by people from other minority ethnic groups including other religious groupings such as Muslims. The Dalai Lama is clear that there could not – and should not – be a return to the authority structures that existed in pre-1950s Tibet, but while the Tibetans continue to include the outer areas in their claim for independence there may be little scope for negotiation over the Tibet Autonomous Region itself.

A different but potentially more significant problem is the future of the institution of the Dalai Lamas. The Dalai Lama is the most senior lama in the Tibetan tradition. Second to him in importance is another lama with a venerable lineage, the Panchen Lama. When a Dalai Lama dies the Panchen Lama is responsible for leading the search to find his successor. When a Panchen Lama dies it is traditionally the Dalai Lama who leads the search for the new Panchen Lama. The tenth Panchen Lama died in 1989, before which date he had been living in China. The Dalai Lama instigated a search for the new Panchen Lama and a child was identified in Tibet. However, the Chinese government ignored this process and set about choosing its own candidate. You can see the method they used for their final choice in the film 'Panchen Lama' on the DVD Video. Notice how subdued and uncomfortable the Tibetans look at the ceremony. For them the process used to select the Panchen Lama is a travesty of their traditional system, and this ceremony is not validated by the skills and knowledge of the Dalai Lama. Gedhun Choekyi Nyima, the boy identified by the Dalai Lama, was not included for consideration at the Chinese ceremony and his whereabouts are unknown to the Tibetan government in exile. Their choice is kept from them and under the control of the Chinese regime. This has important consequences for the office of the Dalai Lama. The Panchen Lama chosen by the Chinese will not be recognised by the Tibetan government in exile. They will not regard him as the legitimate incarnation and he will therefore be unable to lead the search for a new Dalai Lama when the time comes. The fourteenth Dalai Lama has already warned that he may not be reborn as the Dalai Lama, and indeed it is currently difficult to see how there could be a

*The film 'Panchen Lama' lasts less than five minutes.*

Figure 7.9   The Dalai Lama's birthday celebrations inside contemporary Tibet. Image taken from Melvyn C. Goldstein, *The Snow Lion and The Dragon: China, Tibet, and the Dalai Lama*, University of California Press, 1997. Used with the permission of the University of California Press. The 6 July is a holiday in Lhasa. These Tibetans are throwing roasted barley flour at one another.

fifteenth Dalai Lama in any way that is meaningful for the Tibetan people.

The ethnic, cultural and national identity of the Tibetans is tied inextricably to their religious identity and has as its focus the person of the Dalai Lama. The Dalai Lama has become the symbol of Tibetan hopes for the future even while they acknowledge that they must operate under the Chinese regime. Meanwhile, the Chinese have forged ahead with modernisation, including road and rail building programmes, and they remain confident that the changes they have implemented in Tibet have brought the Tibetan people nothing but benefit. The Chinese regime presents itself as beneficent by promoting a view of the Dalai Lama that contrasts sharply with his traditional, religious reputation in Tibet and his somewhat romanticised reputation in the West.

## CONCLUSION

The Chinese portray contemporary Tibet as an area where there is freedom of religion. The Dalai Lama's government in exile portrays Tibet as an area where religion has been suppressed. Under these circumstances, the reputation of the Dalai Lama himself varies widely.

As we have seen, the Dalai Lama's reputation in the West is based largely on his personal qualities rather than on his religious status. He is both helped and hampered by the fact that the West is in the middle of a love affair with all things Tibetan based in part on a romantic notion of Tibet, its religion and its people. The American scholar of Tibetan Buddhism, Donald Lopez, sees the romantic notion of Tibet as an issue both for scholarship and for the Tibetan people themselves. He expresses that in this way:

> Tibet's complexities and competing histories have been flattened into a stereotype. Stereotypes operate through adjectives, which establish chosen characteristics as if they were eternal truths. Tibet is 'isolated,' Tibetans are 'content,' monks are 'spiritual.' With sufficient repetition, these adjectives become innate qualities, immune from history. [...] This language about Tibet not only creates knowledge about Tibet, in many ways it creates Tibet, a Tibet that Tibetans in exile have come to appropriate and deploy in an effort to gain both standing in exile and independence for their country.

(Lopez, 1998, p. 10)

**Activity**    What do you think Lopez means when he says that 'Tibet's complexities and competing histories have been flattened into a stereotype'? What example of this have you encountered in this chapter?

**Discussion**    As Lopez points out, when we employ stereotypes we 'flatten' complexities by forcing people or things into fixed mental categories. Life is nearly always more complicated than a stereotype allows. Stereotypes can be misleading because they oversimplify and they are often accompanied by unfair prejudice. As soon as we look beyond an idealised Tibet we find that Tibet and the Tibetans have a complex history which can be told in contrasting ways. Simply by taking the competing recent histories of contemporary Tibet as told by the Chinese and the Tibetan government in exile we find that this is so.

This brings us back to where we started in this chapter. In spite of his modest claims to be a simple monk, the Dalai Lama has a complex role and competing reputations. He is a religious leader, a politician, a negotiator, and the symbol of hope for his people. He is the holder of a traditional, charismatic office with a long history, but he has powerful enemies. After his death his personal reputation will be reassessed and, because of the political situation that continues in Tibet, his office may or may not be continued.

## REFERENCES

Batchelor, S. (1994) 'Buddhism and European culture in Europe', in Gill, S., D'Costa, G. and King, U. (eds) *Religion in Europe: Contemporary Perspectives*, Kampen, Kok Pharos, pp. 86–104.

Dalai Lama (1990) *Freedom in Exile*, London, Cardinal.

Dalai Lama (1996) *The Good Heart*, London, Rider.

Goldstein, M.C. and Kapstein, M.T. (eds) (1998) *Buddhism in Contemporary Tibet: Religious Revival and Cultural Identity*, Berkeley and London, University of California Press.

Lopez, D. (1998) *Prisoners of Shangri-La: Tibetan Buddhism and the West*, London, University of Chicago Press.

Samuel, G. (1993) *Civilised Shamans: Buddhism in Tibetan Societies*, Washington and London, Smithsonian Institution Press.

Soanes, C. and Stevenson, A. (eds) (2006) *Concise Oxford English Dictionary*, eleventh edition (revised), Oxford and New York, Oxford University Press.

Williams, P. (2004) *Songs of Love, Poems of Sadness: The Erotic Verse of the Sixth Dalai Lama*, London, I.B. Tauris.

## RESOURCES

**Reading 7.1**   **1989 Nobel Peace Prize Citation**

The Norwegian Nobel Committee has decided to award the 1989 Nobel Peace Prize to the 14th Dalai Lama, Tenzin Gyatso, the religious and political leader of the Tibetan people.

The Committee wants to emphasize the fact that the Dalai Lama in his struggle for the liberation of Tibet consistently has opposed the use of violence. He has instead advocated peaceful solutions based upon tolerance and mutual respect in order to preserve the historical and cultural heritage of his people.

The Dalai Lama has developed his philosophy of peace from a great reverence for all things living and upon the concept of universal responsibility embracing all mankind as well as nature.

In the opinion of the Committee the Dalai Lama has come forward with constructive and forward-looking proposals for the solution of international conflicts, human rights issues, and global environmental problems.

*October 5, 1990 Oslo, Norway*

Source: www.tibet.com/DL/nobel.html (Accessed January 2008).

**Reading 7.2**   **His Holiness the Dalai Lama's Nobel Prize acceptance speech**

*University Aula, Oslo, 10 December 1989*

Your Majesty, Members of the Nobel Committee, Brothers and Sisters.

I am very happy to be here with you today to receive the Nobel Prize for Peace. I feel honored, humbled and deeply moved that you should give this important prize to a simple monk from Tibet. I am no one special. But I believe the prize is a recognition of the true value of altruism, love, compassion and non-violence which I try to practice, in accordance with the teachings of the Buddha and the great sages of India and Tibet.

I accept the prize with profound gratitude on behalf of the oppressed everywhere and for all those who struggle for freedom and work for world peace. I accept it as a tribute to the man who founded the modern tradition of non-violent action for change Mahatma Gandhi whose life taught and inspired me. And, of course, I accept it on behalf of the six million Tibetan people, my brave countrymen and women inside Tibet, who have suffered and continue to suffer so much. They confront a calculated and systematic strategy aimed at the destruction of their national and cultural identities. The prize reaffirms our conviction that with truth, courage and determination as our weapons, Tibet will be liberated.

No matter what part of the world we come from, we are all basically the same human beings. We all seek happiness and try to avoid suffering. We have the same basic human needs and concerns. All of us human beings want freedom and the right to determine our own destiny as individuals and as peoples. That is human nature. The great changes that are taking place everywhere in the world, from Eastern Europe to Africa are a clear indication of this.

In China the popular movement for democracy was crushed by brutal force in June this year. But I do not believe the demonstrations were in vain, because the spirit of freedom was rekindled among the Chinese people and China cannot escape the impact of this spirit of freedom sweeping many parts of the world. The brave students and their supporters showed the Chinese leadership and the world the human face of that great nation.

Last week a number of Tibetans were once again sentenced to prison terms of up to nineteen years at a mass show trial, possibly intended to frighten the population before today's event. Their only 'crime' was the expression of the widespread desire of Tibetans for the restoration of their beloved country's independence.

The suffering of our people during the past forty years of occupation is well documented. Ours has been a long struggle. We know our cause is just. Because violence can only breed more violence and suffering, our struggle must remain non-violent and free of hatred. We are trying to end the suffering of our people, not to inflict suffering upon others.

It is with this in mind that I proposed negotiations between Tibet and China on numerous occasions. In 1987, I made specific proposals in a Five-Point plan for the restoration of peace and human rights in Tibet. This included the conversion of the entire Tibetan plateau into a Zone of Ahimsa [non-violence], a sanctuary of peace and non-violence where human beings and nature can live in peace and harmony.

Last year, I elaborated on that plan in Strasbourg, at the European Parliament. I believe the ideas I expressed on those occasions are both realistic and reasonable although they have been criticised by some of my people as being too conciliatory. Unfortunately, China's leaders have not responded positively to the suggestions we have made, which included important concessions. If this continues we will be compelled to reconsider our position.

Any relationship between Tibet and China will have to be based on the principle of equality, respect, trust and mutual benefit. It will also have to be based on the principle which the wise rulers of Tibet and of China laid down in a treaty as early as 823 AD, carved on the pillar which still stands today in front of the Jokhang, Tibet's holiest shrine, in Lhasa, that 'Tibetans will live happily in the great land of Tibet, and the Chinese will live happily in the great land of China'.

As a Buddhist monk, my concern extends to all members of the human family and, indeed, to all sentient beings who suffer. I believe all suffering is caused by ignorance. People inflict pain on others in the selfish pursuit of their happiness or satisfaction. Yet true happiness comes from a sense of brotherhood and sisterhood. We need to cultivate a universal responsibility for one another and the planet we share. Although I have found my own Buddhist religion helpful in generating love and compassion, even for those we consider our enemies, I am convinced that everyone can develop a good heart and a sense of universal responsibility with or without religion.

With the ever growing impact of science on our lives, religion and spirituality have a greater role to play reminding us of our humanity. There is no contradiction between the two. Each gives us valuable insights into the other. Both science and the teachings of the Buddha tell us of the fundamental unity of all things. This understanding is crucial if we are to take positive and decisive action on the pressing global concern with the environment.

I believe all religions pursue the same goals, that of cultivating human goodness and bringing happiness to all human beings. Though the means might appear different the ends are the same.

As we enter the final decade of this century I am optimistic that the ancient values that have sustained mankind are today reaffirming themselves to prepare us for a kinder, happier twenty-first century.

I pray for all of us, oppressor and friend, that together we succeed in building a better world through human understanding and love, and that in doing so we may reduce the pain and suffering of all sentient beings.

Thank you.

Source: www.tibet.com/DL/nobelaccept.html (Accessed January 2008).

Reading 7.3    **Invasion and illegal annexation of Tibet: 1949–1951**

After the military invasion of Tibet had started and the small Tibetan army was defeated, the PRC imposed a treaty on the Tibetan Government under the terms of which Tibet was declared to be a part of China, albeit enjoying a large degree of autonomy. In the White Paper, China claims this treaty was entered into entirely voluntarily by the Tibetan Government, and that the Dalai Lama, his Government and the Tibetan people as a whole welcomed it. The facts show a very different story, leading to the conclusion that the so-called '17 Point Agreement for the Peaceful Liberation of Tibet' was never validly concluded and was rejected by Tibetans. The Dalai Lama stated Tibetan Prime Minister Lukhangwa as having told Chinese General Zhang Jin-wu in 1952:

> It was absurd to refer to the terms of the Seventeen-Point Agreement. Our people did not accept the agreement and the Chinese themselves had

repeatedly broken the terms of it. Their army was still in occupation of eastern Tibet; the area had not been returned to the government of Tibet, as it should have been.

**Diplomatic activity and military threats**

Soon after the Communist victory against the Guomindang and the founding of the PRC on 1 October 1949, Radio Beijing began to announce that 'the People's Liberation Army must liberate all Chinese territories, including Tibet, Xinjiang, Hainan and Taiwan.' Partly in response to this threat, and in order to resolve long-standing border disputes with China, the Foreign Office of the Tibetan Government, on 2 November 1949, wrote to Mao Zedong proposing negotiations to settle all territorial disputes. Copies of this letter were sent to the Governments of India, Great Britain and the United States. Although these three Governments considered the spread of Communism to be a threat to the stability of South Asia, they advised the Tibetan Government to enter into direct negotiations with Chinese Government as any other course of action might provoke military retaliation. [...]

In the course of negotiations, the Chinese Ambassador, Yuan Zhong-xian, demanded that the Tibetan delegation accept a Two- point Proposal: i) Tibetan national defence will be handled by China; and ii) Tibet should be recognised as a part of China. They were then to proceed to China in confirmation of the agreement. On being informed of the Chinese demands, the Tibetan Government instructed its delegates to reject the proposal. So negotiations were suspended.

On 7 October 1950, 40,000 Chinese troops under Political Commissar, Wang Qiemi, attacked Eastern Tibet's provincial capital of Chamdo, from eight directions. The small Tibetan force, consisting of 8,000 troops and militia, were defeated. After two days, Chamdo was taken and Kalon (Minister) Ngapo Ngawang Jigme, the Regional Governor, was captured. Over 4,000 Tibetan fighters were killed. [...]

The Tibetan National Assembly convened an emergency session in November 1950 at which it requested the Dalai Lama, only 16 at that time, to assume full authority as Head of State. The Dalai Lama was then requested to leave Lhasa for Dromo, near the Indian border, so that he would be out of personal danger. At the same time the Tibetan Foreign Office issued the following statement:

> Tibet is united as one man behind the Dalai Lama who has taken over full powers. ...We have appealed to the world for peaceful intervention in (the face of this) clear case of unprovoked aggression.

[...]

On 9 September 1951, around 3,000 Chinese troops marched into Lhasa, soon followed by some 20,000 more, from eastern Tibet and from eastern Turkestan (Xinjiang) in the north. The PLA occupied the principal cities of Ruthok and Gartok, and then Gyangtse and Shigatse. With the occupation of all the major cities of Tibet, including Lhasa, and large concentrations of troops throughout eastern and western Tibet, the military control of Tibet was virtually complete. From this position, China refused to re-open negotiations and the Dalai Lama had effectively lost the ability to either accept or reject any Tibet–China agreement. However, on the first occasion he had of expressing himself freely again, which came only on 20 June 1959, after his flight to India, the Dalai Lama formally repudiated the 'Seventeen-Point Agreement' [the formal 'agreement' between the PRC and the Tibetan representatives], as having been 'thrust upon Tibetan Government and people by the threat of arms'.

Source: http://www.tibet.com/WhitePaper/white2.html (footnote omitted) (Accessed January 2008).

Reading 7.4     **Chinese government statement on religious freedom, 1951**

Freedom of religious belief is stated as clear as day in the Common Program and it will not be compromised. However, one must realize that the Common Program is a charter for the era of the New Democracy; and the New Democracy takes as its premises the struggle against imperialism, feudalism and bureaucratic capitalism, the overthrow of the reactionary power of the Kuomintang, and the purge of open and hidden counterrevolutionary forces. Buddhists who do not accept these premises are either reactionaries or backward elements. Reactionaries have no political rights; backward elements do not understand the times and, since in their thinking there is not much trust of the government, the government cannot treat them with the respect and concern that would otherwise be appropriate. Only if they become progressive and join the people of the era of the New Democracy can they fully enjoy all the freedoms of the Common Program. ... Some Buddhists think that, because the Common Program provides for freedom of belief, they can do anything they like and that anyone who corrects their thinking or actions is infringing on their freedom of religion. This is a very big mistake and really is the thinking of backward elements. ... [I]t must be corrected as forcefully as possible.

Source: Goldstein and Kapstein, 1998, pp. 2–3.

Reading 7.5     **Regional ethnic autonomy in Tibet, 20 May 2004**

It must be pointed out that the local government of Tibet headed by the Dalai representing feudal serfdom under theocracy has long since been replaced by the democratic administration established by the Tibetan people themselves. The destiny and future of Tibet can no longer be decided by the Dalai Lama and his clique. Rather, it can only be decided by the whole Chinese nation, including the Tibetan people.

This is an objective political fact in Tibet that cannot be denied or shaken. The Central Government's policy as regards the Dalai Lama is consistent and clear. It is hoped that the Dalai Lama will look reality in the face, make a correct judgement of the situation, truly relinquish his stand for 'Tibet independence,' and do something beneficial to the progress of China and the region of Tibet in his remaining years.

Source: www.chinese-embassy.org.uk/eng/zt/zgxz/t118374.htm (Accessed January 2008).

# AFTERWORD

*Elaine Moohan*

Book 1 and its related materials have introduced you to some of the concepts and skills that are central to your study of the Arts both in this course and beyond. There are two key academic skills to take from this book:

1  how to study and interpret works of art and historical documents
2  how to undertake close reading of a literary text and close listening of pieces of music.

In addition to these core academic skills, you have been given some technical language appropriate to each discipline. You have had the opportunity to practise using these terms in the activities in each chapter, and you will probably have made use of them in your first assignment. In later chapters you will encounter more technical language, and again you will have ample opportunity to practise using this in the activities before being required to use it in assignments.

Throughout this book you have read about how a reputation is acquired, retained, and in some cases developed. Take a few minutes now to reread the questions from the beginning of the book, set out in the introduction: why are some people widely remembered and others not? Exactly what makes a person famous, or infamous? How does someone acquire a reputation? What is the relationship between a figure's reputation and what we can discover about his or her life from the historical record? When you read these questions for the first time in the Introduction you may have had someone well known in mind. As you read the questions again now, which of the people studied in this book comes most immediately to mind? Think about why that person comes to mind. Is it someone you already knew about or someone new? Is he or she from an academic subject that you particularly enjoyed studying?

**Activity**  Take a few minutes now to consider these questions and write a short paragraph in your electronic notebook. Compare this with the paragraph that you wrote in your notebook at the start of this book. How has your attitude to these questions changed?

# GLOSSARY

**accompaniment**   musical support of the solo line(s). This can be instrumental or vocal or a combination of both, and may duplicate the solo line or be independent.

**aria**   italian for 'song', one of the set items of an opera. In general, an aria tends to have a song-like melody and contains some repetition of text, which brings the action to a halt.

**avant-garde**   when applied to artists, writers and musicians, avant-garde serves to identify those considered pioneers in the development of specifically modern forms.

**baritone**   a middle-ranging male voice.

**BCE**   stands for 'Before the Common Era' and is equivalent to BC.

**blank verse**   unrhymed lines of iambic pentameter. Not to be confused with free verse, blank verse was the dominant verse form in early modern drama, favoured by Marlowe, Shakespeare and their contemporaries.

**Bodhisattva**   a **Buddha** to be.

**Bolshevik**   the Bolsheviks were originally a faction within the Russian Social Democratic Workers' Party – the term means 'majority' – who believed that change was best achieved by a tightly disciplined party led by a vanguard of dedicated revolutionaries who would overthrow the Tsarist regime. They became a separate party in 1912, which seized power during the October Revolution in 1917, eventually becoming the Communist Party of the Soviet Union.

**brushwork**   the evidence of the means of application of paint that is left on the **literal surface** of a painting. It is one of the factors that most clearly defines an individual artist's style and technique.

**Buddha**   an enlightened one. Someone who has understood the truth of the way things really are and is no longer tainted by greed, hatred and delusion.

**CE**   stands for 'Common Era' and is equivalent to AD.

**characterisation**   the techniques employed by a writer to create the characters in any given literary text.

**chair**   an alternative term for a professorship.

**Chorus**   an integral part of ancient Greek tragic drama, the Chorus was a group of people which sometimes participated in the dramatic action and sometimes commented on it, giving voice to traditional moral and social attitudes. In early modern English drama the term was used to denote a single performer who delivered the prologue and epilogue to a play and sometimes introduced individual acts, and who often retained something of the Chorus's original role of commentator.

**collectivisation**    a process by which individual farms were to combine and to farm in larger collective units. While individual farmers were legally co-owners of collective farms, and were not paid in wages, but received a share of the collective's profits, land was farmed on an industrial scale, and the differences between the individual farms that made the collectives up disappeared.

**composition**    the techniques and process by means of which the various elements of a work of art are organised into a whole; also, the end result.

**corresponding member**    a class of membership of many organisations, less than full membership, for those living at a distance who were likely to contribute to the organisation through their writing or correspondence.

**delineation**    refers to the representation of shapes and details by means of drawing.

**disco**    a style of dance music very popular in the late 1970s and early 80s, characterised by a strong, lively beat and use of synthesisers. The term is derived from the French *discothèque* – record library – referring to a club where you dance to records.

**dukkha**    an inherent characteristic of life in **samsara** translated as suffering, unsatisfactoriness, incapable of satisfying.

**dynamics**    indication of the volume of music, often relative to surrounding passages. The most common words used are **piano** (softly), **forte** (loudly).

**electronica**    a broad term used to describe any dance-based electronic music created by using computer systems and other electronic devices. Includes many different styles, such as techno, house, trance and trip-hop.

**empiricism**    relying primarily on experimental results.

**enjambement**    a French word meaning 'a striding-over', enjambement occurs when the sense or meaning of a line of verse carries on beyond the end of the line. Also called run-on lines.

**feudalism**    a social system in which people are permitted to occupy and cultivate land in return for allegiance to the state.

**figurative language**    language used in a non-literal way. When we say 'The police combed the grass for clues', for example, we understand that the police did not literally 'comb' the grass; rather, that the verb 'combed' is being used in a figurative manner to convey how closely and systematically the police searched the grass for clues. See also **metaphor** and **simile**.

**forte**    indicates the music is to be played or sung loudly. Abbreviated on printed music to *f*.

**fortissimo**    indicates the music is to be played or sung very loudly. Abbreviated on printed music to *ff*.

**generalisation**    drawing general conclusion from specific examples.

**genre**    the French word for 'kind', a genre is a category or type of art work distinguished from other types by a particular form and conventions; for example, in literary studies, tragedy is a distinct genre of drama, usually characterised by (among other conventions) an unhappy ending; in this respect it is recognisably different from the genre of comedy, which tends to have a happy ending. In the study of art, the term was originally used in the late seventeenth century to refer to different classes of subject matter, such as history painting, landscape, portraiture, still life and scenes from everyday life.

**Great Patriotic War**    the term used in the Soviet Union (and still used in Russia) to describe the Second World War. Contrary to the practice of the United Kingdom and much of continental Europe, it refers only to the period between 1941 and 1945.

**guru**    a religious teacher who deserves the respect and devotion of his followers.

**harpsichord**    early keyboard instrument in which the sound is produced by quills plucking the strings, instead of striking them with hammers as for a piano.

**Hellenistic**    the period of history usually defined as stretching from the death of Alexander the Great in 323 BCE to the battle of Actium in 31 BCE.

**humanist**    relating to an educational movement that started in Italy in the fourteenth century and had made its way to England by the end of the fifteenth century. Renaissance humanism aimed to recover the literature, philosophy and values of classical antiquity and to develop an educational system based on the imitation of the language and style of classical (mainly Latin) texts.

**iambic pentameter**    this is the verse form used by Marlowe, Shakespeare and many other poets. It consists of five iambic feet; an iamb is a metrical unit in which an unstressed syllable is followed by a stressed syllable. So 'The hand' is an iambic foot, in which 'the' is unstressed and 'hand' is stressed. When a poet puts five such feet together, you get an imabic pentameter, as in Marlowe's 'Was this the face which launched a thousand ships?' (*Doctor Faustus*, 5.1.91).

**imitation**   a technique where the music sung by one voice is immediately repeated by a second voice, although the similarity may last only for the first few notes of the phrase concerned.

**induction**   the transfer of an effect from one place to another without an obvious means of transfer. In electric induction a changing current in one wire causes a changing current in a second wire, even when there is no connection between the two wires.

**interpretation**   suggesting explanations for facts and the relationship between facts.

**internal exile**   commonly described as the forced resettlement of an individual within their country of residence. It was a sanction widely applied by Russian courts to revolutionary political activists in the pre-Revolutionary period.

**lama**   the Tibetan equivalent of the Indian word **guru**. A teacher who is worthy of respect and devotion.

**legato**   direction that the music is to be played or sung smoothly.

**line of force**   an imaginary line showing the direction in which an imaginary magnet would move if placed near a real magnet.

**literal surface**   the actual physical surface of an object (for example, a painting).

**madrigal**   a secular (not religious) song cultivated during the Renaissance, intended for domestic entertainment.

**metaphor**   a type of figurative language which describes one thing in terms of another. A metaphor differs from a simile mainly in that it does not make the comparison explicit. So 'My love burns' is a metaphor that draws an implicit link between love and fire, while 'my love is like a fire' is a simile that makes the comparison plain through the use of the word 'like'.

**modelling**   refers to the technical means used to represent figures and objects as three-dimensional. In drawing and painting, modelling involves assuming a direction and fall of light, normally from the side.

**monotheism**   a religious system based on the belief that there is one, and only one, divine being.

**morality play**   a type of medieval religious drama concerned in the main to dramatise the struggle within the human soul between the forces of good and evil.

**natural philosopher**   the term used before the late nineteenth century for what we would now call a scientist.

**opera**   a dramatic work set to music throughout, i.e. with no spoken dialogue.

**ornament**   a device used to decorate a long note, or ending of the last phrase, by dividing it into shorter components.

**patronage**   the support of wealthy or influential people.

**periodisation**   refers to the breaking down of historical time into a series of different periods, for example, 'the Victorian era', or even 'the nineteenth century', and is widely practised when thinking about the past.

**phrase**   part of a melody, of no fixed length. In vocal music it is often defined by the places where the singer must breathe.

**pianissimo**   indicates the music is to be played or sung very softly. Abbreviated on printed music to *pp*.

**piano**   indicates the music is to be played or sung softly. Abbreviated on printed music to *p*.

**picture plane**   the frontier between the virtual world (see **picture space**) and the actual world in which the viewer stands.

**picture space**   in painting, the virtual world, or imaginary depth, within which all of a picture's represented contents are contained.

**pizzicato**   plucking the strings on an instrument that is usually played with a bow.

**pop music**   an umbrella term typically applied to chart music that appeals to a wide audience. Pop music is accessible, commercial, marketable and memorable, with catchy choruses or verses.

**producer**   a popular music producer can have many roles, including choosing the material for the artist, directing the performers, supervising the recording sessions, organising the musical arrangement of the song, and supervising technical processes such as mixing and mastering.

**rap**   a genre of music in which a person talks rapidly over a beat (rapping) in a form of improvised street poetry. Originating in the 1970s among black and Hispanic teenagers in New York's outer boroughs, the genre quickly became one of the most important and influential forms of popular music in the 1980s and 90s.

**recitative**   a style of singing that is close to speech and can rely on speech rhythms. There is no repetition of text, allowing the plot to move forwards.

**representation**   words, symbols, diagrams or pictures used to communicate an idea.

**samsara**   the ever-changing cycle of illness, ageing, death and rebirth in which all non-enlightened beings exist. It is characterised by **dukkha**, ignorance, greed and anger.

**Sandemanian Church**   a Christian, non-conformist, sect, founded in Scotland in the eighteenth century.

**shading**   the technique used to convey the quality of the transition between dark and light, and to distinguish lit from unlit surfaces. It is gradual when the light is subdued and diffused, and abrupt when it is bright and concentrated.

**simile**   a type of figurative language which draws an explicit comparison between two things using the word 'like' or 'as', as in Robert Burns's 'O my love's like a red, red rose'.

**soliloquy**   a speech, often fairly long, in which a dramatic character, while alone on stage, expresses his or her feelings and thoughts. Early modern dramatists like Marlowe and Shakespeare used this dramatic convention often and with great skill.

**soprano**   highest sounding female voice.

**tenor**   highest sounding male voice.

**texture**   the method by which different lines of music are woven together.

**theme**   the central idea(s) examined and explored in a literary text.

**theocracy**   government by the representatives of the prevailing religious system.

**tone**   in pictures, the range from lightest light (pure white) to darkest dark (pure black).

**virtuoso**   a performer of extraordinary technical skill and musical ability; the adjective 'virtuosic' is used to describe such a person, or music that requires a performer with these talents.

**word painting**   illustrating a particular word by a musical device that represents the sound or emotion of that word.

# ACKNOWLEDGEMENTS

Grateful acknowledgement is made to the following sources for permission to reproduce material in this book.

## Chapter 2

'Landscape with the Fall of Icarus' by William Carlos Williams, from *Collected Poems 1939–1962*, Volume II, copyright © 1962 by William Carlos Williams. Reprinted by permission of New Directions Publishing Corp. and Carcanet Press Limited.

## Chapter 5

Khrushchev, N. (1956) 'Excerpts from the Secret Speech Delivered by First Party Secretary at the Twentieth Party Congress of the Communist Party of the Soviet Union, February 25, 1956', *Congressional Record: Proceedings and Debates of the 84th Congress, 2nd Session* (May 22, 1956–June 11, 1956), C11, Part 7 (June 4, 1956), pp. 9389–9403, in *Modern History Internet Sourcebook* (http://www.fordham.edu/halsall/mod/1956khrushchev-secret1.html). Reproduced by permission of Professor Sergei Khrushchev.

Suny, R. G., 'Stalin and his Stalinism: power and authority in the Soviet Union, 1930–53', Kershaw, I. and Lewin, M. (eds.) (1997) *Stalinism and Nazism: Dictatorships in Comparison*, Cambridge University Press.

Scott, J. (1989) *Behind the Urals: An American Worker in Russia's City of Steel*, Indiana University Press.

## Chapter 6

From *An Interpretive Guide to Operatic Arias: A Handbook for Singers, Coaches, Teachers and Students* by Martial Singher. Lyrics by Rossini, translation by Singher. Copyright © 1983 by the Pennsylvania State University. Reproduced by permission of Penn State Press.

Luzzaschi, L., 'I am a young maiden' and 'There will never be a Spring for you', in the CD booklet 'Concerto delle Dame di Ferrara', 2001, reproduced with kind permission of harmonia mundi.

## Chapter 7

Sixth Dalai Lama, 'Verse 17' and 'Verse 53', in Williams, P. (trans.) (2004) *Songs of Love, Poems of Sadness: The Erotic Verse of the Sixth Dalai Lama*, I. B. Tauris & Co. Ltd.

Dalai Lama, '1989 Nobel Peace Prize Citation' (1990) found at http://www.tibet.com/DL/nobel.html and 'His Holiness the Dalai Lama's Nobel Prize acceptance speech, University Aula, Oslo, 10 December 1989' (1989), found at http://www.tibet.com/DL/nobelaccept.html, reprinted by permission of The Office of Tibet (http://www.tibet.com).

'Invasion and illegal annexation of Tibet: 1949-1951' (1996), http://www.tibet.com/WhitePaper/white2.html, reprinted by permission of The Office of Tibet (http://www.tibet.com).

# INDEX

Page numbers in **bold** refer to figures.

Abbot, Benjamin 92

academic skills 230

Academy of Fine Arts, and the Paris Salon 58

Actium, battle of (31 BCE) 7–8, 13, 14, 15

African-American Gospel music, and Madonna 169–70

Afrocentrism, and Cleopatra 25–6

agricultural collectivisation *see* collectivisation policy

Albert, Prince Consort 109, **109**, 111

Alexander the Great 15, 16, 25
in Marlowe's *Doctor Faustus* 46, 48

Alexandria, and Hellenistic culture 16

Alfonso II d'Este, Duke of Ferrara 182, **183**, 184, 188

Altan Khan, Mongol king 207

ancient historians, and the ethical approach to history 8–9

Antony, Mark 6–7
and Augustan poetry 13, 14, 15
and Cleopatra as politician and ruler 18
coin portraits of 23, **24**
image of in Octavian's speech 7–8
meeting with Cleopatra at Tarsus 10–11
in Plutarch's *Life of Antony* 9–11, 14

Apple computers, and the Dalai Lama 202, **202**

Arco, Livia d' 184

arias, operatic 171–3, 174

Aristotle 40, 51
Poetics 52

Art History v, vi
*see also* Cézanne, Paul

artistic development, and technique 58

autobiographies vi

avant-garde art, and Cézanne 62, 63, 83

Baines, Richard 33, 34, 53

Baltic states, and the Nazi–Soviet Pact (1939) 132

Banks, Sir Joseph 91

Barnard, Jane 113

batteries, and Faraday's experiments 98, **98**, **99** 100–1, **100**, **101**, 102, **105**

Baudelaire, Charles
on modernity in art 68–9, 71, 73
on 'scholars' and 'owners' 82–3

Beard, Thomas 33, 34, 53

*Bedazzled* (film) 34

Bell, Clive 63

Beria, Laverentii 136

Bernard, Emile 73

Best, George 175

Bevilacqua, Alfonso 184

biographies vi

black Gospel music, and Madonna 169–70

Blaikley, *Alexander, Faraday delivering a Christmas lecture on gold and silver* **109**, 111

blank verse, and Marlowe's *Doctor Faustus* 35

Bodhisattvas, Avalokiteshvara 210, 211

Bolsheviks
and the building of a socialist society 128–9
and the Russian Revolution 127, 128

Bonnard, Pierre 72

bookbinding, and Faraday's early career 90, 91, 92

Bouguereau, William-Adolphe, pictures of nudes 63–4, 66–8, 70, 71, 78–9

Brande, William 93, 99–100, 113

Britain, and Tibet 216

Brueghel, Pieter, *Landscape with the Fall of Icarus* **40**, 41

brushwork 65–6
Cézanne compared with Bouguereau 66

Buddha
the Buddha of India 200, 204, 207, 208, 210
the Dalai Lama as a living 200, 206, 207, 210–11

Buddhism
in China 216
and enlightened beings 200
and samsara 208–9, 210
and the tradition of the Dalai Lamas 206–15
and the West 201, 204–5
*see also* Tibetan Buddhism

Bukharin, Nikolai 129, 130

Bush, Kate 167

Byron, George Gordon, Lord 34

Caesarion, son of Cleopatra, sculptural relief of 19, 20

Caillebotte, Gustave 72

Callas, Maria 163, 164, 174–82, 189
biography 174–5, 192–3
prestige and the opera house 180–181
and Puccini's *Tosca* 175–80, **176**, **177**, 181
and tragedy 164, 175, 181
voice 177–8

Calvinist doctrine, and Marlowe's *Doctor Faustus* 44–6

Cantor, G.N. 96, 97, 110

Carreras, José 174

Castagnary, Jules-Antoine 81–82

Catholic Church, in Marlowe's
*Doctor Faustus* 43, 46–7

Caucasus, deportation from the 134

Cézanne, Paul v, vi, 55–84
and artistic techniques 63–6
and avant-garde art 62, 63, 83
background and education 57–8
Basle exhibition of (1989) 60
drawing of Hortense with a spray
of hydrangeas 67
financial value of paintings by
57, 81
*The House of the Hanged Man at
Auvers* **59**
and Impressionist exhibitions
59–60, 63
and landscape painting 72–6
and modern art 63, 67–8, 71
*A Modern Olympia* 69–70, **70**, 75
painting of Leda and the Swan 61
and the Paris Salon 58–9, 63,
67–8
pictures of bathers 60–2, 64, 72,
76–7
compared with Bouguereau
66–8, 78–9
*The Three Bathers* **64**, 71–2
reputation 83
Salon d'Automne exhibition
(1907) 71–2
shaded drawing of male model 64
still lifes 78–81
*Jug and Fruit* **78**, 79
*Still Life, Curtain, Jug and
Compotier* 57, **57**, 78, 80–1
*The Three Bathers* **64**

Chapman, Tracy 167

Chardin, Jean-Siméon 80

charisma, and the legitimate
authority of the Dalai Lama
214–15

China
creation of the communist
state 132
and the Dalai Lama 200
the Dalai Lama's reputation in
216–22
and the Panchen Lama **218**, 220

and Tibet 201, 214, 216–22, 225,
226–8

Chinese porcelain, and still-life
paintings 79

Christianity
and Buddhism 205
and Marlowe's *Doctor
Faustus* 42, 44–6

classical Greece
and Marlowe's *Doctor Faustus*
42
and the nude in art 61,
69, 70–1

Classical Studies v, vi
*see also* Cleopatra

Cleese, John, and the
Dalai Lama 215

Cleopatra v, vi, 1–28
and Afrocentrism 25–6
appearance 9–10, 21–4
hairstyle 23
jewellery 23
'Cleopatra' DVD Video vi,
4–5, 6
facial features 21, 22
as a Hellenistic queen of Egypt
15–17, 25
in Hollywood 3, 4–5, **4**, 25
images of herself 18–24
on coins 18, 21–4, **21**
marble portraits **22**, 23
sculptural relief at the
Temple of Hathor 18,
19–21, **19**, 24
impressions of 3
personality 9–10
as politician and ruler 17–18
reassessment of 24–6
and Rome 5–15
in Augustan poetry
11–15, 28
meeting with Antony at Tarsus
10–11
in Plutarch's *Life of Antony*
9–11
'spin' and the construction of
Cleopatra 6–9
suicide 11, 14

coin portraits
of Antony 23, 24, **24**
of Cleopatra 18, 21–4, **21**

collectivisation policy

in Soviet Russia 130–1, 135
assessing Stalin's reputation
146
and the myth of Stalin 137,
138, 140
in Tibet 216

composition, and picture plane 65

Conquest, Robert, *Stalin: Breaker of
Nations* 147–8, 149, 152–3

Cook, Peter 34

Correggio (Antonio Allegri),
painting of Leda and the Swan 61

Crimea, deportation from the 134

Crosse, Cornelia, first visit to
Faraday's home 94, 118–19

the Dalai Lama v, vi, vii, 197–229
birthday celebrations in Tibet **221**
and charisma 214–15
doll **203**
DVD Video
'Chinese Incursion' 218
'Panchen Lama' 220
'Searching for a Reincarnated
Lama' 209–10
the fourteenth (Tenzin Gyatso)
199, 201, 223
as an ecological activist 200
as an enemy of the People's
Republic of China 200
birthplace 216
and Buddhism 204
as Chenresig 208–11, 212–13,
215, 219
and the continuation of
the office 220–1, 223
discovery of 210
education and training
210, 211
*Freedom in Exile* 206–7,
211
as a god-king 206, 207,
208, 211–15
in India **201**, **212**, 215,
216–18
as leader of the Tibetan people
200, 208
as a living Buddha 200, 206,
207, 210–11
in New York **206**
as a Nobel Peace Prize
winner 200, 202–4,
216, 224–6

reputation in China 216–22
as a Tibetan Buddhist monk
200, 207
the Great Fifth (1617-82)
211, 213
origins of the title 207
the sixth (Tsangyang Gyatso)
213–14
the thirteenth (Thupten Gyatso)
210, 211, 213
tradition of the Dalai Lamas
206–15
and the West 201–5, 222
*see also* Tibet

Davies, Sarah 142

Davy, Sir Humphrey
and applied science 107–8
and Faraday's early career 90–1,
92, 93
and the Royal Institution 91, 93
'Great Battery' at 98

Degas, Edgar 59, 72

delineation 64
Cézanne compared with
Bouguereau 66

Dendera, Egypt, sculptures at the
temple of Hathor 18, 19–21, 24

Diana, Princess of Wales 175

dictatorship of the proletariat 128

Dietrich, Marlene 163

Dio, Cassius, and Roman views of
Cleopatra 7–8, 14, 15

the diva v, 161–196
defining a diva 163
the Ferrarese ladies' vocal
ensemble 163, 164, 182–8, 189
Madonna 163, 164, 165–71, **166,**
**167,** 189, 190–1
Maria Callas 163, 164, 174–82,
**176, 177,** 189
modern-day divas 163
training to become a diva 164,
173–4

Domingo, Placido 174

drawing terms and techniques 64–5

Dudley, William, *The 1587 Rose
Theatre: A Cutaway View* **48**

dukkha in Buddhism 208

DVD material vi

eastern Europe, and post-war
Stalinism 132

Ecclestiastes, biblical book of, and
Vanitas paintings 79

Edward II, King 33

Egypt
and Cleopatra
in Augustan poetry 13–15
as Hellenistic queen of 15–17
Octavian's speech on 7–8
as politician and ruler 17–18
sculptural relief at the
Temple of Hathor 18,
19–21, **19,** 24

Einstein, A. 99

electric generators 100, **100,** 108,
111

electric lighting 108

electric motors, and Faraday's
experiments 98, 101, **101**

electricity, Faraday's experiments
with 97–102, 111–12, 121–2

electromagnetic forces, Faraday's
experiments on 100–1, 103–6, 108

Elizabeth I, Queen, and Marlowe's
*Doctor Faustus* 46–7

*Encyclopaedia Britannica* 90

English literature v
canon of 33
*see also* Marlowe, Christopher

enjambement, in Marlowe's *Doctor
Faustus* 49

ethnic minorities, deportation in
Soviet Russia 134

*Everyman* (medieval morality
play) 36

the Faraday Cage **102**

Faraday, James 89, 90
optical glass experiments 108

Faraday, Michael v, vi, 85–122
as corresponding member of the
Paris Académie de Science 99

death 113
DVD ROM of 113
early life 89–90
education 90, 91
experiments 97–106
the Faraday Cage **102**
induction 100–1, **100**
lines of force 103–6, 111
rotations 97–9, **98, 99,** 101
and generalisation 88
and the Haswell Colliery
explosion (1844) 108
and interpretation 88
marriage 93
nervous breakdown 94
obituary in *The Times* 88–9, 92,
115–17
and the practical application of
science 107–8
reasons for fame 88–9
religious beliefs 88, 95–7
influence on scientific work
97, 101–2, 108, 113, 119
and the Royal Military
Academy 108
on scientific method 119–20
*see also* Royal Institution

Faraday, Sarah (formerly Barnard)
93, 94, 95, 96, 113

the Faustbuch (*The History of the
Damnable Life and Deserved
Death of doctor John Faustus*) 34,
36, 37

Ferrara, court of vi
ladies' vocal ensemble 163, 164,
182–8, 189
'I'mi son giovinetta' 186–8
vocal abilities 188
and Luzzaschi 182–3
Orazio Urbani's visit (1581) 195
visit of Duc de Joyeuse
(1583) 195

feudal serfdom, and the
Dalai Lama 219

Fiennes, Joseph 31

figurative language, in Marlowe's
*Doctor Faustus* 38

Fiquet, Hortense 67

First World War, and the Russian
Revolution 127, 128

Fitzgerald, Ella 163

Fitzpatrick, Sheila 154

forte/fortissimo 172

Fragonard, Jean-Honoré 61

Franklin, Aretha 163

French bourgeoisie, and literary and artistic culture 82–3

French Revolution (1789) 82

Fuller, John 101


Galen (Greek medical authority) 40

Gandhi, Mahatma 200, 201, 224

Garland, Judy 163

Gaveston, Piers 33

generalisation, and Faraday's life and work 88

genre
    of bathers in European painting 60, 61
    of Marlowe's Doctor Faustus 37

Georgia
    Stalin's early life in 127
    Victory Day in Tbilisi (1997) **144**

Germany, and the Nazi–Soviet Pact (1939) 131–2

Giacosa, Giuseppe 178

Gobbi, Tito 177, 178

Goethe, J. von, Faust 34

Gonzaga, Margherita 184, 185

Grana, Cavalier 186, 195

Great Patriotic War (1941-45) 131–2, 134–5

Greece, ancient Greece and the Ptolemy rulers of Egypt 15–17, 25

Greek drama, and Italian opera 180

Greek tragedy, the Chorus in 37

Guarini, Anna 184

Guarini, Giovanni Battista 184

Guys, Constantin 69


Hancock, Tony 175

Handel, Georg Friedrich, Serse 174

harpsichord music
    accompaniment for madrigals 186
    and Luzzaschi 182

Hastwell, Margaret 89

Haswell Colliery explosion (1844) 108

Hathor, Egyptian goddess, sculpture 19, 20

Hawkins, Stan, on Madonna 168, 171, 190–1

Healy, Thomas 48–9

Heaney, Seamus, translation of Sophocles' Antigone 37

Helen of Troy
    and Leda and the Swan 61
    in Marlowe's Doctor Faustus 48–9
    Rosetti's painting of **50**

Hellenistic period, and the Ptolemy rulers of Egypt 15–17, 25

Hello magazine, and the Dalai Lama 202

Heywood, Thomas 33

Highgate Cemetery, Faraday's burial in 113

Himalaya (BBC series), the Dalai Lama in 215

History
    defining 126–7
    ethical approach to, and ancient historians 8–9
    and myth 125, 126–7
    see also Stalin, Josef

History of Science v
    see also Faraday, Michael

Hollywood, Cleopatra in 3, 4–5, 25

Horace, Ode 1.37 12–15, 28

Hulsdonck, Jacob van 79

Humboldt, Alexander von, latitude and longitude charts 103, **104**


iambic pentameter, and Marlowe's Doctor Faustus 35

Icarus myth
    Brueghel's painting of **40**, 41

in Marlowe's Doctor Faustus 38, 39

Illica, Luigi 178

imitation, in madrigals 186, 187

Impressionists
    brushwork 66
    and Cézanne's pictures of bathers 72
    disagreements over the virtues of 81–2
    independent exhibitions 59–60, 63, 69, 73
    and modernity 72–3
    see also Cézanne, Paul

India
    the Buddha of 200, 204, 207, 208, 210
    the Dalai Lama in **201**, **212**, 215, 216–18

induction, Faraday's experiments on 100–101, **100**, 108

industrialisation in Soviet Russia 129, 130, 135, 137
    assessing Stalin's reputation 146
    Magnitogorsk and the impact of the purges 148–9, 155–9

internet vii

interpretation
    and Faraday's life and work 88
    of the Stalin era 125, 126, 145–9

iron filings, and Faraday's experiments on lines of force 104, **105**

Italy, and the opera house 180, 181


Jews, and Buddhism 205

Johns, Jasper 72

Joyeuse, Duc de, visit to Ferrara (1583) 195

Julius Caesar 6–7, 13
    Cleopatra's first meeting with 17–18

Justinian, Roman Emperor 40


Kennedy, Jacqueline 175

Khrushchev, Nikita, speech to the Twentieth Congress of 136–7, 151–2

Kirov, Sergei 131

Klutsis, Gustav Gustaovich
    posters
        'Metro' 137, **139**
        'Shock Workers to the Fields,
        to the Battle for Socialist
        Construction' 137, **138**

Korea, creation of communist state
in 132

Kyd, Thomas 32–3, 34

landscape painting, and Cézanne
72–6

Leda and the Swan (classical
mythology), paintings of 61

legato melodies 171–2, 173

Lenin, V.I. 127, 128, 129, 130
    and the myth of Stalin 136–7,
    145, 151

Lewin, Moshe 137, 154

light and magnetism, Faraday's
experiments on 87, **87**, 103

lightning conductors, Faraday work
with 108

lighthouses, Faraday and electric
lighting 108

lines of force, Faraday's experiments
on 103–6, 111

literary texts vi

Lombardini, Alessandro 195

London
    City Philosophical Society 90, 91
    National Gallery 62
    Rose theatre 48
    Royal Military Academy,
    Woolwich 108
    Tate Britain 62
    Tate Modern 62
    see also Royal Institution

Lopez, Donald 222

Luzzaschi, Luzzasco 182–3, 189
    'I'mi son giovinetta' 186–8, 196

lyric poetry, ancient 12

McClary, Susan, on Madonna
166–7, 190

Mackerras, Sir Charles, description
of the diva 163, 188

Madden, John 31

Madonna 163, 164, 165–71, 190–1
    as author-producer-entrepreneur
    166–7, 190
    and black Gospel music 169–70
    image/persona 167–8
    images of in concert **166, 167**
    'Like a Prayer' 165, 168–70, 171
    Like a Prayer 190
    Like a Virgin 165, 190–1
    'Material Girl' 165, 169
    and music video 168, 171, 190–1
    'Open Your Heart' 171
    'Papa Don't Preach' 171, 190
    as pop diva 165, 171, 189
    song lyrics 168–9
    True Blue 190
    voice 165, 169

madrigals
    and the court of Ferrara 182–3,
    188, 189
    'I'mi son giovinetta' 186–8, 196

magnetism, Faraday's experiments
on 87, **87**, 97–9, 100–1, 103–6

Malenkov, Georgi 136

Manet, Edouard 81
    Olympia 69, 70, 74–5

Mann, Thomas, Doctor Faustus 34

Mantua
    and the court of Ferrara 184
    and madrigals 186

Mao Zedong **218**, 227

Marcet, Jane, Conversations in
Chemistry 90

Marlowe, Christopher 29–54
    biography of 31–2, 36
    Corpus Christi portrait of **32**
    death 31, 32
    Doctor Faustus v, vi, 31, 34–54
        Act 1 36–43
        Act 2 44–6
        Act 3 46–7
        Act 4 47–9
        Act 5 46, 49–51
        Audio CDs of 35, 40, 43, 46
        characterisation in 36
        Chorus in 36–7, 37–40,
        43, 51

comic scenes in 43
        Epilogue 36, 51, 52
        Faust's last soliloquy
        49–51
        Faustus as court magician
        in 46–7
        Faustus and God in 44–6
        Faustus's first speech in 40–3
        figurative language in 38
        genre of 37
        Good and Evil Angels in 36,
        42, 45–6
        Helen of Troy in 48–9
        historical context of 43
        Icarus myth in 38, **39**, 40
        and Marlowe's reputation
        52–4
        as a morality play 36–7, 51
        the Old Man in 46, 48–9
        performance-related issues
        47–9
        principal theme of 42
        Prologue 36, 37–40, 42, 51
        as a Renaissance play 34–6
        title page of the 'B' text
        of **53**
        as a tragedy 51–2
    investigation for heresy 32
    posthumous literary reputation
    32–4
    in Shakespeare in Love 31, 33

Marx, Karl 128

mathematics, and Faraday's
experiments on lines of force 103

Matisse, Henri 62, 71–2, 75

Maverick production company 165

Maxwell, James Clerk 106

media, and the diva 164

meditation, and Buddhism 205

metaphors, in Marlowe's
Doctor Faustus 38

Mitchell, Joni 167

modelling, in drawing and
painting 64–5

modern art
    and Cézanne's bathers 63, 67–8
    and the nude 68–71
    and 'scholars' and 'owners'
    82–3

Molotov, V. 131, 136

Molotov–Ribbentrop Pact (1939) 131–2

Molza, Tarquinia 184, 189

Monet, Claude 59

monotheistic religions 205

Monroe, Marilyn 175

Monte Saint-Victoire, Cézanne, Paul's paintings of 73, 75–6

Moore, Dudley 34

Moore, Harriet, *Faraday in his Basement Laboratory* 106, **107**

Moore, Henry 72

morality plays, and Marlowe's *Doctor Faustus* 36–7, 51

Morisot, Berthe 59

Mozart, Wolfgang Amadeus, *The Marriage of Figaro* 173–4

Music v, vi
    *see also* the diva

music video, and Madonna 168, 171, 190–1

musical terms
    aria 174
    dynamics 172
    forte/fortissimo 172
    legato 171–2, 173
    ornament 172
    phrases 172
    piano/pianissimo 172
    pizzicato accompaniment 172, 173
    recitative 174
    texture 172

myth
    and history 125, 126–7
    and religion 199
    of Stalin 136–45

Napoleon, and Davy's tour of the Continent 92

nationalisation, in Soviet Russia 129

natural philosophy, and Faraday 88, 90, 91

Nazi–Soviet Pact (1939) 131–2

NEP (New Economic Policy), in Soviet Russia 130

Nicholas II, Tsar of Russia 128

NKVD (People's Commisariat for Internal Affairs) 133

Nobel Peace Prize
    and the Dalai Lama 200, 204, 224
        acceptance speech 202–3, 216, 224–6

nudes
    Cézanne's paintings of bathers 61–2, 64, 72, 76–7
        compared with Bouguereau 66–8
    and the classical world 61, 69
    and modern art 68–71

nymphs, paintings of 61

Octavian (later Augustus, Roman emperor) 6–7, 16
    Augustan poetry and Roman views of Cleopatra 13–14, 14–15
    speech before the battle of Actium 7–8, 27

October Revolution (1917) 127, 128, 137

Oersted, Hans Christian 97, 98

Onassis, Aristotle 175

opera
    and the diva 163, 164
    opera houses 181–2, 183
    operatic arias 171–3, 174
    Royal Scottish Academy of Music and Drama, Opera School 164, 173–4
    the 'Three Tenors' 174
    *see also* Callas, Maria

optical glass, Faraday's experiments on 108

Ovid 61

*Oxford English Dictionary*, definition of 'myth' 126

painting terms and techniques 64–6
Palin, Michael 215
the Panchen Lama **218**, 220
Paris
    Académie de Science 99
    Musée du Petit Palais 72

Salon 58–9, 63, 67–8, 69, 75, 81–2
    Salon d'Automne exhibition (1907) 71–2, 77

Parma, Prince of, in Marlowe's *Doctor Faustus* 43, 46

patronage, and Faraday, Michael's early career 91

Pavarotti, Luciano 174

Peel, Robert 108

Peele, George 33

Peverara, Laura 184

Piaf, Edith 163

piano/pianissimo 172

Picasso, Pablo 62, 71, 75

picture plane/picture surface 65, 74–5

Pissarro, Camille 59, 72, 73, 83

pizzicato accompaniment 172, 173

Plutarch
    on Cleopatra's first meeting with Julius Caesar 17–18
    *Life of Antony* 9–11, 14, 15

poetry vi, 11–12
    blank verse 35
    Cleopatra in Augustan poetry 11–15, 28
    iambic pentameter 35
    lyric 12

Poland, and the Nazi–Soviet Pact (1939) 131–2

Pollock, Juliet, account of Faraday's lectures 110

pop music 163, 164

porcelain, and still-life paintings 79

portraiture, and picture plane/picture surface 74–5

Pourbus, Frans the Younger, *Portrait of Margherita Gonzaga* **185**

Poussin, Nicolas 73–4, 75

predestination, doctrine of 45

Presley, Elvis 175

Protestantism, and Marlowe's *Doctor Faustus* 43, 44–6, 46–7

'Prouvaire, Jean' (art reviewer) 59–60, 62

Provençal landscape, and Cézanne's paintings 72–3, 75–6

Ptolemy rulers of Egypt, and Cleopatra 15–17, 25

Puccini, Giacomo
*Tosca*
extract from libretto 193–4
and Maria Callas 175–80, **176**, **177**, 181

*Quarterly Journal of Science* 93

religion
China and religious freedom in Tibet 219, 222, 228
defining religion 199
impact of 200–1
monotheistic religions 205
myth and religion 199
religious meaning of charisma 214, 215
Religious Studies v, 199
*see also* Buddhism; the Dalai Lama

the Renaissance, and Marlowe's *Doctor Faustus* 34–6, 41–2

Renoir, Auguste 59, 72

representations, and Faraday's experiments on lines of force 103

reputations v, 230

Riebau, George 90

Rilke, Rainer Maria 72, 77, 78, 80, 83

Rinpoche, Khensur, abbot of Drepung monastery 209

Rivière, George 60, 63, 68, 70

Rodin, Auguste 72

Rogers, Catharine 173–4

Romantic movement, and the artist 58

Romantic poets, and Marlowe 33–4

Rome
and Cleopatra 5–15
in Augustan poetry 11–15
in Plutarch's *Life of Anthony* 9–11

as politician and ruler 17–18
propaganda and image of 6–9, 18
and the veristic style of portraiture 23

Rose theatre, London 48

Rossetti, Dante Gabriel, *Helen of Troy* **50**

Rossini, Gioacchino, *The Barber of Seville*, 'Una voce poco fa' 171–3, 191–2

rotation experiments (Faraday) 97–9, 101, **101**

Royal Institution
additional facade to the building 112
and Davy 91, 93, 98
Faraday's appointments
Director of the Laboratory 99, 110
laboratory assistant 91
Professor of Chemistry 89, 99–100
Faraday's lectures 89, 92, 109–12, **109**, 120
'Chemical History of a candle' 111–12, 121
Christmas lectures 111–12
early observations on 117–18
'Experimental researches in electricity' 111–12, 121–2
Friday Evening Discourses 87, **87**, 103, 110–11
Faraday's living quarters 92, 93–4
foundation 93
Fullerian Professorship of Chemistry 101
laboratory 92, 93, 94, 97, 106–7, **107**, 109–11
lecture theatre 87, **87**, 93, 109–10, **109**
library 93
presidency 96, 113

Royal Scottish Academy of Music and Drama, Opera School 164, 173–4

Royal Society, and Faraday 91, 96, 99

Russian Federation, and Stalin's reputation 134

Russian Revolution (1917) 127, 128, 137

Sabata, Victor de 178

samsara, Buddhist cycle of 208–9, 210

Sandemanian Church, and Faraday 89–90, 93, 94–7, 108, 110, 113, 119

Sardou, Victorien 178

science
and the Dalai Lama 203, 208
*see also* Faraday, Michael

Scott, John, *Behind the Urals: An American Worker in Russia's City of Steel* 148–9, 155–9

Scott-Kilvert, I. 9, 10

Second World War
and Stalin 125, 131–2, 134–5
victory parades 142, 143–4, **143**
'Victory Vase' 139–40, **141**

shading, in drawing and painting 64

*Shakespeare in Love* (film) 31, 33

Shakespeare, William
*Antony and Cleopatra* 9, 24
and Marlowe 31

Shelley, Percy Bysshe 33–4

Shepherd, Thomas Hosmer, *The Royal Institution* **112**

Shuker, Roy 168

Siberia, Stalin's internal exile in 127

similes 38

Sinfield, Alan 44

Sisley, Alfred 59

Smith, Paul 81

socialist state-building, in Soviet Russia 128–9

soliloquies, in Marlowe's *Doctor Faustus* 41, 44, 45, 49–51, 52

Sophocles, *Antigone* 37

Soviet Union
and the Bolsheviks 127, 138–9
collectivisation policy 130–1, 134, 135
posters 137, **138**, **140**
First Five-Year Plan 130, 139, 148

and the Great Patriotic (Second
World) War 131–2, 146
Moscow Victory Parade **142**,
143–4, **143**
'Victory Vase' 139–40, **141**
industrialisation 129, 130, 135,
137, 146
Magnitogorsk and the impact
of the purges 148–9, 155–9
maps of
(1922) **129**
(1945) **133**
Molotov–Ribbentrop Pact (1939)
131–2
Moscow metro 137, **139**
National Economic Plans 138–9,
140–1
NEP (New Economic Policy) 130
and the rise of Stalin 130
Shakhty Trial (1928) 130, 131
and 'Socialism in
One Country' 130
and socialist state-building
128–9
*see also* Stalin, Josef

spirituality, and Buddhism in the
West 204

Stachniewski, John 44

Stalin, Josef v, vi, 123–59
and the Bolsheviks 127, 128
cult of personality 131, 136,
137–145
death 132, 136
early life 127
historical evaluation of 125
interpretation of the Stalin era
125, 126, 145–9
myth of 125, 136–145
and Khrushchev's speech to
the Twentieth Congress
136–7, 145, 151–2
as a wise leader 142–4
and work campaigns
137–40
periodisation of the Stalinist era
130–2
and the purges 131, 137, 146
historians' assessments of
146–9, 152–5
impact of in Magnitogorsk
148–9, 155–9
reputation 133–6
assessments of 125, 145–9

in the current Russian
Federation 134
and the Great Patriotic War
134–5
and politically motivated mass
murder 133–4
and social transformation of
the Soviet Union 135
revolution from above (1928-34)
130–1, 131
rise of 130
and the Russian Revolution
(1917) 127, 128
and the Second World War 125,
131–2, 134–5
Moscow Victory Parade 142,
143–4, **143**
'Victory Vase' 139–40, **141**
setting in context 127–32
and 'Socialism in One
Country' 130
and the Soviet Union as
superpower 125
and Stalinism 128, 132
*see also* Soviet Union

Steenwyck, Harmen 79, 80

stereotypes, and Tibet 222

still-life paintings 78–81
as allegories 79
and exotic possessions 79, 80

Streisand, Barbra 163

Striggio, Italian composer, visit to
Ferrara (1584) 186, 188, 196

string instruments, pizzicato
accompaniment 172, 173

suffering, and Buddhist doctrine
202, 205, 208–9

Suny, Ronald Grigor, 'Stalin and his
Stalinism: power and authority in the
Soviet Union' 147–8, 149, 153–5

TAR (Tibet Autonomous Region)
216, **217**, 220, 228–9

Tasso, Torquato 184

Taylor, Elizabeth, in *Cleopatra* 3,
4, 25

technique, and artistic
development 58

Thomson, William 106

Tibet
and Britain 216
and China 201, 215, 216–22, 225,
226–8
and the Dalai Lama as a
'god-king' 211–15
ethnographic Tibet 216,
**217**, 220
and the Panchen Lama
**218**, 220
and stereotypes 222
TAR (Tibet Autonomous Region)
216, **217**, 220, 228–9
*see also* the Dalai Lama

Tibetan Buddhism
and China 216
and the tradition of the Dalai
Lamas 206, 207–8, 209–11
and the West 204, 205

tone, in drawing and painting 65

tragedy
and Maria Callas 164, 175, 181
and Marlowe's *Doctor Faustus*
51–2

transformers, and Faraday's
experiments 101

Trinity House lighthouses 108

Trotsky, Leon 129, 130, 131

Trotti, Ercole 184

Tsering, Tashi 210

Turco, Count Annibale 184

Tyndall, John 113

unemployment, in Soviet Russia 130

United States, and the Cold War 132

Urbani, Orazio, visit to Ferrara 195

urbanisation, in the Soviet Union 135

Vanitas paintings 79

Vecchio, Palma 61

*verism* (Roman style of portraiture)
and Antony 23, 24
and Cleopatra 23

Verona, Roman amphitheatre
180, **181**

Victoria, Queen, and Faraday
89, 113

virtuoso soloists, and black Gospel music 169

Vollard, Ambroise 71, 76

Volta, Alessandro 98

Wales Millennium Centre **182**

Wang Qiemi 227

Warner, R. 17

Watts, Isaac, *Improvement of the Mind* 90

Wert, Giaches 184, 189

Whitney, Geoffrey, 'Fall of Icarus' from *Choice of Emblemes* 39

Williams, Paul 213

Williams, William Carlos, poem about Brueghel's painting of the fall of Icarus 41

word painting, in madrigals 186, 187

Yuan Zhongxian 227

Zola, Emile 58, 67